An Irish Statesman and Revolutionary

The Nationalist and Internationalist Politics of Seán MacBride

ELIZABETH KEANE

BLOOMSBURY ACADEMIC

LONDON · NEW YORK · OXFORD · NEW DELHI · SYDNEY

For my family – Dennis, Patricia, Nancy,
and Catherine Keane

BLOOMSBURY ACADEMIC
Bloomsbury Publishing Plc
50 Bedford Square, London, WC1B 3DP, UK
1385 Broadway, New York, NY 10018, USA

BLOOMSBURY, BLOOMSBURY ACADEMIC and the Diana
logo are trademarks of Bloomsbury Publishing Plc

First published in Great Britain by I.B. Tauris 2006
Paperback edition published by Bloomsbury Academic 2020

A catalogue record for this book is available from the British Library.

A catalog record for this book is available from the Library of Congress.

ISBN: HB: 978-1-8451-1125-0
PB: 978-1-3501-7538-9
ePDF: 978-0-7556-3223-7
ePub: 978-0-7556-2860-5

Series: International Library of Historical Studies, vol. 39

To find out more about our authors and books visit
www.bloomsbury.com and sign up for our newsletters.

Contents

Acknowledgements

This book began as a PhD thesis in the Faculty of History at the University of Cambridge. Therefore, my first debt is to my supervisor Dr. Eugenio Biagini for his excellent guidance, perceptive criticism, and endless patience.

In the process of researching and writing this volume, I have greatly benefited from the kind and generous assistance of many people and institutions. Thanks especially to Seamus Helferty and the exceptionally helpful staff of the University College Dublin Archives, the staff of the National Archives, Ireland, Liz Safly and Randy Sowell at the Harry S. Truman Library, Oliver House at the Bodleian Library, Oxford, the staffs of Churchill College Archives, Cambridge and the Cambridge University Library and Faculty of History, Sunniva O'Flynn at the Irish Film Archive, the staff of the National Library of Ireland, David Sheehy at the Dublin Diocesan Archives, and the staff of the National Archives, Kew. Thanks to Michael McEvilly for suggesting helpful secondary sources, Caitriona Lawlor for allowing me to see some of Seán MacBride's personal correspondence, Declan Costello for giving me permission to access the papers of John A. Costello, and François Danis, Secretary General at the Fondation Paul-Henri Spaak and Ghislain Malette at the National Archives of Canada for finding and sending relevant documentation.

I am grateful to the Royal Historical Society, the Cambridge University Faculty of History's Prince Consort and Thirwell Trust Fund and Sara Norton Fund, and to Fitzwilliam College, Cambridge for various travel grants. Thanks to the Master of Fitzwilliam, Prof. Brian Johnson, and my graduate tutors Dr. Bill Allison and Dr. Ghassan Yassin for helping out in that regard. Thanks again to Fitzwilliam and to the Cambridge University Board of Graduate Studies for providing extra funding to allow me to complete my degree.

Dr. Brendan Simms and Prof. Peter Clarke reviewed earlier drafts of this work and I am appreciative of their valuable commentary and suggestions. Thanks also to my *viva voce* examiners Prof. Joseph Lee and Dr. Colin Barr for their insight and help. While the final product has greatly benefited from the many comments, suggestions, and criticisms I have received along the way, final responsibility for the historical analysis presented is mine alone.

Thank you to Dr. Lester Crook, Elizabeth Munns, Carolann Martin, and the staff at I.B. Tauris for their professionalism and dedication.

For advice, guidance, and friendship during the thesis and beyond; much gratitude to Jane Goundrey, Sonia Osman, Saydan Osman, Stuart Snaddon, Sasha LeGeros, George and Katie Brennan, Matthew McCann, Noel Shields, and Annaleese MacNamara.

Thanks to Roberta Hamilton, Aurora Gaxiola, Sarah Skinner, James Suter, Charlie Farquharson-Roberts, Adrian Joyce, Christopher Clark, David Weaver, Roman Roth, and Carrie Roth-Murray for making my time in Cambridge much more than I expected or hoped. Thanks also to Claire Hawkins and the wonderful staff at Indigo Coffee House for ensuring that I had enough caffeine and onion bagels to sustain me. To Fergus McGuire for being his perceptive and contrary self – *go raibh míle maith agat, mo chara*.

Finally, to my family for their support, love, and ability to tolerate my frenetic state of mind over the last few years – thanks to my grandparents, E. Richard and Helen Hoffman and Clifton and Bernice Keane, my sisters Nancy and Catherine, and my parents Dennis and Patricia Keane. This volume is dedicated to them.

Abbreviations

AI	Amnesty International
CAB	Cabinet Records
CEEC	Committee for European Economic Cooperation
CIA	Central Intelligence Agency
CO	Commonwealth Office
DO	Dominions Office
ECA	Economic Cooperation Administration
ERP	European Recovery Programme
ESB	Electricity Supply Board
FO	Foreign Office
GNR	Great Northern Railroad
HSTL	Harry S. Truman Library
HSTP	Harry S. Truman Papers
ICJ	International Commission of Jurists
IMA	Irish Medical Association
IPB	International Peace Bureau
IRA	Irish Republican Army
NAT	North Atlantic Treaty
NATO	North Atlantic Treaty Organisation
NSC	National Security Council
OECD	Organisation of Economic Cooperation and Development
OEEC	Organisation for European Economic Cooperation
PREM	Records of the Prime Minister's Office
PRO	Public Record Office, Kew
PRONI	Public Record Office, Northern Ireland
PSF	President's Secretary's File
SDLP	Social Democratic and Labour Party
TD	Teachta Dála, a Deputy to the Dáil
UNESCO	United Nations Educational, Scientific, and Cultural Organization
UTA	Ulster Transport Authority

Nomenclature

Throughout the text, I have left intact any irregular spellings that appear in quoted documents, particularly American English spellings, for example 'favor' instead of 'favour'. The Irish acute accent mark, or fada, is included on Irish proper names and words in the Irish language where required, for example Seán MacBride and Dáil Éireann, except when the fada is not used in a direct quote. I have employed the term *sic* in brackets for misspellings or odd usage in the original text.

As for the rather murky business of place names: 'the Irish Free State', 'Éire', and 'the Republic' refer to the 26 southern Irish counties. 'The Six Counties', 'the North', and 'Northern Ireland' refer to the northern counties currently within the United Kingdom. 'Ireland' may refer either to the Republic or the entire island, depending on context.

Introduction

'If people have a creed to preach, a message to expound, they can go before their fellow citizens and preach and expound it. But let the appeal be to the mind, to reason rather than to physical fear. They cannot have it both ways. They cannot have the platform and the bomb.'[1]

Kevin O'Higgins

Despite O'Higgins' assertion, the history of Ireland contains a mixture of these two elements, the platform and the bomb, and many Irish politicians have successfully used both. Daniel O'Connell and Charles Stewart Parnell, though outwardly disapproving of force in their respective movements, may not have met with the success they did if not for the implicit threat of violence behind them. During the War of Independence, Sinn Féin relied on violence to force the British to negotiate. At the time O'Higgins was speaking, anti-treaty forces violently protested the legitimacy of his Free State government, believing that the treaty negotiators had failed to secure the desired Irish Republic. Among the anti-treaty supporters was Seán MacBride, whose family history made a career in Irish politics almost predestined.

MacBride's mother was indefatigable revolutionary and muse of William Butler Yeats Maud Gonne and his father John MacBride was executed for his role in the 1916 Easter Rising. Shortly after his birth in 1904, Gonne received a telegram sending congratulations to the 'future President of Ireland'. His baptism was observed by the police because of the expected nationalist turnout and prominent Fenian John O'Leary was asked to be godfather. MacBride's contemporary C.S. Andrews described his upbringing: 'he was brought up in situations where he only met the important people in the Independence movement. He behaved from boyhood as if he were one of them. He was accepted as such by everyone he met.'[2]

His parents' marriage ended acrimoniously when MacBride was very young. He remained with his mother in Paris until 1918, which left him with a distinctive French accent he would retain all his life. At age 14 he joined Fianna Éireann, a training ground for the IRA. In 1920, he became a member the Irish Volunteers, lying about his age. He was assigned to the Third Battalion of the Dublin Brigade during the War of Independence. He also managed to obtain a law degree from University College Dublin. He came to the attention of Michael Collins and was his bodyguard and courier during the Treaty negotiations in 1921.

MacBride did not accept the settlement and joined the anti-treaty forces during the Irish Civil War. He was arrested during the attack on the Four Courts and imprisoned at Mountjoy for 16 months. He escaped en route while being transferred to Kilmainham Jail. MacBride refused to join the anti-treaty leader Éamon de Valera after he split from Sinn Féin and formed Fianna Fáil in 1926. In that same year he married Catalina Bulfin, whose father William edited the Buenos Aires based *Southern Cross* newspaper and introduced hurling to Argentina, and whose brother Eamonn fought with Patrick Pearse during the Easter Rising. MacBride became the IRA's director of intelligence in the late 1920s then Chief-of-Staff in the mid 1930s. The group was losing political significance; reduced in size they fought a sporadic terrorist campaign with little success. They realised that they would need a political arm to attract republicans drawn to Fianna Fáil. In 1931 MacBride founded Saor Éire, a republican/socialist party; it and the IRA and were declared illegal in the Free State. Like all decent republican parties, it was denounced by the Catholic Church and its members were excommunicated. The party soon dissolved.

In 1932, Fianna Fáil came to power and the conflict between the party and the IRA grew. In 1936 the government banned the IRA and imprisoned its leading activists. After de Valera introduced the new Constitution in 1937, MacBride spent the next few years focusing on his legal career, mainly defending political prisoners.

He came to believe that more could be accomplished by constitutional methods than through violence, perhaps following de Valera's own example. In 1946 he founded and developed the political party Clann na Poblachta, whose platform stressed ending partition, establishing an Irish republic, improving social welfare especially health services, monetary policy, and forestry. MacBride was elected TD for Dublin South-West in the by-election of 1947. In the 1948 General Election, 10 Clann TDs were elected to the Dáil and the party helped form Ireland's first inter-party government. MacBride took the position of Minister of External Affairs.

Despite having little experience as a cabinet minister, MacBride became an accomplished statesman and diplomat. Though the government fell in 1951, MacBride was re-elected as TD in 1951 and 1954, but was never again to hold a position of political importance in the Republic.

After his defeat in 1957, MacBride became disillusioned with Irish politics and began to broaden his perspective. His diplomatic experience allowed him to begin a new vocation and he would hold a number of high-level international positions. He became a United Nations Roving Ambassador in the early 1960s, helped to found Amnesty International in 1961, served on the International Commission of Jurists (ICJ) from 1963 to 1970, and worked as the United Nations Commissioner for Namibia from 1973 to 1976, gaining the title Assistant Secretary General.

In 1974, MacBride was the first Irishman to win the Nobel Peace Prize, the culmination of his conversion from bomb to platform, considering his position as a former IRA Chief-of-Staff. He also won the prize at a time when conflict in the North was intensifying. MacBride is the first individual to claim both the Nobel Peace Prize and the Lenin Peace Prize, showing just how universal his later concerns became.

Despite it international scope, his later career also had an impact on Ireland. In the 1980s, he resumed practice at the Irish Bar, defending political prisoners in Irish law courts. In 1983, Fine Gael, Fianna Fáil, Labour, and the SDLP met to review their position on the national question. MacBride attended the New Ireland Forum Public Session to communicate his views on the partition issue and the continuing violence in the North. He also became an active supporter of the Irish National Caucus, an American lobby formed to fight discrimination against Catholics in the North. He lent his name to a series of conditions known as the MacBride Principles for American companies operating in Northern Ireland to follow in order to prevent discrimination. MacBride's participation in the ICJ and his role in founding and developing Amnesty International served as a counterpoint to growing tensions in the North. His transition from leading a political party that many believe was influenced by the IRA to actively renouncing revolutionary methods and participating in organisations that denounced violence serves as a parallel to the evolution of the Irish state developing into a democracy within in lifetime.[3]

This volume concentrates on the politics and policies of MacBride with a focus on his impact on Irish foreign policy, both while in government and after his departure from Irish party politics. MacBride was involved in many significant events taking place in the emerging Irish Republic and his influence can be clearly seen in the realm of foreign policy. While MacBride was Minister for External Affairs during the first inter-party government, his responsibilities included the 1948 repeal of the External Relations Act, officially removing Ireland from the British Commonwealth, attempts to draw worldwide attention to the partition issue, NATO and Marshall Plan negotiations with the United States, and expanding Ireland's role in Europe by joining the Organisation of European Economic Cooperation (OEEC) and the Council of Europe.

This enquiry will involve close study of his tenure as Minister of External Affairs, where MacBride had the most direct influence on foreign policy. His re-emergence as elder statesman and humanitarian, the culmination of his conversion from bomb to platform, had a positive effect on Irish foreign policy and how the world perceived Ireland at a time when conflict in the North was intensifying. His short-lived but productive political career in Ireland and the development of his role in human rights issues are of major importance as Ireland also finds its niche within the larger European community.

Despite having one of the most extraordinary and varied lives of any Irish figure of the twentieth century, there is only one biography of Seán MacBride, written by Anthony Jordan in 1993. Jordan's work is hampered by a very limited use of primary source material; there are surprisingly few references to either the private papers of members of the inter-party government or the Department of Foreign Affairs files located in the Irish National Archives. There is not much analysis of MacBride's life or career; Jordan calls MacBride a 'kaleidoscopic' man while only tersely demonstrating why.[4]

Even with the recent diversity of secondary works, Seán MacBride's impact on Irish foreign policy has merited relatively brief attention.[5] The present study differs in that it aims to present a fuller, more definitive examination of his contribution to the formulation of the foreign policy of the newly independent Ireland and how this policy impacted the shaping of the Irish nation. Not only is there a lack of study on MacBride, but general misconceptions also exist about Irish foreign affairs, one of which is that the period from 1946-1955 was an inactive one in Irish foreign policy. Such perceptions serve to diminish MacBride's contribution. Though foreign affairs were somewhat overshadowed by the partition problem, Ireland did play more of a role in international relations than is sometimes credited and MacBride deserves praise and blame for helping to shape foreign policy in its formative stages.

One of the first Irish politicians to write his memoirs, Noël Browne's *Against the Tide* provides a valuable look into Clann na Poblachta politics and the Mother and Child controversy. Described by J.J. Lee as 'etched in vitriol' yet quite plausible,[6] Browne harbours an obvious bias toward MacBride even in retrospect. Browne makes clear in his preface that *Against the Tide* was written to correct certain inaccuracies about his political career. Browne describes MacBride as insecure and somewhat manipulative. He delves into MacBride's personality, especially his upbringing, and finds his later peace campaign difficult to reconcile with his former violent ways.[7] Browne feels that MacBride was dominated by a formidable mother and needed to find some way to fulfil his destiny as an important political figure. When he lost his cabinet post, his Dáil seat, and Clann na Poblachta, he had to find another role, another way to achieve.[8] Browne's wife, Phyllis, recently wrote a memoir *Thanks for the Tea, Mrs. Browne: My Life With Noël* where she echoes her husband's assessment of MacBride, positing that his unstable childhood left him cold and aloof.

Politician and historian Conor Cruise O'Brien's memoir provides a more balanced view. Cruise O'Brien worked in the Department of External Affairs at the beginning of the inter-party government, coming into contact with MacBride almost daily. Like Browne, Cruise O'Brien feels that MacBride's upbringing led him to strive for recognition. For the first twelve years of his life, his mother taught him to fear his father, going so far as to speak only French to MacBride so he and his father would be unable to communicate. But Gonne's image of her former husband was transformed after his execution in 1916, as she wrote to Yeats, 'Major MacBride by his Death has left a name for Seagan to be proud of. Those who die for Ireland are sacred. Those who enter Eternity by the great door of Sacrifice atone for all.'[9]

This must have been an unexpected change for twelve-year old MacBride, but his mother brought him up as a fervent nationalist, so perhaps he could process and accept such a change. Cruise O'Brien makes the point that MacBride was striving to please 'ghosts', his mother's reputation and his father's martyrdom, rather than a sincere desire to be a politician. He delves into the complexities of the relationship between MacBride and de Valera, who MacBride disliked at times, yet tried to emulate.[10] Cruise O'Brien maintains that there were few immediately perceptible changes as a result of MacBride's tenure, but the Department of External Affairs became larger in the national consciousness. On a personal level, Cruise O'Brien felt that when MacBride was no longer involved in Irish politics, he was more spontaneous and relaxed – he no longer had to appease those ghosts.[11]

As of now, MacBride's papers are not available for consultation. He willed his library at Roebuck House to his personal assistant Caitriona Lawlor, who is still in possession of the papers and has not yet made them available, although she did allow me access to certain documents pertaining to his time in government as well as releasing a memoir written by MacBride describing his time in the IRA and his participation in the first inter-party government.

There is still an extensive amount of primary source material available to appraise MacBride's influence and impact on Irish policy. Therefore this study utilises a variety of sources.

The Seán MacBride Collection at Iona College, New York reveals what MacBride's later concerns were.[12] The Dáil Éireann debates from 1948-1951 when MacBride was a cabinet minister are an important source of information as well as a record of repartee between MacBride and de Valera. The Irish National Archives, which is in dire need of an organised database, contains cabinet minutes and the Department of Foreign Affairs papers and harbours loads of information for those with the time and patience to sort through the files. The Canadian National Archives contained information which shed light on Taoiseach John Costello's Ottawa Declaration, examined in chapter two. *Our Nation*, the Clann na Poblachta periodical which includes their platform, offers clues to how the public was supposed to perceive the new party. *Our Country*, the Clann's 1948 election film, provides an absorbing look at conditions in Ireland and the Clann's social welfare policy as well as MacBride's rather exotic accent.

United States Secretary of State Dean Acheson's papers contain summaries and minutes of meetings he had with MacBride regarding NATO, the Marshall Plan and the partition issue. Paul G. Hoffman helped administer Marshall Plan aid during the Truman administration and his papers feature information about Marshall loans to Ireland. Harry Truman was President of the United States during NATO and Marshall Plan negotiations and his papers are quite extensive, including diaries, correspondence, meeting minutes, and official files relating to Ireland joining NATO and receiving Marshall aid, and assessments of the partition issue as well as personal, Central Intelligence Agency (CIA) and National Security Council (NSC) appraisals of MacBride.

Clement Attlee, the British Prime Minister at the time the Irish government repealed the External Relations Act, left papers containing information regarding repeal and Ireland's relationship with the

Commonwealth. The papers of Foreign Secretary Ernest Bevin and Secretary for Commonwealth Relations Philip Noel-Baker provide insight into the workings and priorities of both Labour foreign policy and Commonwealth affairs.

University College, Dublin has an extensive archival collection containing the papers of most of the government officials in office with MacBride including Frank Aiken, Seán MacEntee, Seán MacEoin, Patrick McGilligan, and Richard Mulcahy, as well as Éamon de Valera, the leader of the opposition during the inter-party government as well as the centre of political life in Ireland for over forty years. The John A. Costello papers, opened in January 2005, contain valuable information regarding the two events the inter-party government is most remembered for; the repeal of the External Relations Act and the Mother and Child scheme.

The recently opened papers of John Charles McQuaid, Archbishop of Dublin and a leading figure in the Mother and Child controversy provided a useful insight into both the Irish Catholic Church's influence on health care in Ireland and the relationship between McQuaid and MacBride.

This volume is organised in primarily chronological fashion, beginning with Clann na Poblachta's participation in the inter-party government, MacBride's influence within that government as Minister of External Affairs, and his later role in human rights movements.

The first chapter describes the beginnings of Clann na Poblachta and their policies. The party was concerned with social welfare as well as being staunchly republican and offered respite from sixteen years of Fianna Fáil domination. It was the first party with strong republican feeling not to come out of Treaty politics and show the influence of European Christian Democracy, a change in Irish political identity. What did MacBride hope to accomplish and how did he plan to do it? This chapter also briefly describes the formation of the government and their policy priorities.

Chapter two studies MacBride and Clann na Poblachta's paramount goal; the declaration of an Irish Republic, which some, like Anthony Jordan, believed was the most important achievement of the coalition, while others, like Nicholas Mansergh, saw Ireland's removal from the Commonwealth as a disadvantage. Was the repeal of the External Relations Act a truly radical change in Ireland's identity at home or within the Commonwealth or was it merely a confirmation of existing conditions? Did it benefit the country or was it ultimately detrimental toward unity with the North? Why did a pro-Commonwealth Fine Gael dominated government decide to take Ireland out of the Commonwealth? Was MacBride's presence in government a factor?

Chapter three examines the second aspect of Clann na Poblachta's party platform, the desire to end partition. The anti-partition campaign was a priority of MacBride's and though it was not successful, the movement and propaganda agencies created had an enormous impact on Irish foreign policy and affected relationships with both Britain and the United States. The government's 'sore thumb' strategy worked to their detriment, sacrificing foreign policy gains in order to publicise the issue as well as alienating the North. This behaviour was a direct result of the Irish political characteristic of not appearing 'soft' on the issue. Were there alternatives the inter-party government could have pursued to end partition?

The United States is at the centre of chapter four. MacBride was involved in negotiations with President Truman's government regarding Marshall Plan aid and Ireland's proposed entry into NATO. Ireland had always laid claim to a special relationship with the United States, but the combination of Irish neutrality during World War II, the escalating Cold War, and the Irish government's fixation on the partition issue would greatly affect that relationship. MacBride's virtual dominance in Marshall Plan negotiations, despite such negotiations being within the domain of the Department of Finance, gave the Department of External Affairs a more prominent profile and participation in the Marshall Plan forced Ireland to consider both economic planning and its position on European integration. Participation was generally beneficial for Ireland, however NATO negotiations proved to be counterproductive and haphazardly handled by the Irish government.

The present volume argues that Ireland's growing participation in an integrated Europe is where MacBride's most substantial foreign policy contribution lies and his role is the focus of chapter five. By taking part in the OEEC and the Council of Europe, MacBride was attempting to create a new identity for Ireland within Europe, one that would be independent of Britain while still enabling Dublin to maintain Irish neutrality. Institutions like the Council of Europe allowed Ireland an international forum to seek support for ending partition, but his seeming obsession with the topic led to the impression that partition was all the country cared about.[13] Yet Ireland did make positive contributions to those organisations and MacBride's attempt to internationalise Irish politics would play a great part in shaping his later career.

The first inter-party government is chiefly remembered for two events, the declaration of the Republic and the Mother and Child controversy. While declaring the Republic benefited MacBride and the Clann, his role in the Mother and Child controversy split his party and led to the end of his career in Irish politics. The infamous Mother and Child controversy and the fall of the inter-party government are explored in chapter six. What did the controversy really demonstrate about church-state relations in Ireland? The handling of the issue sheds light on MacBride's shortcomings as a party leader, the Roman Catholic Church hierarchy's attitude toward women, and ultimately provides another example of the reactive nature of the inter-party government.

Chapter seven concentrates on MacBride's later vocation. His legal career, fluency in French, and his diplomatic experience made it possible for him to take up a new international role as a spokesman for human rights issues. MacBride soon became a respected diplomat, co-founder and sometime chairman of Amnesty International, and winner of the Nobel Peace Prize. Despite gaining fame outside Ireland, he continued to impact the country, returning to the Irish bar in the 1980s, participating in the New Ireland Forum, and sponsoring the MacBride Principles to prevent discrimination against Catholics in the North.

The involvement of Ireland in international history and international relations has propelled the study of Irish history from being a rather restricted investigation to one of international importance and Seán MacBride's career reflects this remarkable development. I hope to supply a comprehensive portrait of his influence on Irish politics and to underscore the importance of MacBride to both the development of the Irish nation and global concerns. Moreover, I hope to draw attention to evolution and change in a country sometimes perceived as stagnant.

1

Man of Destiny: Seán MacBride and Clann na Poblachta

'Remember I never liked politics. I just hated politics from beginning to end. I hate the ballyhoo of politics.'[1]

Seán MacBride

The political climate of the 1940s provided a promising atmosphere for the founding of a new party. Since coming to power in 1932, Fianna Fáil had gradually moved to the centre, losing much of its original radicalism and leading to disenchantment among some former supporters resulting in a sense of inertia and complacency. While in power, Fianna Fáil adjusted their interpretation and application of republican ideology as well as their social welfare policies. Taoiseach Éamon de Valera's, and consequently Fianna Fáil's vision of the Irish state, was summarised in his St. Patrick's Day speech in 1943. He famously described the ideal Ireland as

the home of a people who valued material wealth only as the basis for right living, of a people who were satisfied with frugal comfort and devoted their leisure to the things of the spirit – a land whose countryside would be bright with cosy homesteads, whose fields and villages would be joyous with sounds of industry, with the romping of sturdy children, the contests of athletic youths and the laughter of comely maidens, whose firesides would be forums for the wisdom of serene old age.[2]

Yet the Ireland that de Valera governed did not correspond with this vision. At a time when, in Noël Browne's words, 'they [the Fianna Fáil government] had offered nothing but unemployment, much human distress, and mass emigration,'[3] de Valera at best seemed to be progressing backward; at worst appeared to have completely lost touch with reality. However, in the general election that followed that speech, de Valera was returned to office and was again victorious in yet another election the following year largely because there did not seem to be any other promising alternative. As a result of the long period of Fianna Fáil dominance and a lack of able party organisation and dynamic leadership, Fine Gael seemed poised for a slow descent into obscurity. In several important by-elections in 1945, the party could not find candidates, failing to profit from any ennui with the Fianna Fáil government. The Irish Labour Party, never a real threat to the two major parties when united, split in the 1940s. Even without the division, Labour in 1940s Ireland proved too afraid of being labelled socialist or communist to develop a strong left-wing programme that could benefit from Fianna Fáil's lack of direction in the realm of social welfare policy. Clann na Talmhan, a farmer's party founded in 1938, seemed too small and specialised to pose a threat to Fianna Fáil. Thus, Fianna Fáil seemed the best possible choice.

In addition to the apparent stagnancy in the party system, Ireland's neutrality policy during World War II also affected the political climate. F.S.L. Lyons famously compared post-war Ireland to the inhabitants of Plato's Cave, who, after spending a long time seeing only shadows of the world beyond, are suddenly thrust into sunlight.[4] As the *Times* editorialised in July of 1948, Ireland resembled 'a sleeping beauty who has slept through a long winter and is now stirring her limbs to life.'[5] Neutrality possessed a positive side; the policy saved the country from war, emphasised the consciousness of sovereignty, gave the Irish a sense of confidence and common dedication to a national purpose - which went far in mollifying Civil War divisions - and it marked the beginning of an independent foreign policy.[6] However, the debit side proved to be harsh; neutrality led to an inactive economy, a sense of apathy in politics and society, increased emigration, and isolation and insularity from a quickly changing world. Post-war modernisation came later to Ireland than other Western European nations because she did not directly suffer from the war and was not in need of rapid rebuilding.

Food and fuel rationing continued after the war and a sluggish economy, poor housing conditions, poverty and illnesses associated with it like tuberculosis, a depressed agricultural sector, high prices, low incomes, an increasing rate of emigration, growing industrial unrest, and a series of strikes, most notably (and ultimately quite beneficial for Clann na Poblachta) a teachers' strike in 1946 undermined confidence in the government and began to drain support from Fianna Fáil. The mood of the country was shifting as well; Ireland had 'passed the honeymoon period of national independence and are wondering how best to manage their everyday bread-and-butter affairs.'[7] The harsh treatment of political prisoners under the Fianna Fáil government, notably Seán McCaughey, an IRA prisoner who died on hunger strike in Portlaoise prison, served as a catalyst for a diverse group of people to create a constitutional alternative to Fianna Fáil.[8]

Clann na Poblachta officially came into existence on 6 July 1946 in Barry's Hotel in Dublin; the first mention of the Clann in the press appeared on the front page of the *Irish Times* on 8 July 1946. Most of the party's Provisional Executive, like MacBride, were lawyers. MacBride was best known in Dublin as a barrister specialising in the defence of republicans; elsewhere in Ireland as the son of Maud Gonne and John MacBride. Why, especially considering MacBride's aversion to 'the ballyhoo of politics,' did he choose to form and lead a political party? MacBride's republican background assured that his entrance into politics would be taken seriously; perhaps he craved the recognition that being the leader of a successful party would bring. He may have been conditioned by his mother's belief that he was destined for greatness and encouraged by reminders of his father's contribution to Irish republicanism. As Conor Cruise O'Brien believes, MacBride was continually 'appeasing ghosts.'[9] Perhaps the most likely reason is that MacBride was guided by the pattern within Irish politics of the movement from violent action to constitutional methods typified by the movements of Daniel O'Connell, Charles Stewart Parnell, and more recently, de Valera himself. MacBride found himself frustrated with the IRA and was willing to endure the ballyhoo in order to to accomplish objectives that he thought would improve the Irish nation. MacBride echoes journalist Brian Inglis, who felt that becoming politically conscious was essential to the Irish character; 'I must find a way to embrace Irishness; and the obvious one was to join a political party.'[10]

Clann na Poblachta would prove to be the most serious challenge to complacent Fianna Fáil power in the 1940s, taking Fianna Fáil to task for their failure to tackle severe social and economic problems and resolve the problem of partition while also claiming to be the more sincere republicans. Ian McCabe maintains that the Clann was the only party that benefited from the post-war apathy.[11] The party possessed an instant nucleus of support from those, like MacBride, who had been republican activists in the 1930s and 1940s.

The Clann's support came from 'elements of the IRA, dissatisfied members of Fianna Fáil, and from ordinary voters.'[12] Capitalising on post-war frustration and winning over discontented supporters from all parties, the trick for Clann na Poblachta was 'to sound more nationalist (or "national") than de Valera but less nationalist than the IRA.'[13] They succeeded in mobilising almost all of the remaining extra constitutional republicans, former IRA members and those disenchanted with Fianna Fáil's move toward the centre. Clann na Poblachta contained people of diverse ideological backgrounds that managed to remain intact due to the prospect of electoral success, the idea of defeating Fianna Fáil, and the excitement of campaigning. The party attracted republicans disheartened by the widespread imprisonments of the 1930s. Noel Hartnett, MacBride's junior counsel in many defences of IRA prisoners, became disillusioned by Fianna Fáil's move away from republicanism, especially in regard to the government's treatment of political prisoners. Clann na Poblachta also attracted those concerned with social welfare like Noël Browne, who according to his wife Phyllis was unfamiliar with MacBride's political background, joining the party because of his desire to eliminate tuberculosis. Peadar Cowan, Clann na Poblachta's director of finance, was an executive member of the Labour Party. Inglis calls the Clann 'vaguely progressive', maintaining that it was merely a disparate group linked only by dissatisfaction with Fianna Fáil and thus did not promise to be stable.[14] An accurate assessment, but in 1946 such dissatisfaction was enough to gel such a varied collection of people.

There is little comment from the press after the Clann's initial meeting. No editorials or letters followed and they did not publicly issue any new or more detailed policy statements. For the moment, de Valera and Fianna Fáil possessed a comfortable majority in the Dáil and the latest splinter parties, National Labour and Clann na Talmhan, had posed no real threat. Fianna Fáil had introduced an Electoral Amendment Bill in the Dáil on 2 July, four days before the Clann was officially founded, so this extra cushion would give them even less to fear from the new party. In 1946, Clann na Poblachta had not formulated any specific policies or programmes and a general election would not be necessary until May 1949. As Eithne MacDermott indicates, nothing about the Clann appeared in Fine Gael leader Richard Mulcahy's correspondence until the general election of 1948.[15] It seems that although Clann na Poblachta made an impression on individual discontented party members, it did not initially have a significant impact on their rival parties.

The Party Programme

Clann na Poblachta translates to 'family of the republic,' though 'clann' can also mean 'children', 'people', or simply 'clan'. It was the only Irish political party to refer to a republic in its name; both Fine Gael ('Tribe of the Gaels') and Fianna Fáil ('Soldiers of Destiny') used past mythology choosing their names whereas Clann na Poblachta looked toward the future with its choice.[16] As the republic did not formally exist yet, their name made it obvious where the Clann stood. Despite the republican emphasis, the party aimed to be broadly based, and to concentrate on social and economic problems. MacBride wanted to win a wide measure of popular support for his party by promising a fresh, objective approach to politics. As MacDermott points out, very little about the party was totally innovative: 'it looked new, and radical, and challenging, and different, without really being many of these things.'[17] Clann na Poblachta cannot be termed truly extreme in any sense; the claim to radicalism must be judged in the context of Irish political and social traditions. In a country with a strong Catholic and democratic culture, it was radical in a 'thoroughly safe, unthreatening manner, sculpting its proposals around the traditional framework of Catholic social teaching.'[18]

The party was influenced more by Catholic social principles and the new trend of Christian Democracy in Europe than by any staunch socialist philosophy. While deciding on the Clann na Poblachta programme, MacBride may have been influenced by the current trends in European politics. Christian Democracy, as Kees van Kersbergen posits, was not merely a political party, but a political movement.[19] MacBride never publicly compared Clann na Poblachta to Christian Democrats, but his desire to cultivate a European perspective and the similarities in his party's programme, for example the belief that economic policies must go hand in hand with social policies assuring that members of society had equal opportunities for self-development, demonstrate that he was somewhat influenced by Christian Democracy.

The philosophy of Christian Democracy contained a recognisable doctrine broadly based on Catholic social thought, but individual parties covered a wide range of political opinion and practice. For the most part, continental Christian Democracy pursued a post-war middle course between socialism and liberalism, what could be labelled 'moderate conservatism'. The first significant Christian Democratic party, Mouvement Republicain Populaire, was founded in France where MacBride was born and spent much of his early life. In Belgium the Christelijke Volkspartij replaced the Catholic Party in 1945 but was supported by the Church. From 1943 the Democrazia Cristiana dominated Italian government for more than fifty years, mostly in coalition. Led by Alcide De Gasperi, Democrazia Cristiana favoured Catholic morality, representative democracy, anti-communism, a commitment to the capitalist system, and special attention to the *ceti medi* and the family. MacBride was very familiar with Italian Christian Democracy; one of the inter-party government's first forays into foreign policy involved MacBride, the government and the Irish Catholic Church collecting contributions to stop the Communist Party from winning a majority in Italy's 1948 general election.[20]

Joseph Walshe, the Irish ambassador to the Holy See, warned the government of an imminent Communist victory in Italy in the elections of April 1948, 'a communist victory in Italy, according to the best minds I can contact, will be followed by Communist penetration of the whole of Western Europe.'[21] Believing this dire prediction, MacBride urged the Archbishop of Armagh, John D'Alton and the Archbishop of Dublin, John Charles McQuaid to publicly appeal for funds. Contributions came from religious organisations like the Knights of Saint Columbanus, the Ancient Order of Hibernians, and the Legion of Mary as well as wealthy Catholic individuals – MacBride himself sent a personal contribution. Collections were taken at churches, shops, and factories throughout Ireland. As the *Irish Times* editorialised on 14 April,

> all true democrats must hope for a Communist defeat for the sake not alone of Italy, but all of Europe. Ireland, by virtue of her historic attachment to the Holy See, has a particular interest in the outcome, in which the position of the Vatican is immediately involved.

48.5 percent of the vote went to the Christian Democrats, giving them over half the seats in the Chamber of Deputies. The win was an immediate success for MacBride, but as Dermot Keogh points out, the victory was ultimately dangerous for the Irish government as it 'brought the Catholic Church into the domain of political decision making' in Ireland.[22]

Clann na Poblachta was similar to European Christian Democracy in their vigilance about the defence of Catholic doctrine and institutions and their belief in an integrated Europe. MacBride was a 'Europeanist' before the concept existed.[23] He was a strong supporter of the embryonic European economic, political, and military integration and he wanted Ireland to participate. However, there were notable differences between

Clann na Poblachta and the continental Christian Democrats. On the continent, cooperation with other Christian denominations was seen as the way forward. In Germany, Catholics abandoned the Centre Party and gave support to the Christian Democratic Union. Yet, in Ireland, which possessed a homogenous religious environment where the 'special position' of the Roman Catholic Church was enshrined in the Irish Constitution, 'all sorts of forces were at work to make Ireland a more totally Catholic state than it had yet become.'[24] Archbishop McQuaid wielded immense religious, political, and social power and this power was used to build up an intensely conservative Catholic-dominated state in which dissention of any sort was not welcome. The inter-party government was overtly Catholic and one of the first actions the government took was to send a message to Pope Pius XII authored by the Taoiseach affirming

> on the occasion of our assumption of office and of the first Cabinet meeting, my colleagues and myself desire to repose at the feet of your Holiness the assurance of our filial loyalty and of our devotion to your August person, as well as our firm resolve to be guided in all our work by the teaching of Christ, and to strive for the attainment of a social order in Ireland based on Christian principles.[25]

MacBride himself wrote to McQuaid on the day of his election to the Dáil on 30 October 1947, stating that 'I hasten, as my first act, to pay my humble respects to Your Grace and place myself at Your Grace's disposal,' and would 'always welcome any advice which Your Grace may be good enough to give me and shall be at Your Grace's disposal should there be any matters upon which Your Grace feels that I could be of any assistance.'[26] McQuaid replied that 'I shall not fail to take advantage of your generous suggestion that you are at my disposal for any matters in which you could assist,' but promised to do so only if 'the good of the faith was in question.'[27] After the 1948 election, MacBride again promised that he would as, 'a Catholic, a public representative and the leader of a party' welcome 'any advice or views' which McQuaid might express 'officially or informally.'[28] The correspondence provides an excellent example of the deference the inter-party government demonstrated to the Catholic hierarchy. The two letters that MacBride wrote to the Archbishop were handwritten on Roebuck House stationery, not Department of External Affairs or Clann na Poblachta letterhead; presumably MacBride only intended for McQuaid to see the letters, as there are no other copies on file except in McQuaid's papers. John Bowman pointed this out in his *Irish Times* article of 13 November 1999, questioning the wisdom of giving such 'blank cheques' to the hierarchy.[29] Bowman felt that MacBride's supporters could excuse the initial letter, as MacBride was politically inexperienced, but his repetition in 1948 is inexcusable. As MacBride wrote in a tone 'wholly inappropriate for a leader with Clann na Poblachta's roots, policies, and membership,' Bowman concludes the article by wondering if he wasn't a bit of a hypocrite.[30] J.T. Morahan, a Clann candidate in North Tipperary stated at a public meeting in Ballinrobe that the Clann 'were Christians and Catholics before they were Irishmen... The better Catholics they were the better Irishmen they were.'[31]

Catholics in other parts of Europe began leaning toward the socialist tradition; Austria's Catholic Party entered a coalition with socialists as did Christian Democrats in the Netherlands and France, whereas Clann na Poblachta was careful not to be equated with politics that were too left wing, fearing any suspicion that they would sympathise with communism, despite the lack of any socialist or communist movement in Ireland. Experiences of world war had made Ireland's development in relation to Christian Democracy different from that of the rest of Europe.[32] The continent had been bombed, fought over, and occupied by enemies, which led to barriers and established patterns being broken down. Resistance movements brought diverse people together and encouraged cooperation. In neutral countries that did not have these experiences, including Portugal, Spain, and Switzerland as well as Ireland, the post-war passion for cooperation that influenced Catholics in other parts of Europe seems to have been missing or subdued. As J.H. Whyte points out, rather than trying to find common ground with other traditions, post-war Irish Catholics were emphasising their distinctive customs, making Irish Catholicism appear comparatively more right wing.[33]

Regarding the early steps toward European integration, MacBride and the Clann's position could be construed as 'radical' within Ireland simply because such ideas were not in keeping with de Valera's concept of neutrality or Fine Gael's desire to remain tied to the British Commonwealth. MacBride himself had gained a reputation as a radical, or at least a liberal, which probably originated from his concern with civil rights evolving from his legal practice. However, such a reputation is very hard to sustain in light of MacBride's deference to the Church at the start of the inter-party government, the decision to go into government with

Fine Gael, and the disastrous outcome of the Mother and Child controversy.

Radical or not, the genesis of Clann na Poblachta was notable because it was the first broadly-based political party in Ireland not to come out of Treaty politics, taking the republicans to task for preventing political development. The initial statement of the founding members demonstrates this attitude:

> For many years a large section of republican opinion has felt that republicans should take an active part in the political life of the Nation. It was felt that it would be possible to work for the achievement of republican ideals by purely political means. It was felt that the cycles of repression and violence that marked the history of the last quarter of a century could provide no solution and could weaken the national effort. Various causes combined to prevent political development. Not least of these was the low standard of political morality set by those who in the name of republicanism secured office. The continual inroads on elementary personal rights (quite apart from Emergency legislation) also rendered it difficult to instil in republicans confidence in political action... The Nation is being weakened by the forced emigration of its youth. A small section has been enabled to accumulate enormous wealth while unemployment and low wages, coupled with an increased cost of living, are the lot of the workers... It has been apparent that if these evils, and the system responsible for them, are to be ended there must arise a strong political party that will set up an ideal before the nation and a new standard of political morality in public life.[34]

The reference to a 'new standard of political morality in public life,' alluded to recent Fianna Fáil scandals, notably the suspect sale of Locke's Distillery which received considerable press attention during the 1947 by-elections. MacBride's thoughts were that 'political life in this country had got into a rut and Clann na Poblachta had been founded to stem the decadence and set a clean ideal for the nation.'[35] An early election manifesto for MacBride declared

> Seán MacBride is fighting your battles for a right to live in reasonable comfort in your own country; for a lower cost of living; for food subsidies and price controls; for increased old age pensions; for free secondary education for your children; for decent housing; for proper

social services; for municipally owned transport; for a Christian state in reality, not merely in name.[36]

The Clann also represented the first major attempt since 1932 to create something more republican and more concerned with social welfare than anything offered by Fianna Fáil at that time; here was a challenge to Fianna Fáil on their own territory. The similarities between early Fianna Fáil and Clann na Poblachta are ironically demonstrated by Fianna Fáil Minister for Local Government Seán MacEntee's labelling of Clann na Poblachta as communists, which is exactly the response Fianna Fáil once elicited from their opponents in the 1920s and 1930s. During the 1932 general election, Cumann na Gael's Ernest Blythe, Desmond FitzGerald, and William Cosgrave alluded to communist doctrine in Fianna Fáil; Blythe stating that Fianna Fáil was full of people 'infected by Communist propaganda.'[37] A 1932 newspaper advertisement read 'How will you vote tomorrow? The gunmen are voting for Fianna Fáil. The Communists are voting for Fianna Fáil.'[38] As Fianna Fáil candidate Michael O'Clery stated in the *Irish Times*, the 1932 election 'was going to be fought, not on vague treaties or personalities, but on the policies of the parties,'[39] a sentiment that MacBride echoes in both the 1947 by-election and the 1948 general election. In addition, the Fianna Fáil government of 1932, having never been in power, could criticise the present long-standing government; Clann na Poblachta would later have a similar privilege.

An obvious divergence existed within the party, with one side favouring nationalist-political issues and the other emphasising socio-economic goals; the republican aspect competing with the social programme for prominence within the party. In a 1946 handbill, the Clann's first pledge was 'to reintegrate the whole of Ireland as a Republic' but went on to state that, though this was the ultimate objective, it was also the intention that Clann 'should take an active and independent part in the political life of the Nation.' The most urgent problem was 'political decadence' and it was necessary to address social security, emigration via a scheme of national planning, improving rural life, cultural aims including preserving the language, then plans for ending partition. As T. Desmond Williams stated, 'politics at any time is merely one aspect of a people's life.'[40] Everyday struggles were of more consequence; a vague concept of 'republic' may not be the first priority of someone with relatives in an underfunded tuberculosis sanatorium. In a speech at Mansion House, MacBride declared that 'if we get a Republic in name, it would mean nothing unless it ensured economic and social freedom for all the people of the country.'[41] Clann na Poblachta also promised to remove taxes on beer, tobacco, cinema seats, and greyhound racing, which was sure to be popular with most of the electorate.

Were such statements merely populist rhetoric designed to win votes? How committed was MacBride to social welfare issues in general? Peadar O'Donnell commented that he was clever, 'but on political matters he was almost an amateur and had no real contact with life or living problems.'[42] Clearly if the party hoped to succeed, the day-to-day concerns of the voting public had to be addressed: in a letter to the *Irish Times* on 27 January, MacBride wrote that although the republic was the ultimate aim, 'problems in the economic and social spheres... are of paramount importance and... require immediate attention.' He knew he could not make a 'politics, not personality' plea without addressing socio-economic issues. MacBride also recognised the localist character of Irish politics. Though as Phyllis Browne observed, 'MacBride was really more of a diplomat than a politician,'[43] he knew it would be necessary to please his constituency and work within the broker/client relationship of Irish politics if only to insure re-election.[44]

For a party so linked to republicanism, Clann na Poblachta did show a genuine and vigorous concern for domestic issues. MacBride's own speeches focused to a large degree on the general economic situation and his final speech before the by-election concerned moving Ireland away from British sterling. Most early speeches concentrated on domestic reform; especially halting emigration and improving the situation of Irish workers. As MacBride said, 'The Christian State must be based on the family unit; but to-day the family is being broken up by forced emigration.'[45] He believed that Ireland's problem was a fall of production caused by the enforced emigration of Irish workers to England because of higher wage rates in that country. The plan to limit emigration was to provide jobs by developing Ireland's natural resources, particularly afforestation and hydro-electricity, as well as housing and 'other constructional works of national or social importance,' faintly echoing the American New Deal. MacBride would later ask McQuaid's opinion regarding a government ban on the emigration of women under the age of 21.[46]

The Clann supported the Bishop of Clonfert's scheme for a national health insurance closely following Catholic teaching, a proposal that Seán MacEntee had rejected as too costly. MacBride cited the example of New Zealand and Sweden as models for successful social insurance schemes. He believed that the state should take responsibility for the employment of those who were unemployed and hoped to eliminate 'the wasteful and harmful system, whereby those who are unable to secure employment have to exist on doles and public charity, while essential work remains undone.'

This essential work would help provide the funds necessary to implement his party's proposed programme. MacBride pledged to make Ireland self-supporting; to electrify rail transport, create a deep-sea fishing fleet, provide state forests, and adequate housing with a kitchen and bathroom in each dwelling. As well as developing the country's resources, national planning would provide the funding for the proposed economic policies. MacBride suggested the establishment of a National Monetary Authority to 'equate currency and credit to the economic needs of full employment and full production' and to provide 'credits free of interest for full employment and national development of industry and agriculture.' 'Our Party will support a policy of economic development of our natural resources and full employment to return to full production.'[47] He wanted to use the money invested in British banks and securities to develop forestry and education.[48] Forestry was worthwhile because land was available, it would provide employment, and the product could be used for timber, fuel, paper, and alcohol. As MacBride pointed out in a meeting in Tuam, Ireland possessed 2 million acres of wasteland that could be utilised.[49] He claimed that Ireland had the best tree-growing climate in Europe, yet planted fewer trees than any other European country, preferring to use the land for agriculture, which provided a more immediate return on the investment.

Culturally, the Clann wanted to get rid of the 'alien, artificial and unchristian concepts of life,' to establish a national theatre and film industry, to extend the Irish-speaking Gaeltacht, and create a council to help spread knowledge of music and the arts. Another council would be set up to coordinate all branches of education, to build additional schools and modernise the existing ones. Such decentralisation, 'instead of concentrating vast armies of civil servants in Dublin,' would secure the development of civic responsibility as well as reduce inefficiency and bureaucracy. Admission to universities would not only be regulated by aptitude, but also by the needs of the country in different professions – though this part of the programme would only be successful if emigration rates among graduates declined considerably, and would be nearly impossible to implement in a free society. An *Irish Independent* editorial of 2 February 1948 praised the Council of Education idea and agreed with raising the leaving age, but nothing was mentioned regarding university admission, and surprisingly educators from the National University or Trinity College Dublin did not respond to the proposal.

Clann na Poblachta also claimed to be dedicated to the special concerns of women, a claim which amounted to keeping prices of consumer goods and food down and limiting the emigration of women to Britain. One of the Clann's initial pamphlets 'You and the Future' focused on social insurance, price controls, and improving the economy. Problems like inadequate medical care and a high cost of living probably had more immediate resonance with voters. As Browne noted, 'There were many of my age with a general radical outlook who were weary of the gross incompetence of a succession of civil war generation politicians.'[50]

The division within the Irish Labour Party helped Clann na Poblachta. Labour had suffered a bitter split between leader Jim Larkin and General Secretary of the Transport Union William O'Brien. O'Brien, claiming that the Labour Party had been infiltrated by communists, formed the National Labour Party. J.J. Lee's assessment that the division had more to do with personality conflicts between Larkin and O'Brien than politics, that O'Brien was 'the type of man, only too common in Ireland, who prefers to wreck a movement rather than lose control of it'[51] was more likely than any alleged communist influence. Labour Party members who did not want to involve themselves in such political minefields but desired, like Noël Browne, to ally with a party concerned with social welfare, found an outlet in Clann na Poblachta.

Clann's policies sounded good on paper and on the platform, but the price tag seemed very steep. If the plan was to lower taxes, how could all of these social welfare programmes be funded? Minister for Finance Frank Aiken commented that the proposed social insurance scheme, modelled on Sweden and New Zealand, would have likely required an income tax increase, as taxation per head in Sweden was £22 and New Zealand £54 compared to Ireland's £20.[52] Aiken criticised the Clann's unemployment insurance scheme, wryly observing that 'the weekly stamp necessary to pay benefits on this scale would be so heavy on the men at work that there would be a definite and positive inducement for them to get into the ranks of the unemployed.'[53] However, if income taxes were reduced, money could come from several alternative sources; an Excess Profits Tax and a proposed tourist tax collected either on arrival into the country or added to hotel bills. Yet these revenues would not cover all that Clann had planned. As the 11 November editorial in the *Irish Independent* posited, 'We seem in many directions to allow our ideas to outstrip our needs, and to propose plans more suited to an imperial standard than to the strictly-limited resources of the people.'

Through generally praising the party, an *Irish Times* editorial of 1 November 1947 stated that Clann na Poblachta's 'economic programme scarcely deserves to be taken seriously,' and *The Economist* predicted after the by-elections that 'a Coalition Government of the Republican Party and Labour now becomes a real possibility. Such a combination would be less likely to follow a rational trade and economic policy than Fianna Fáil.'[54] Perhaps MacBride, not an economist, was naïve about how a free market economy functioned and saw the evils of communism only in terms of religion, not economics. It is very likely that he did not have time to properly work out his policies or the foresight to see their consequences and may have realised this later on. In an RTÉ radio interview with John Bowman in 1980, MacBride posited that 'we lost in the last ten days of the election campaign... Our economic policies frightened the people... I could feel the people being scared that last ten days.'[55]

The Clann and the IRA

Lyons sums up the party philosophy as an 'apparent combination of republican orthodoxy with social radicalism.'[56] The orthodoxy was not always comfortably compatible with the radicalism. Though MacBride's and Clann na Poblachta's commitment to social welfare issues was sincere, the IRA element continued to dominate the party.' The basis of the party, after all, was the committees formed to help republican prisoners and the party organisation retained similarities to the IRA structure. For example, the national executive and standing committees of the Clann had considerable power over candidate selection which, in other Irish parties at the time, was the duty of the constituency convention of a party; the Clann's executive could determine how many candidates a constituency convention could nominate as well as imposing additional candidates over the heads of the constituency convention. The standing committee could also refuse to ratify the nomination of a particular candidate. Such checks and balances show a restraint similar to the workings of paramilitary organisations, not political parties.[57] Cruise O'Brien maintains that MacBride's connection with the IRA had not been fully severed. MacDermott points out that over time, MacBride fell out with nearly every senior member of Clann na Poblachta - Noel Hartnett, Noël Browne, Jack McQuillan, and Peadar Cowan - whose immediate ancestry did not lie with the IRA.[58] Perhaps this is because MacBride was used to taking command of a revolutionary organisation, not constitutional politics. Cruise O'Brien recalls that MacBride was pleasant to work for 'except that he expected you to be available at all hours, whenever required, like a member of a revolutionary organisation... There were always distant semi-revolutionary overtones when he was around: a rather somnambulistic obeisance to the Pearsean call.'[59]

MacBride's attitude may have been akin to the leader of a revolutionary movement, yet he did not want the Clann to be seen as another IRA party rather than one for social change, a 'party of protest' rather than a 'party of government.'[60] Was he taking care to emphasise social welfare to distract from the Clann's IRA background? The choice of Noël Browne as cabinet minister seems to bear this theory out; Browne was 32, a young age for a government minister, had no IRA connections or controversial political past, and was obviously committed to social welfare, particularly the eradication of tuberculosis. Browne's position in the cabinet would demonstrate that the Clann was sincere in breaking away from the past and was not merely a party of IRA dissidents.

Yet social issues were tied to the Clann's foreign policy concerns. MacBride pointed out that 'one of the realities that has to be faced is that until we set up social services and an economic system that are at least as good as those offered to the people of the Six Counties by the British Labour government, no serious advance can be made towards the ending of partition.'[61] Perhaps MacBride was trying to persuade extreme republicans that a focus on improving social welfare would be useful in achieving the ultimate goal of a united Ireland.

Despite MacBride's stance that economic and social problems required immediate attention, solving the problem of partition and proclaiming Ireland's independence from Britain superseded issues of social welfare for many party members. Such a dichotomy could eventually prove harmful to Clann na Poblachta, but in 1947 the prospect of defeating Fianna Fáil provided the necessary cohesiveness between the two groups.

The By-elections of 1947

Three vacant Dáil seats in Dublin, Tipperary, and Waterford became available in October 1947, giving Clann na Poblachta its first campaigning opportunity. In that same month, the cabinet approved an Electoral Amendment Bill that increased the number of three-member constituencies from 15 to 22, as the *Irish Independent* wrote, loading 'the electoral dice in favour of the big party. Moreover, there seems to be no good reason, in geography, population, or convenience, for some of the groupings now proposed.'[62] Under proportional systems with the single transferable vote, large constituencies tend to favour smaller parties; yet in three-member constituencies, the largest party typically wins two of the three seats leaving the third to be fought over by the smaller parties. Thus Fianna Fáil's solution was to break up the number of large constituencies to ensure a Dáil majority. The Dáil grew from 138 to 147 members despite a fall in population. Here was a sign that Fianna Fáil was worried about the increasing popularity of Clann na Poblachta.

Clann na Poblachta fought both the 1947 by-elections and the 1948 general election on the basis of social welfare proposals first and a militant republican stance second, roughly adopting the programme of early Fianna Fáil as its own. But unlike Fianna Fáil in the 1930s, the Clann desired to dispense with the political and social divisions defined by treaty politics, end any residual bitterness of the Civil War and the 1930s, and begin a new type of political discourse. Thus policy differences rather than personality debates played an enormous role in the 1947 and 1948 elections; '"Home front" policies have provided the main issues for the political orators during the past few weeks. The cost of living has loomed largely with agriculture and housing supplying equal good material for political discussion and argument.'[63] MacBride tried to keep to the issues, limiting broad nationalist rhetoric. As MacBride later told MacDermott, 'I had campaigned very strongly on the basis that people should be appointed in government irrespective of their past political affiliations, and that had a progressive political viewpoint, and were capable of trying to change conditions in the country.'[64] MacBride, in a speech at Roscrea on 26 October 1947 suggested 'that they [government ministers] were subject to the influence of their political and personal friends in the granting of licences involving vast sums of money to trading concerns.'[65] Roddy Connolly, the son of James Connolly, wrote in the *Irish Times* that Clann na Poblachta 'is looked upon by the people as a battering ram to break the power and privilege of the present government and that combined with Labour and Clann na Talmhan would contribute largely to the overthrow of Fianna Fáil.'[66]

During the by-election campaigns, the Clann went on the offensive, baiting the government, and attempting to grab attention and get public support. MacBride's letters most often appeared on the pages of *Irish Times*, a paper supportive of his campaign or at least antagonistic to Fianna Fáil and the *Irish Press*, which was seen as an unapologetically pro-Fianna Fáil paper while the *Irish Independent* was partially, but not overtly, favourable to Fine Gael.[67] MacBride and Seán MacEntee engaged in a letter-writing duel; as the radio was government-controlled and television had yet to become widespread, letters to newspapers were the main method by which political arguments could take place and spread to a wider audience.[68] During the general election campaign, MacBride suggested that, due to the inclement weather which prevented the electorate from attending open meetings, radio time be given to political parties. The Secretary to the Taoiseach Maurice Moynihan replied that 'it is not considered desirable to depart from the long standing rule that the national broadcasting service should not be used for the purpose of political party controversy.'[69] MacEntee referred to MacBride half-heartedly supporting the Germans during World War II 'sitting on the fence waiting to see what side would triumph in the end,' and accused MacBride of 'a singular lack of judgment, foresight and political sagacity... He has always been among those who have chosen to exploit the difficulties which confronted the nation in order to advance their own political views,' and later stated that 'I am doing my utmost to secure the defeat of Mr. MacBride and his fellow-candidates.'[70] In his reply, MacBride facetiously began, 'Mr. MacEntee is a Minister of State. He therefore has plenty of leisure at his disposal,' and is 'afraid to face the actual issues involved in the present by-elections,' instead resorting to 'invectives and personal abuse... Mr. MacEntee's accusations and innuendoes in so far as they conflict with my views as stated in this letter, are as inconsistent with each other as they are untrue.'[71] The 'Letters to the Editor' served as a venue for political debate; replies to letters usually appeared a day or two after the original. In his letters, MacBride tried to dispense with 'flag-waving "national records" and personalities,' writing that 'what is needed is a policy based on realities. Instead of recriminations and self-glorification based on past events, the need is vision and planning for the future.'[72]

The by-elections took place on 29 October. Two of the three candidates including MacBride, running in Dublin, were successful. Both Tipperary and Waterford were considered Fianna Fáil strongholds. Fianna Fáil did manage to hold on to Waterford, which was expected. The larger rallies were disappointing in size and 'other meetings generally were small and little enthusiasm was evidenced.'[73] Before the Tipperary election, the *Irish Independent* commented that the 'general impression throughout the country is that [Clann candidate Patrick Kinnane] will upset the ordinary gauge of the Tipperary election by taking votes from each of the other four parties.'[74] MacBride and Kinnane's main support came from those affected by economic depression rather than those with a strong republican agenda; Kinnane's election 'showed very clearly the trend of feeling in the country. It showed that the people of Tipperary only wanted a lead to show their desire to get back to the old track again.'[75] The *Irish Times* noted that 'this totally illogical development is a sign of the times.'[76] An *Irish Independent* editorial of 1 November theorised,

> we venture to think that a high proportion of those who voted for Clann na Poblachta were former supporters of Fianna Fáil who have been disillusioned. Whatever may be the people's views of the policy of the new party, it has certainly aroused the interest of many young citizens in public affairs at a time when apathy was a disturbing feature of political affairs.

After the election results were announced, MacBride declared that he was pleased to be the 'first spokesman of a new movement in Ireland.'[77] The success in the by-elections led to an atmosphere of optimism and more prominent people willing to join, for example Kathleen Clarke, wife of 1916 martyr Thomas Clarke, Joseph Brennan, a key civil servant in the early years of the state, and ex-IRA activist Dr. Patrick McCartan. The general reaction to the by-elections in London was chiefly about how it would affect the ongoing Anglo-Irish trade talks.[78]

MacBride entered the Dáil on 5 November 1947. The first issues he addressed were the desirability of an inquiry regarding the proposed sale of Locke's Distillery[79] and the necessity to reduce cost of living, thus preventing emigration by making it more cost-effective to live in Ireland:

> In other words, in Britain at all times the increase in wages and salaries was twice the increase in the cost of living... The fundamental cause of emigration here is that we allowed a position to develop whereby the wage earners, the small farmers, the agricultural labourers, were unable to earn an economic living in this country, whereas they were able to go across to England to earn an economic living there which enabled them to send money home. Therefore, if we really want to stop emigration, we must reduce the cost of living to at least the level which prevails in the neighbouring island.[80]

In the Dáil, MacBride proved to be well-prepared and spoke more about domestic issues than foreign policy; from 5 November 1947 until 11 December when the Dáil was dissolved, he did not mention partition or the republic at all. The topics he addressed included fishing rights, sanatoriums, amnesty for political prisoners, taxation, emigration, and decreasing the cost of living.

The General Election of 1948

Though an election was not necessary until May 1949, de Valera had promised to call an early general election if Fianna Fáil candidates were not successful in the by-elections, a move that the 29 October *Irish Times* editorial called 'petulant'. He kept his promise and called a general election for February 1948 in the hope of securing power and curbing the Clann's development by embroiling them in a nationwide contest before they were ready. The ploy was clever; Clann na Poblachta had no breathing space and did not have the time to build up and strengthen their organisation or fine-tune their policies. De Valera's move denied Clann na Poblachta the time necessary to organise itself properly. At the time of the election, the party had no established structure and skeletal organisational systems in many parts of the country.

As MacBride said during the by-election campaign, he would not be in a position to alter government policy or bring about a change of government if elected. But the general election now offered the chance of government removal and formation. Campaigning began in late November and one advantage the party did have was excellent public relations and advertising, largely due to the efforts of Noel Hartnett. All competing parties ran small advertisements in the newspapers. Fine Gael highlighted specific candidates like Liam Cosgrave and Richard Mulcahy. Fianna Fáil's 'information series' were packed with small print expounding on election issues and using the tagline 'These are Facts.' Fianna Fáil was also the only party not to ask for funds. Clann na Poblachta's ads were succinct; focusing on their platform, their diverse membership and, notably, answering their critics:

> We serve no duce, no marshal, no fuehrer, no dictator, no taoiseach… but Ireland. If Clann na Poblachta has converted Blueshirts – is it to be called Fascist? If it has converted Leftists, is it to be called Communist? If it has converted De Valerites, is it to be called Fianna Fáil? That would be the last straw.[81]

Clann na Poblachta produced an eight-minute film *Our Country*, addressing rural depopulation, poverty, urban deprivation, emigration, shortages, and unemployment. As cameraman Brendan Stafford remembered, the footage was genuine; 'If we showed bare-footed newsboys, there were bare-footed newsboys – we didn't ask them to take their shoes off.'[82] However, MacDermott spoke to one of the actors, Liam Ó Laoghaire, who pointed out that very few people went barefoot in Dublin in December and that a young man was given sixpence to remove his shoes. However, Ó Laoghaire also said that the shortages and depictions of the slums were indeed accurate.[83] Browne was interviewed regarding tuberculosis. MacBride was also interviewed, declaring, 'it's your country' and only the voters themselves could change the situation, presumably by changing the government. Noel Hartnett acted as narrator, commenting, 'Communism will not solve these problems. State control will not solve these problems. Only you, the people, can solve them.' The film never mentioned 'Clann na Poblachta' at all, but the point had been made. Browne found it 'an enlightened effort in the political education of an electorate whose politics were of the crudest emotive civil war tribal variety.'[84]

MacBride attempted to concentrate on politics, asking voters in Clare (de Valera's constituency) to 'vote for a policy rather than a personality.' According to Inglis, MacBride 'spoke... of matters which were hardly calculated to grip the audience; the repatriation of Ireland's external assets was one theme, reforestation another.'[85] MacBride was attempting to break the 'cult of personality' and so tried to keep his focus on prosaic concerns, 'little has been heard of their [republican] policy on the hustings.'[86] MacBride was not a dynamic speaker; he disliked shows of spontaneous enthusiasm and preferred to speak seriously about relevant issues. A major memory of the campaign for Liam and Colm Ó Laoghaire was MacBride solemnly lecturing some dishevelled slum youngsters about 'the incompatibility of sterling' with Irish economic independence.[87] At the final speech on the eve of the general election, there was excitement, but no wild cheering; yet the *Irish Times* concluded that 'the crowds were thinking, instead of bursting into enthusiasm for a single individual.'[88] Such a lack of showmanship may have been MacBride wanting to avoid a 'cult of personality' by attempting to focus on issues.

This strategy may have proven difficult because the party platforms were not very diverse. There was no tangible difference between Fine Gael and Fianna Fáil; the parties agreed on the methods for solving domestic issues such as improving agriculture, industry, education, housing, and healthcare, increasing the standard of living, and lowering taxes. Labour and Clann na Poblachta had similar social welfare programmes; the difference lay in Labour's emphasis on the workers and trade unions and Clann's more republican stance. During the election,

Labour seemed to accept that it would not gain a majority and looked to support or coalesce with a suitable party. In such a political climate, candidates must find some way to make themselves or their party stand out. With a lack of real distinction between the competing parties, the focus shifts to symbolic rather than substantive issues. Thus, the questions of Ireland's connection with Britain and which party were the true republicans were dealt with. However, repeal of the External Relations Act was not a major theme in the election campaign.

MacBride and Clann na Poblachta continued avoiding relying on past glory, pointing out the dangers of doing so; 'Political issues have for the last quarter of a century been judged on the basis of past affiliations rather than on their merits. Likewise, public life has largely been the monopoly of persons whose only qualifications were derived from their associations with events that occurred 20 or 30 years ago.'[89] In a speech during the 1948 election, Browne stated that 'we are sick and tired of hearing about 1916 and 1922 and of the futile wrangling about the past. There are present social and economic evils which need resolution.'[90] Browne's sentiment certainly could be interpreted as radical; it was nearly impossible in the environment of Irish politics to escape from the rhetoric of 1916/1922 especially while part of a party called the 'family of the republic.' Yet, the heckling cry of 'Where were you in 1916 and 1921?' was replaced by 'Where will you be tomorrow?' Of course, such sentiments were easier for MacBride to articulate, as his republican lineage was firmly established.

The election focused on the shortcomings of Fianna Fáil and the Clann had the advantage of being able to chide Fianna Fáil for not carrying their policies out.[91] As MacBride stated in a speech in Tralee,

> the Fianna Fáil party have been 15 years in office. They claim that they have done everything that could be done. They claim there is no remedy for emigration, poverty, squalor. They are satisfied with existing conditions. As that is their attitude then let them stand out of the way and let the people with faith in the future take over.[92]

Government corruption, stagnancy, and failure to achieve proposed goals in both the domestic and foreign spheres provided Clann na Poblachta with election material. As the British Representative to Ireland, John Maffey, later Lord Rugby reported, support for Clann na Poblachta originated from 'a strong gesture of disgust with the de Valera Government for the usual economic grievances of failing to satisfy popular demand to keep prices down.'[93] Moreover, Fianna Fáil did not take the opportunity to seriously rebut the Clann's economic policies, nor did the other parties.

Public perceptions of MacBride himself varied. *The Observer* cynically commented before the election, 'MacBride has caught hold of the popular imagination... His following is composed of extreme chauvinists or incorrigible Celts, disgruntled IRA, a few ex-communists, and some political adventurers.'[94] Brian Inglis kept a diary of Clann na Poblachta progress during the election for the *Irish Times*. To Inglis, Seán MacBride seemed refined and modest, yet 'not impressive on the platform. His face, skull-like in its contours, split rather than relaxed by his rare smile, was a little intimidating, and the foreign inflection was not as attractive on the hustings as it could be in conversation... MacBride did not have the personality needed to create a revolution in voting habits.'[95]

However most observers felt differently; 'Unfortunately for his party, it has not been organised sufficiently long to enable it to select or attract many candidates who have either Mr. MacBride's popular personality or background.'[96] MacBride's speeches and rallies were well attended, including the largest public meeting in Ballina for years on 11 January, complete with torchlight processions and bonfires.[97] At the high point of the campaigning, MacBride was speaking at up to four meetings a day in inclement weather which strained his voice. Both the *Irish Times* and the *Irish Independent* refer to 'huge gatherings' where MacBride received an 'attentive hearing.' The *Irish Independent* estimated that MacBride had attended 100 meetings over 3,000 miles and 'the appearance of his party created an interest not apparent since 1932.'[98] At one rally in Cork,

a tumultuous welcome awaited Mr. MacBride when he arrived at Cork from Cobh. He was met at the entrance to the city by a cheering crowd of several thousand people who mobbed his car. He was later driven to the scene of the meeting – said to be the biggest election meeting ever seen in the city.[99]

John A. Murphy writes that the exotic element of MacBride's personality provided 'an additional attraction in an Irish political chief'[100] and Ronan Fanning credits MacBride with personifying 'the impulse for change in Irish politics and he had the advantage, more unusual in politics than is commonly realised, of knowing what he *wanted* to do.'[101]

The Irish papers continued to receive 'Letters to the Editor' from both MacBride and MacEntee. In a speech at Kilrush on 15 January, MacBride claimed that MacEntee was engaged in 'a campaign of lying and personal vilification.' MacEntee, in a letter to the *Irish Times* on 16 January once again labelled Clann na Poblachta as communist, citing MacBride's organisation of Saor Éire in 1931, a worker's movement within the IRA. An *Irish Times* editorial of 17 January called MacEntee a 'political Don Quixote, tilting gaily at Communist windmills and smelling Bolsheviks behind every bush,' and further stated that 'many voters who are sick of the ancient feuds between the older parties will be tempted to give the "new man" [MacBride] a chance.'

Clann na Poblachta nominated 93 candidates, which vastly overstretched their time and resources. Though MacBride's speeches were cautious and restrained, some of his followers boasted of repeating the 1918 Sinn Fein landslide. MacBride himself mused that the party could gain an overall majority.[102] Ultimately, Clann na Poblachta won ten seats; 13.2 percent of the national vote. This number did not meet expectations but a young political party winning ten seats in its first general election in a conservative Irish political climate could be seen as very promising.[103] If not for the previously mentioned Electoral Amendment Act, Clann na Poblachta would have won 19 seats based on the proportion of votes the party acquired. Over-ambition made the 1948 election feel like a failure, yet 13.2 percent was, after all, the highest ever won by minor party in their first general election, and in the long-term, Clann na Poblachta was able to cause a break in the conventional pattern of the treaty-based pattern of voting. Their numbers provided enough presence to help form the Dáil's first inter-party government, dominated by Fine Gael and united mainly to keep Fianna Fáil from returning to power.

Formation of the Inter-party Government

As a result of the election, Fianna Fáil lost their overall majority but remained the largest single party in the Dáil. De Valera would not enter a coalition as a rule, but he believed he would have the support of National Labour and Dáil Independents. Instead, at the impetus of Fine Gael leader Richard Mulcahy, the opposition parties agreed to form a coalition government. In an *Irish Times* interview with Michael McInerny in 1979, MacBride recalled, 'I think I was the first to enunciate policy. I was aware at the time that this was awaited anxiously by Fine Gael and others.' [104] The four points MacBride put forth were more public investment in Irish resources, increased forestry planning, release of Hospital Trust Funds to build hospitals and sanatoria, and increases in social welfare benefits. 'There was a sigh of relief because I had not mentioned the External

Relations Act or the political prisoners, although I had campaigned on those issues in the election. Everybody around the table agreed to the points I had proposed.' MacBride did not raise those issues because 'while I had campaigned on those issues the others had not, and I felt it would be putting an impossible strain on them to ask them to agree to things for which they had not campaigned.'

1948 was one of the most unusual elections since 1932-1933 not only because it ushered in the first inter-party government, but it also led to the electoral trend of Fianna Fáil versus the rest. Clann na Poblachta had campaigned with the slogan 'Put Them Out' and now they had their chance, even if it meant joining a Fine Gael-led government, proving Ronan Fanning's assertion that coalition governments in Ireland 'have more to do with taste, temperament, and environment than with party labels.'[105] The question of whether to enter a coalition proved to be divisive and may have been the beginning of end for the party, as many within Clann na Poblachta could not stomach the party serving in a pro-Treaty, pro-Commonwealth Fine Gael government. The reasons for entering the inter-party government may have been more pragmatic than just the desire to oust Fianna Fáil; the Clann was largely financed through loans and may have been unable to fight another election if de Valera returned to power and called another election right away.

MacBride could not agree to Mulcahy becoming Taoiseach, as he had been commander of the Free State forces during the Civil War. Mulcahy offered to stand down, a gesture MacBride admitted was 'magnanimous,' and John Costello, who had not been involved in the Civil War, was chosen to be Taoiseach. The fact that Mulcahy and MacBride could serve in the same government after being on opposite sides in a bloody, contentious, and recent Civil War showed that tensions had abated and that the desire to stop Fianna Fáil from forming another government was quite fervent. The lack of strong ideological differences among the parties also made it easier to form a coalition.

As the first inter-party Taoiseach, Costello found himself in a bind. As Ernest Blythe put it, 'possibly you have been elected to something more like a bed of thorns than a bed of roses.'[106] He was not the party leader, his party did not have a Dáil majority, and due to the compromise situation of coalition, he was only able to make one senior governmental appointment. MacBride managed to secure two ministries for Clann na Poblachta, External Affairs for himself and Health for Noël Browne. Due to the wide range of interests MacBride had demonstrated as TD, it is not implausible that he could have been given Finance or Lands. Yet he was content with External Affairs because the Ministry would provide him with a way to further Clann na Poblachta's aims and would keep the party (and himself) in the public eye. The cabinet also consisted of Labour leader William Norton as Tánaiste, Clann na Talmhan leader Joseph Blowick as Minister for Lands, Independent James Dillon as Minister for Agriculture, and Mulcahy as Minister for Education, completing what Dermot Keogh called a 'cabinet of talent, temperament and torpor.'[107] Despite being from different parties, the cabinet members all had close ties; MacBride and Costello moved in the same legal circles and MacBride and Dillon had gone to school together.

In his first radio speech as Taoiseach, Costello stated that his government believed the main challenges were of a socio-economic nature rather than a political-constitutional one, affirming that the new government was 'primarily concerned with the problems of making ends meet... these economic considerations must take priority over all political and constitutional matters'[108] but did claim 'as a priority' the reunification of the island. As party leader, MacBride continued to pontificate on social welfare issues in the Dáil, yet it would be in foreign policy that his influence would be most clearly seen.

2

The Harp Without the Crown: Ireland's Repeal of the External Relations Act and the Declaration of the Republic

'What does independence consist of? It consists fundamentally and basically of foreign relations. That is the test of independence. All else is local autonomy. Once foreign relations go out of your hands into the charge of somebody else, to that extent and in that measure you are not independent.'[1]

Jawaharal Nehru to the Indian Parliament, 8 March 1949

The repeal of the External Relations Act and the establishment of an Irish Republic have been lauded as the most important achievement of Ireland's first inter-party government. Both initiatives demonstrate Seán MacBride's influence within that government, although repeal ultimately benefited John Costello and Fine Gael at the expense of MacBride and Clann na Poblachta and cemented the partition of Ireland, which Clann na Poblachta had vowed to end. Despite those circumstances, Ireland did gain from repeal by being able to ensure continued Commonwealth benefits while also making an important psychological claim to true independence.

Because the motivation and execution of Ireland's leaving the Commonwealth is controversial, the event is discussed in both the significant surveys of Irish history[2] and in specific writings on Irish foreign policy.[3] The revisionist controversy is reflected in the debate about repeal and the revisionist aim to question received wisdom or supposedly indisputable assumptions concerning well known events should be applied here due to the tendency to view Ireland's departure from the Commonwealth, as Anthony Jordan does in his biography of MacBride, as the single most important act of the coalition government.[4] Though a patriotically potent sentiment, it actually does a disservice to the government, which did accomplish more, though not on such a grand or public scale. However the available evidence, although some is contradictory or circumstantial, points to a different interpretation, bringing about a need for a more critical approach to the events concerned and their impact.

Recent writings by Eithne MacDermott and Ian McCabe examine the repeal of the External Relations Act and the declaration of the Republic in detail. MacDermott's *Clann na Poblachta*, which analyses the party's contribution to Irish political life, is particularly strong on the both the beginnings and spectacular end of the party and delves into repeal and the effect on Clann na Poblachta, but there is no intense analysis of the wider implications of leaving the Commonwealth. McCabe's *A Diplomatic History of Ireland 1948-1949* is thorough and extensively researched, yet some of his conclusions come into question, especially his assertion that there was no prior cabinet decision to repeal the act, because of contradictory recollections by participants in the events he examines. The focal point of McCabe's book is on the 'announcement' and its immediate effect on the Anglo-Irish relationship. However there is little detail on MacBride's role and the long-term consequences of Ireland's leaving the Commonwealth. Neither work includes Taoiseach John Costello's recently released private papers. Taking these studies as a starting point, this chapter re-examines the reasons for leaving the Commonwealth, emphasising MacBride's influence both on the decision and the method by which it was executed and explores the wider implications for Ireland, Britain, and the Commonwealth.

Ireland's move away from the Commonwealth was a gradual one. In 1931, the Statute of Westminster gave Commonwealth members the legal right to revoke treaties and to withdraw from the Commonwealth if they so wished. Upon becoming President of the Executive Council a year later, Éamon de Valera took advantage of the Statute and proceeded to remove the oath of allegiance to the British monarch from the Constitution. The link with the Commonwealth was further weakened after the abdication of King Edward VIII in 1936. De Valera's government recognised the abdication and took the further step of omitting the king and the governor general from the Irish Constitution. He then decided to reappoint the king's successor by making him nominal head of External Relations. Britain accepted this External Relations Act as a sufficient link to retain Commonwealth membership. In 1937, de Valera authored a new Constitution asserting in Article 1 that Ireland 'hereby affirms its inalienable, indefeasible, and sovereign right to choose its own form of Government, to determine its relations with other nations, and to develop its life, political, economic and cultural, in accordance with its own genius and traditions.' The Constitution omitted the passage stating that 'the Irish Free State is a co-equal member of the community of Nations forming the British Commonwealth of Nations.' De Valera informed the British that this omission did not mean that Ireland would no longer be a member; it was because he had assured his followers that when the new Constitution came into existence, it would be written so as to not require an amendment if it was later decided to leave the Commonwealth.[5] Again, there was no protest from the British government.

For de Valera and Fianna Fáil in 1932, the goal was to win power, then remove the restrictive features of the 1921 Treaty they fought against. The main problems that de Valera had with the Treaty were that it did not provide the Irish Republic (merely a 'Free State') and it necessitated an oath of allegiance to the British monarch. In the 1920s, Britain would never have considered accepting a republic associated with the Commonwealth, as 'it simply did not form part of their mental framework or constitutional furniture.'[6] De Valera removed the oath of allegiance after the Statute of Westminster, but hesitated in declaring Ireland a Republic, largely because he believed that such a declaration would strengthen partition and if he declared the Republic, he would do so for 32 counties, not 26. However, some would argue that he held back more out of a sense of political timing and a wish to avoid direct challenge to Britain than his professed concerned for the ending of partition.[7]

When asked in the Dáil whether he intended to officially proclaim Ireland a Republic, he replied that 'we are a democracy with the ultimate sovereign power resting with the people—a representative democracy with the various organs of State functioning under a written Constitution, with the executive authority controlled by Parliament, with an independent judiciary functioning under the Constitution and the law, and with a Head of State directly elected by the people for a definite term of office.'[8] De Valera thus maintained that Ireland already functioned as a Republic and proceeded to read out dictionary and encyclopaedia definitions of the word 'republic' to prove the point.

De Valera's reluctance provided the impetus for MacBride's newly formed Clann na Poblachta to make the claim that they were the true republican party. De Valera and Fianna Fáil had 16 years in office to declare Ireland a republic; the fact that they had not bolstered the Clann's claim that tedium had set in. In a letter to the *Irish Times*, MacBride criticised the notion of a 'dictionary republic' which 'in no way satisfies the traditional aspiration of the republican section of our own people' and stressed his party's desire for a *de jure* rather than *de facto* Republic.[9]

Clann na Poblachta had pledged to establish an Irish Republic during the 1948 general election. Having secured only ten seats in the Dáil, MacBride admitted that his party could not

> claim that in this election we secured a mandate from the people that would enable us to repeal, or seek to repeal the External Relations Act and such other measures as are inconsistent with our status as an independent republic. These, therefore, have to remain in abeyance for the time being.[10]

Fine Gael, the party with the majority of seats in the new government, had campaigned on retaining the Commonwealth connection. In an interview with the Irish-American paper *Advocate* in March of 1948, Costello declared that members of the government were in agreement to assert the right of the Irish nation to territorial and absolute freedom, but their immediate goal was to find solutions to economic, social and educational problems. After the first Dáil session, the *Irish Times* editorialised 'we may assume, therefore, that so long as the new Government remains in office there will be no interference with the existing condition of affairs.'[11]

The Declaration of the Republic

Despite the government's assertion that declaring Ireland a Republic would have to wait, Costello announced that the government would be doing so after a mere seven months in power. The eventual repeal of the External Relations Act itself was expected, but the time and place of the announcement led to conflicting rumours and interpretations.

It was becoming obvious within the government that Ireland planned to leave the Commonwealth at some stage. As MacBride stated in July, 'The Crown and outward forms that belong to British constitutional history are merely reminders of an unhappy past that we want to bury, that have no realities for us and only serve as irritants.'[12] A letter from Assistant Secretary of External Affairs Frederick Boland to the High Commissioner in Canada John Hearne dated 21 August 1948 reads 'it is generally accepted here now that the days of the External Relations Act are numbered... you will probably have deduced as much from the

Minister's statement when introducing the External Affairs Estimate in the Dáil.'[13] While Taoiseach, de Valera had prepared draft bills for repeal in November 1947 and in January 1948. The *Irish Times* reported during the 1948 campaign that 'MacBride hints darkly about the repeal of the External Relations Act,' former Fine Gael TD James Dillon stated in the Dáil that 'I observe that Deputy MacBride contemplates a long postponement of some objectives near his heart [achievement of the Republic], but I am more optimistic than he.'[14]

It may have been apparent that Ireland's days in the Commonwealth were coming to an end, but it was not clear as to whether a formal cabinet decision had been reached to officially remove Ireland from the Commonwealth. As McCabe points out, there is no record of any decision made in cabinet meetings prior to Costello's trip to Canada, where the official announcement was delivered. According to an interview Nicholas Mansergh had with Boland, the inter-party government had unclear views on repeal until the summer of 1948 when the issue of attendance at the October meeting of the Commonwealth Prime Minister's conference led to discussion on Ireland's role within the Commonwealth.[15] In contrast to McCabe, F.S.L. Lyons believes there had been a prior cabinet decision to repeal the act but uncertainty remains about when such a decision was reached.[16] The discussion could have taken place at a cabinet subcommittee meeting, as there were no minutes taken at such meetings. Both Costello and MacBride maintained that a decision was reached that summer. It can be surmised that an 'unofficial' decision had been made and there is evidence that Ireland's connection to the Commonwealth was on the government's mind. Issues of citizenship legislation were under discussion between London and Dublin and the accredation of the new Argentinian Minister directly to the president of Ireland rather than the King appeared to be another small but important severance in the Commonwealth connection.

On 21 July Independent (former Clann na Poblachta) TD Peadar Cowan stated in the Dáil that 'we in this House should make it perfectly clear that we do intend to take the steps that will establish this country as an independent Republic, whatever those steps may be, and whatever sacrifices may be necessary in the process.'[17] On 6 August, Tánaiste William Norton put the question to de Valera, now leader of the Opposition:

An Tánaiste: I said it then and I repeat it again now… I think it would do our national self respect good both at

home and abroad if we were to proceed without
delay to abolish the External Relations Act.

Mr. de Valera: Go ahead... You will get no opposition from us.[18]

It is reasonable to say that by August the scene had been set. On 10
August 1948 at a cabinet meeting, MacBride recommended that Ireland
should not attend the October Commonwealth conference.[19] Yet there
was no sign of preparation for an upcoming declaration and repeal of the
External Relations Act was not on MacBride's proposed agenda for the
October cabinet meeting; instead ending partition, the elimination of
'Ireland' from the monarch's title, and the substitution of diplomatic titles
for title of high commissioner were listed. There is no record of MacBride
seeking any type of preliminary forum to discuss leaving the
Commonwealth with either Britain or any Commonwealth countries. Thus
the cabinet had informally decided on repeal, but had made no substantial
plans.

Not only was there controversy regarding any official cabinet decision,
but the choice of venue for the public announcement has been the subject
of some debate, as vastly conflicting versions exist of what, why, when,
and how the announcement happened. As Costello said later,

the most extraordinary, fantastic and completely unfounded
statements were issued from various sources, generally to the effect
either that I had without any consultation or authority from my
colleagues in the government "declared the Republic in Canada" or
else in a fit of pique at something that is supposed to have happened at
a function.[20]

The Taoiseach was invited by the President of the Canadian Bar
Association to attend a gathering in Montreal from 31 August to 4
September. The Canadian government then invited Costello to be their
'official guest' for the duration of his visit and several receptions were held
in Costello's honour. Yet the trip was not an 'official' or state visit; he was
there in the capacity as a barrister who happened to be Taoiseach of
Ireland.[21] It was Costello's first trip abroad in an unclear capacity; he was
not yet fully confident of his role, and he was there without MacBride or
any departmental 'minders'. According to Costello, when drafting his
speech for the Bar Association dinner entitled *Ireland and International
Affairs*, he was aware that a government decision had already been taken to

repeal the External Relations Act, and the process was supposed to begin when the Dáil resumed in October.

Costello delivered the speech on 1 September. He criticised the 'lack of a precise and formal definition of legal and constitutional relationships' between Britain and Ireland, declaring that 'the harp without the Crown symbolised the ideal of Irish independence and nationhood... the whole purpose of our national struggle was to free ourselves from those British institutions which, as the inevitable consequence of our history, had become associated in our minds with the idea of national subjection.'[22] The talk was well-received and Costello prepared to attend several dinners in his honour.

Problems began due to issues of diplomacy. Costello was asked in Montreal by Louis St. Laurent, the Canadian Minister for External Affairs, if a toast to the King would cover him as well. Costello attempted to explain, 'I had to argue, that it did not, because we were not real members of the Commonwealth,'[23] but he was not positive that the distinction was clear. A dinner with the Governor-General Lord Alexander was planned in Ottawa on 4 September and the Irish Embassy had previously 'indicated to the Department that the Taoiseach would not attend the dinner unless the toast of the President was honoured. At 6 p.m. the Governor General's Private Secretary confirmed by 'phone that the procedure regarding toasts would be observed as agreed with the Department of External Affairs.'[24] However, the Governor-General did not toast the President, a serious breech of protocol. The King was honoured and Costello complied, but was disconcerted by the slight. He was not enraged, however, and seemed to believe that the toast situation was a confirmation of the confusing status of Ireland within the Commonwealth.

According to Minister of Health Noël Browne, Costello felt there was 'a certain coolness' at the reception. The Governor-General was not a 'talker', and seemed standoffish in his few exchanges with the Taoiseach, including snubbing him at a garden party at McGill University in Montreal.[25] Costello was unhappy with the seating arrangement at the banquet table, and the replica placed in front of him of 'Roaring Meg', a cannon used by Protestants against Catholics in the Siege of Derry in 1689 bearing the legend 'The walls of Derry and no surrender.' It is likely that the placement was an oversight: a Canadian External Affairs briefing reported that the replica 'is constantly used by the Governor General as a centerpiece on the dining room table at formal functions.'[26] Costello was annoyed, but according to his assistant Patrick Lynch, he was restrained and polite to his hosts.[27] He made no comment during dinner but later asked John Hearne what should be done, as, at the time, he believed that the Governor-General's actions were intentional; 'I was of the opinion for some considerable time that the failure to honour the Toast of the President was a deliberate action on the part of the Governor General. I am now convinced that for some reason, whether through negligence or otherwise, the Governor General was never informed.'[28] As for Roaring Meg, Costello merely remarked that the replica was in 'very bad taste,' but not a deliberate insult.[29] Hearne reported later that

> I have got no explanation on why the Governor General did not give the toast of the Uachtarán. As I told you I had mentioned the matter of toasts to the Chef de Protocol... I have not asked why the Governor General did not give it; nor whether he was asked why he had a particular replica as a centre-piece on his table when you were his quest of honour. But I shall not leave Canada without letting Pearson know how we felt about it.[30]

In his autobiography, Noël Browne wrote that Costello simply lost his temper and declared that Ireland was leaving the Commonwealth in a burst of anger and Boland confirms this observation.[31] Mansergh calls Costello an 'impulsive and somewhat inexperienced' politician who took umbrage at his treatment in Canada.[32] He further states that ill-temper is the only way to explain the odd timing of the announcement. However, these assessments seem inaccurate, as Costello did not make the announcement until three days after the dinner, which would have given him time to consider such a move. In those three days, he could have calmed down, communicated with the cabinet and carefully considered his position. British Prime Minister Clement Attlee believed the announcement was spontaneous and once Costello declared that Ireland was leaving, he could not retreat from what he had said, [33] similar to Cortes burning his ships upon reaching the New World. Yet it seems unlikely that he delivered an impromptu speech, later realised its consequences, and then felt he could not back down. Lyons' personal impression of Costello was that he was an admirable chairman equipped with tact and patience who made the coalition harmonious – hardly someone who would commit to a rash course of action without considering the outcome.[34] After being chosen as Taoiseach, the *Ottawa Journal* observed that 'Mr. Costello, said to be a philosopher, possesses that patience which is the greatest ingredient of statesmanship.'[35] He was a skilled lawyer who had experience on the international stage and was not easily tempted into indiscretion. The American Minister to Ireland George Garrett agreed: 'Mr. Costello is inclined to be a prudent, conservative lawyer not given to irresponsible statements.'[36] In any case, it is not clear that Costello took the Ottawa slight very seriously at the time. Indeed, David Johnson of Canada's Department of External Affairs, wrote that 'on the numerous times that I have seen Mr. Costello... he has never made any reference to these slights or given the impression that he was upset by any incident that happened in Canada.'[37] In fact, there is another very plausible explanation to account for the strange timing of the announcement.

Costello was pushed into an awkward situation; on 5 September, the *Sunday Independent* reported that the government intended to repeal the External Relations Act. When Canadian journalists inquired about the article, he responded with 'no comment.' But a press conference had been arranged two days later in Canada's House of Commons, where the question was sure to come up again.

Costello suspected someone with insider information had leaked the story (which assumes there was a story to leak), but the author of the article Hector Legge assured him that he had no inside source, that he just drew astute conclusions based on what was said in the Dáil and on MacBride's recent press release quoting parts of Costello's speech. The *Sunday Independent* was known as a Fine Gael paper. Its editor was friendly with members of the party; therefore suspicion would fall not only on MacBride, the staunch republican, but also on other, equally likely sources, such as James Dillon. However, Louie O'Brien, MacBride's secretary, would later reveal that MacBride was the source, though she claims that she herself did not know it at the time.[38] However she learned this information through a third party, whose identity she did not reveal and is not specific on details. In a conversation with Mansergh in 1952, Costello revealed that he believed MacBride was indeed the source.[39]

Had MacBride grown impatient with the progress being made towards repeal of the External Relations Act, even though he recognised that the inter-party government did not have a mandate for such an act? Did he use the opportunity presented by Costello's Canadian tour to hurry legislation along? Legge has consistently denied that a leak occurred[40] and after the article appeared, MacBride telegraphed Costello immediately instructing him to say 'no comment.' Advising Costello not to say anything is a strange response if MacBride had been the leak. It is more than likely that he would encourage Costello to confirm it and comment on the government's plans. The British Representative to Ireland John Maffey, later Lord Rugby, assessed MacBride by writing, 'in office he so far shows restraint and a strong sense of responsibility.'[41] If Maffey's opinion is correct, surreptitiously leaking the information appears out of character. MacBride had no ostensible reason for wanting a republic declared so quickly; it would be wiser to wait and ensure that he and his party could claim credit.

Costello gave consideration to how he should respond; he could either take the lead in movement toward repeal or run the risk of having to give way to a rival within his own government. According to Patrick Lynch, Costello has discussed the repeal of the Act with Hearne and himself on the 6th of September, the day before the press conference and had also spoken to MacBride. Costello decided not to comment, but before going to bed, he had made up his mind to say something, 'as he feared that if he equivocated Mr. de Valera would take the initiative.'[42] Ultimately the newspaper article forced the decision much more so than the diplomatic slights.

Costello did not follow MacBride's directive. He believed that issuing a 'no comment' though 'well intentioned, was one that I felt would not be permitted by my questioners to adopt.'[43] At the press conference on 7 September, he confirmed the accuracy of the report and revealed that the cabinet 'unanimously agreed' to repeal the External Relations Act on resumption of the Dáil.[44] In an *Irish Times* interview in 1967, Costello said that the announcement had nothing to do with the diplomatic slights in Canada, but had been brought about from questions arising from the newspaper article. As he wrote to Norton, 'It was really the article in the *Sunday Independent* that decided me, although I had intended to tell Mr. Mackenzie King [the Canadian Prime Minister]… of our intentions in that regard.'[45] He did not want people to believe that he had 'without any consultations or authority in a fit of pique… on my own responsibility declared the intention of my colleagues and myself to repeal the External Relations Act and declare a Republic in Canada.'[46] He had been bludgeoned with examples of the ambiguities in both the External Relations Act and in the relationship between Ireland and the Commonwealth during his trip and since he was sure that a cabinet decision, however unofficial, had been made, there was little reason not to verify the story.

Most commentators then and now agree that repeal itself was not an unexpected development. Despite its inevitability, the announcement was badly timed, leading to the thought that 'a crucially important constitutional decision had been made in an arbitrary fashion several thousand miles away.'[47] Costello obviously felt that he had to address the *Independent* article, but as Lyons writes, the Irish people deserved to have the proclamation made on their soil.[48] The announcement made international news and Costello was the guest of honour at official dinners as the Canadian government tried to ascertain what was happening.

Apparently, Costello's decision to announce impending repeal came as a surprise to some cabinet members like Browne, James Dillon, and perhaps MacBride, who was informed while at dinner at the Russell Hotel with Maffey. He stated that MacBride appeared surprised at the news, 'I certainly get the strong impression that he was a little surprised – indeed perturbed – by this sudden unconventional development.'[49] MacBride appeared to express shock, but later in two separate interviews with the *Irish Times* said that he was not surprised, that 'this was no surprise to me or to any other Minister.'[50] This is incorrect, as many of the ministers were indeed surprised. He stated that

Lord Rugby may have been quite right when he says that I looked surprised when, on the night of September 7th, 1948, I received copies of news agency reports indicating that our intention to repeal the External Relations Act was being treated as an unexpected sensation. I *was* astonished that anyone should be surprised, particularly in view of the speeches made for some months and the banner headlines which had appeared in one of our leading newspapers only four days before.[51]

Certainly MacBride would not want to admit that he was not aware of what was happening in Canada, as this not only implied a lack of control over his department but also represented Costello usurping an issue the Clann had made their own. He may have been nonplussed that Costello did not follow his advice not to comment on the situation.

According to Browne, after he returned from Canada, Costello told ministers he had decided on repeal while attending a government dinner in his honour. Apparently, he later realised that he had no authority to make the statement and was distressed. He called a cabinet meeting to explain and apologise and offered to resign. As MacBride was not present, Browne spoke for Clann na Poblachta and told Costello not to resign, as the Clann was glad to see the act go.

Whether this meeting ever took place provoked yet another controversy. When Browne made this charge in a radio interview in 1976,

Dillon, Daniel Morrissey, MacBride, and Patrick McGilligan claimed that no such meeting ever happened. But in 1983, Browne reviewed Ronan Fanning's *Independent Ireland* and again stated that Costello held a cabinet meeting after Canadian trip and offered to resign as well as reassuring Fanning, who had found no papers relating to repeal in the cabinet papers, that 'no Cabinet decision or papers could exist since no formal Cabinet decisions had taken place.'[52] Within days, MacBride once again countered Browne's claim about the aftermath of Costello's Canadian trip, 'there was no such Cabinet meeting and Mr. Costello did not offer his resignation.'[53] When MacBride, in the process of writing his memoirs, asked Lynch what his recollection was, Lynch replied that

> On Tuesday 7 Sept. at 10:30 am Taoiseach gave press conference. He announced Government's intention to repeal the External Relations Act and said 'yes' to a question relating to Ireland's leaving the Commonwealth... I have no recollection of any meeting of Ministers in Mr. Costello's own house during the week after his return from Canada as alleged by Dr. Browne.[54]

Browne's account may have some basis in fact; minute-taking at meetings was notoriously careless, Boland agreed with his account, and Browne did stand in for MacBride when he was away. A vulnerable cabinet had to present a united front at the time and may have continued to do so long after the government was in power. An unrecorded cabinet meeting may have taken place on 7 October.[55]

Yet Browne's attendance at cabinet meetings was admittedly erratic; he missed the 19 August 1948 meeting where the cabinet discussed attendance at the Commonwealth Conference. Meetings themselves departed from the normal administrative convention. Due in large part to MacBride's suspicion of civil servants, Chief Whip Liam Cosgrave took notes and, as Lynch recalls,

> Often there were ad hoc meetings of Ministers: these could be tantamount to government meetings because they frequently took decisions. Not all Ministers need be present at any government meetings... and if Mr. Cosgrave were not present the procedure for recording a decision for transmission to the Secretary to the Government could easily be overlooked.[56]

Not all decisions were fully and accurately recorded which led to the suggestion that repeal and Republic were Costello's personal decisions.[57] MacBride would always maintain that the decision was a cabinet one with the implication that the impetus came from Clann na Poblachta.[58]

The cabinet did meet on 9 September immediately after Costello's press conference. Six members did not attend, including Cosgrave, so there is a question of who took the minutes. Because of the slipshod nature of recording and the persistence of conflicting memory, with everyone equally definite that their version is correct, the exact sequence of events will remain unclear. MacBride quickly drafted a bill transferring the functions of the King to the President of Ireland. A month passed before a meeting attended by all government ministers formally and retroactively approved the action taken by Costello in Canada, thus averting any constitutional crisis, and another month elapsed before the government finally considered their repeal legislation in detail.[59]

The Commonwealth Party Takes Ireland out of the Commonwealth

Attlee commented that one of the ironies of Ireland's declaring the Republic was that de Valera, thought to be the extremist republican, did not sever ties, but Costello of Fine Gael still seen as the 'pro-Commonwealth' party, did.[60] As Tim Pat Coogan indicates, Costello was 'one of the least republican figures in the Cabinet, at least in public perceptions.'[61] After the announcement, those who voted for Fine Gael felt betrayed. As Garret FitzGerald recalled,

Joan and I had canvassed for Fine Gael from door to door in Mr. Costello's constituency of Dublin Townships (now Dublin South-East). My understanding... was that Fine Gael supported Commonwealth membership, and Joan and I canvassed accordingly, we particularly remember reassuring the inhabitants of Waterloo Road on that point.[62]

Senator J.W. Bigger remarked during the Seanad debates on the Republic of Ireland bill,

I and thousands of others in this country voted at the last election for Fine Gael, confident that the Leaders of that Party were honest men, upon whose good faith we could rely. It was believed that their policy might be taken on its face value and not subject to legal quibbles. The statements upon which I chiefly relied were those of General Mulcahy and of Mr. Costello. When General Mulcahy was elected President of Fine Gael he said:— 'We stand unequivocally for membership of the British Commonwealth.' That plank in the Fine Gael Party programme, as far as I am aware, has never been withdrawn.[63]

Bigger was correct; there was no mention of repeal by any Fine Gael cabinet members during the campaign. MacBride was also correct about the lack of a mandate for leaving the Commonwealth. Maffey observed, 'They [Fine Gael] are all somewhat bewildered by their own sudden illogical iconoclasm and must now find high sounding phrases to justify it.'[64] The press focused considerably on the accountability of Fine Gael: 'many thousands of Fine Gael's electoral supporters are thoroughly disgusted at the whole business' wheras MacBride and Clann na Poblachta 'have at least been consistent.'[65]

Why did Fine Gael, who, only a few years earlier extolled the benefits of belonging to the Commonwealth, decide to take Ireland out of it? Frustrated with the imprecise definition of status, Costello himself found the External Relations Act 'untidy and inadequate.' He knew it had been a divisive issue since the Civil War and solving it would justify breaking with Fine Gael tradition. As Nicholas Mansergh wrote, dominion status 'evoked only misgiving in Irish minds. They craved, whether wisely or not is beside the point, for precise, logical definitions.'[66] The nature of the link between Britain and Ireland remained vague, despite de Valera's attempts to define it through 'external association,' sovereignty in internal affairs but associated with the Commonwealth for the purposes of external concerns.

In addition, the balance of parties in coalition made the Dáil highly susceptible to initiative from what Costello called 'some person not well disposed to the government' for example, someone like Peadar Cowan introducing his own bill in the Dáil, and an absence of any agreed government policy could mean the end of the coalition. All the parties had in common was a desire to oust Fianna Fáil and to end partition, but since ending partition was not immediately possible, repeal may have 'appealed as something to which all might subscribe without the straining of some few tender consciences.'[67] The inter-party government was especially vulnerable on the republican flank, especially in light of de Valera's recent anti-partition tour through the United States. Repeal could help the government prove its worth on the all-important national question. Some may have felt betrayed by the change in Fine Gael policy, by (as Seán

MacEntee called them) 'Republican wolves masquerading as Commonwealth sheep,'[68] but the party did strengthen their position in the 1951 general election, gaining nine seats in the Dáil so perhaps the disappointment had worn off.

The Republic accomplished a great deal for Fine Gael; it gave them the opportunity to best Fianna Fáil, it helped reinvigorate a fading Fine Gael's image as a serious party whose patriotism was just as fervent as their competition. As his son-in-law Alexis Fitzgerald wrote to Costello, 'by one stroke of genius, politically, you have placed Fine Gael back in the centre of the national tradition right where Mick Collins had it.'[69] Fine Gael would no longer be seen as pro-British or anti-national; they were 'in government doing things rather than an ageing party of sterile opposition living on its memories.'[70] Repeal signalled both the first steps toward Fine Gael's political ascendancy and MacBride's inability to safeguard his ideological territory.[71] Not only did it benefit Fine Gael, it helped Costello to assert his authority as Taoiseach and showed him to be a clever political tactician. He gained the upper hand, both by declaring the Republic in Canada away from his cabinet and without MacBride's approval and by introducing the Republic of Ireland Bill in the Dáil. Though declaring the Republic was largely accidental and forced by circumstance, Costello managed to take control and make the issue his own. He 'took the gunman out of Irish politics' by pacifying the IRA, who were probably pleased that de Valera could not take credit for establishing the Republic. The Republic of Ireland Act showed MacBride's clout, therefore it would be supported by the IRA, where Conor Cruise O'Brien believes he and the Clann still had ties.[72]

Seán MacBride's Influence

MacBride's possessed the highest public profile of any cabinet member. Due to his lineage and prior career, his republican credentials were incontestable. Dermot Keogh referred to him as a 'rival Taoiseach' and after the first cabinet meeting, Richard Mulcahy commented that 'we [he and Thomas O'Higgins] both looked at one another and it was as if the two of us said together, "another de Valera."'[73] His appointment as Minister of External Affairs guaranteed that the issue of repeal would come up; the Clann had put repeal of the External Relations Act and declaration of the Republic at the forefront of their programme during the election campaign. However, as the *Irish People* reported four days before the election, 'Mr. MacBride has already offered ... to coalesce with any party which would endeavour to unseat Fianna Fáil.'[74] This could only mean that MacBride was willing to join Fine Gael, whose manifesto stated that the party did not 'seek to alter the present constitution in relation to external affairs.' If in a coalition with Fine Gael as the dominant party, MacBride must have realised that secession would not happen. Therefore he appeared sincere about his expressed intention of waiting to secede from the Commonwealth.

Did MacBride directly influence Costello to declare the Republic? The Secretary of Commonwealth Relations Philip Noel-Baker believed so, as he said to High Commissioner of Ireland John Dulanty on 7 September, 'My own guess is that Sean put him up to it.'[75] Yet Costello denies that he made the statement because of pressure from MacBride who was allegedly under pressure from the IRA. Repeal was not a price paid by Costello for MacBride and his party's support in government; the confusing situation of a Republic at home and a monarchy abroad had provided the impetus for Costello's decision, a decision made without formal cabinet consultation and apparently without consulting his own party. Costello later stated, 'Sean MacBride did not influence me in the slightest... I must give him full credit that while it was an issue of his party's policy, he never at any stage tried to influence me in that direction.'[76] But Costello, without MacBride, may not have pushed issue of repeal as far as it would go. The *Clann na Poblachta Bulletin* of 1950 encapsulates this opinion:

> Sean MacBride generously gave the Government...whole credit for this Republican step. But does anyone seriously imagine that the Act would have been repealed if Clann na Poblachta had never existed? Fine Gael was a Commonwealth party. Fianna Fáil had passed the External Relations Act, thereby helping to drive genuine Republicans to extreme measures.[77]

Whether MacBride 'generously' gave credit to the government is debateable; it seems that he merely made the best of Costello's appropriation. However, Costello's repeated denials that repeal was the 'pound of flesh' owed to MacBride for his party's continued participation in government paradoxically demonstrates that he did influence the situation even if he did not directly use repeal as a bargaining device.

Brian Farrell, in *Chairman or Chief: The Role of the Taoiseach in Irish Government*, theorises that the Minister of External Affairs cannot be regarded as a key ministry in the cabinet, mainly because Britain had always been the most important element in Irish foreign policy and the Taoiseach took charge at critical stages. Farrell points out that de Valera held the post from 1932-1948 when he was Taoiseach.[78] Yet MacBride, due to the coalition situation, was in a position to exert more influence and he proved to be a highly active minister both in terms of expanding his department and adopting policy initiatives.[79] Although Costello eventually overshadowed him, MacBride's name will always be closely linked with the decision to repeal the External Relations Act. As Cruise O'Brien wrote in his *Leader* piece on MacBride, 'His main achievement – apart from giving the Fianna Fáil Government a short holiday – was to get the Commonwealth party to take Ireland out of the Commonwealth.'[80]

Costello announced on 13 November that he, not MacBride, would introduce the Republic of Ireland Bill to the Oireachtas, stating that he wanted 'to place the question of Irish sovereignty and status beyond dispute or suspicion or guesswork.'[81] Normally, MacBride, as Minister of External Affairs, would have introduced the bill. Costello may have decided to proceed in this way because of his impatience with the ambiguities of External Relations Act and his determination not to have any uncertainties with the bill or to show his resolve 'to assert his position as the principle source of foreign policy in the government.'[82] MacDermott posits that Costello wanted to assert authority over MacBride, who he suspected of backing him into a corner.[83] It may have been done to placate pro-Commonwealth Fine Gael supporters: as Fitzgerald advised him, 'people [must] be taken behind the scenes of your own mind before you made the decision and that your justification when the Act is introduced by you (as you must insist it should be) should have regard to your own Fine Gael origins.'[84] Costello's introduction of the bill in the Dáil made a statement; that he was the one in charge. He asserted his position at the expense of MacBride and even Browne, hardly a fan of MacBride, thought the usurpation ungracious.[85]

In the second reading of the Bill in the Dáil, Costello stated,

> this Bill will end, and end forever, in a simple, clear and unequivocal way this country's long and tragic association with the institution of the British Crown and will make it manifest beyond equivocation or subtlety that the national and international status of this country is that of an independent republic.[86]

The bill was passed by the Seanad on 15 December 1948 and signed six days later by President Seán T. O'Kelly in a ceremony attended by Costello and MacBride. MacBride stated publicly that the Bill 'will enable Ireland to be regarded internationally as a republic, and will thus enable her to play her part in international affairs.'[87] The Republic would be inaugurated on Easter Monday 1949, thirty-three years after the Easter Rising. Goodwill messages were received from all world leaders, except those from communist countries.

According to Browne, MacBride protested his diminished role by not appearing at the Easter Monday celebrations. Actually, he did not attend because he was in the United States at a State Department Conference.[88] This is confirmed in an interview with Ian McCabe on 6 January 1987 where he denied he missed the celebrations deliberately.[89] As Maud Gonne MacBride attended, it does not seem likely that MacBride was exceedingly irritated.[90] No matter what his reasons for not attending, MacBride failed to capitalise on this symbolic turning point which, at a later stage, would be remembered as an act of great statesmanship. De Valera and Fianna Fáil boycotted the festivities, stating that celebrating was out of place as long as partition still existed. Instead, he spent the day at Arbour Hill, praying for the men of 1916. A barman commented at the time, 'Sure, it's all politics. Costello and his crowd have wiped Dev's eye and now Dev is trying to get his own back on them.'[91] As the *Times* reported a day after the celebrations, 'the truth is that the people are not greatly enamoured of Mr. Costello's republic. They regard the introduction of the repeal of the External Relations Act as a piece of rather cute politics on the part of Mr. Costello... They believe that the declaration of the republic will make little constitutional change and that it is intended largely as window dressing and as an attempt to embarrass Mr. De Valera.'[92] Brian Inglis wrote in 'An Irishman's Diary,' 'There were loud cheers, but they were the cheers of people tired of just standing there waiting for something to happen.' The Irish Grand National at Fairy Racecourse competed with the celebrations, which not only may explain the absence of huge crowds but also the priorities of the Irish people. There was a noted lack of genuine warmth in Easter festivities; Inglis quotes a spectator:

Who did you expect to do the cheering? Not Costello supporters after the way he went back on them after the Commonwealth link. Not de Valera after the way he has taken it himself, and not the Clann; they won't start cheering until we get back the six other counties. I don't know who you thought was going to cheer.[93]

The British and Commonwealth Response

If members of the Irish cabinet were surprised by the announcement, the British government had even less warning. They may have believed that repeal would happen in the future, but were not aware of any firm immediate plans. In a report dated 17 August, Noel-Baker stated that Anglo-Irish relations were friendly and that he did not expect any action before the Dáil resumed at end of the summer recess.[94] As Browne recalled, 'no conversation had taken place' between the Irish and British governments and the decision 'came as a painful surprise to the British.'[95] Foreign Secretary Ernest Bevin wrote to John Hearne that he 'regretted the declaration of the Republic and that it was a great surprise to him when Costello went that far.'[96]

Yet there were hints that the British were not terribly enthusiastic about the idea of external association. Ireland's role within the Commonwealth was ambiguous, as Maffey wrote to Sir Eric Machtig before the general election:

Personally I should not be sorry to see this strange device removed. The Irish have handled it in such a way as to discredit it. Furthermore, it is now clear that it will not provide the bridge to closer association, as was once hoped. Indeed, it may well be that its removal will make closer association easier. The relationship between the United Kingdom and Eire is now based on facts, not on sentiments, and we must adapt our policies to this principle.[97]

In Bevin's own papers, there is a notable absence of material relating to Ireland's repeal of the External Relations Act. But then Bevin did not believe the Foreign Office should take responsibility for Irish business.[98] The Commonwealth Office was responsible but Secretary Noel-Baker left no personal letters or correspondence regarding Ireland in his papers, just a few newspaper clippings. Attlee's own memoirs include only a brief treatment on Ireland leaving the Commonwealth.[99]

There are several explanations for the absence of extensive material relating to Ireland. Many other matters were preoccupying the British at the time. The need to convert from a wartime to a peacetime economy and to restore the balance of the British economy, an almost continuous succession of currency and trading crises, and the division of global politics into hostile, competing Cold War camps kept Attlee's government busy during the late 1940s.

In the area of colonial policy, Labour did not yet have a coherent political philosophy linking attitudes of colonial issues with socialist policy.[100] Imperial/colonial policies were not an obvious or impressive aspect of Labour policies before World War II[101] and their 1945 election manifesto, *Let Us Face the Future*, contained little detail on colonial proposals, showing dominion policy to be a peripheral concern. However, Britain still retained control of an enormous amount of territory including large blocks of Africa and the Middle East as well as scattered territory, from the Fiji Islands to Hong Kong to the Falklands. So in addition to solving Britain's post-war crises and establishing the welfare state, Attlee had to deal with the changing structure of colonial relations and help Labour formulate and nurture a consistent colonial policy.

Thirdly, keeping Ireland within the Commonwealth was not all that vital. The negotiations following Costello's announcement seem similar to an amicable divorce with some squabbling over property. If Britain could continue a beneficial economic relationship, still retain territory in the North for defence purposes and could guarantee the constitutional status of the North, then Ireland's presence within the Commonwealth was not crucial. In any case, domestic problems came first at the time. Indeed, even the much more momentous independence of India in 1947 had elicited little public concern: as Kenneth O. Morgan writes, 'so riveted was public attention at that time by the financial crisis over convertibility and the Cabinet's convulsions over steel nationalization, that Indian independence seemed anti-climatic.'[102] The resolution of India's role in the Commonwealth took on far more importance than Ireland's imminent departure. One of the ironies of the situation was that as Ireland left, efforts were being made to ensure that India could remain within the Commonwealth even though the new government was determined to establish a Republic.

In order to assess Britain's lack of serious preoccupation with keeping Ireland in the Commonwealth, it is helpful to recall the backdrop of Commonwealth affairs. Wider imperial interests, especially the potential loss of India and its army, helped Ireland to become a republic. A rigid position concerning Ireland may have increased Indian mistrust of British intentions. Being amenable would help in regard to Britain's relationship with dominions contemplating secession, particularly South Africa, India, and Pakistan.

Additionally, the Commonwealth nations affirmed that they would continue close relations with Ireland after she seceded. With the possible exception of Canadian Prime Minister Mackenzie King, Commonwealth ministers had no advance information and the secession of Ireland was decided apart from the Commonwealth, but members, especially those with large Irish populations like Canada, New Zealand, and Australia respected Ireland's decision. In a letter from Boland to Hearne dated 21 August, Boland posited that repeal would present 'no difficulty at all' and that Commonwealth governments may welcome an end to the ambiguity.[103] The Canadian government seemed to feel that 'the repealed External Relations Act would only formalize what for some time had been the de facto situation.'[104] A communiqué from T.J. Kiernan, the Irish Minister in Australia to External Affairs, dated 11 February 1949 reported that 'it seems clear that the attitude, all around, to Ireland is unchanged by the legislation... they have no difficulty understanding the different historical background in Ireland and the objectivity and absence of rancour in our declaring the Republic.'[105] New Zealand passed the Republic of Ireland Act, stating that New Zealand law would operate toward Ireland 'as it would have if the Republic of Ireland had remained part of His Majesty's dominions.'[106]

Commonwealth countries without substantial Irish populations also supported Ireland's decision; India looked to Ireland as a model in arranging their own situation within the Commonwealth. Jawaharal Nehru had travelled to Ireland in the summer of 1910 after finishing his law studies at Inner Temple and became fascinated with Sinn Féin, empathising with the Irish struggle against the British. As Nehru's biographer has commented, 'to many Indians in those days Ireland was as infectious and inspiring an ideal as the Italy of Garibaldi and Mazzini.'[107] Obvious parallels existed between Ireland and India; religious differences helped lead to partition of both countries, both inherited a British character and construction in their political institutions, but their paths diverged in relation to independence. India chose to remain within the Commonwealth because it offered a sense of stability and peace without limiting independence and Ireland's experience in the 1930s and 1940s had demonstrated that there were methods of declaring sovereignty while still securing Commonwealth benefits.

After Costello announced that Ireland was seceding, the British wrung their hands a bit, but in actuality did not modify the existing relationship. Chancellor of the Exchequer Sir Stafford Cripps told John Dulanty that there were two boxes, 'in one you had Commonwealth countries, in the other you had foreign countries – there really was no intermediate stage,' but that there was nevertheless a desire to find some accommodation between the two countries.[108] The conversations between Dulanty and

Noel-Baker reveal a strange pattern. At first the Commonwealth Office seemed to be trying to frighten the Irish government; Noel-Baker hinted on 23 September to Dulanty that trade preferences may be modified and that Ireland had caused the British Government, himself in particular, a great deal of work and worry.[109] Regarding the rights of Irish citizens in Britain, Noel Baker said if Britain had realised that Ireland was not a true member of the Commonwealth, they would have not secured the passing of the Nationality Act, which gave Irish citizens privileges but not the status of British subjects, and that Act too may have to be altered.[110] Later in November, Noel-Baker seemed to change tactics by acting unconcerned, telling Dulanty that the Commonwealth Office was looking for a solution, but the 'Ministers concerned were all overwhelmed with work of real importance and of pressing urgency.'[111] Perhaps this attitude was punishment for not keeping Britain informed of Ireland's plans.

The Dáil recommended that Ireland should attend the October Commonwealth conference, but the invitation had been withdrawn and the government then had to 'angle' for an invite and persuade Commonwealth leaders to ensure they received it. MacBride was in Paris for an OEEC meeting from 3 to 9 October which gave him a chance to interact with other members of Commonwealth. He and the Minister for Finance Patrick McGilligan attended the Commonwealth conference on 17 October at Chequers as 'observers'. The challenge for the Irish government was to preserve the advantages that had been Ireland's while severing the symbolic ties that bound the two countries.

Britain's overseas dominions had a significant influence in Britain not taking a hard line about repeal. The Chequers meeting was arranged on the initiative of Canada, Australia, and New Zealand's representatives and would not have gone so well for Ireland without Commonwealth support. Lord Chancellor Jowitt stated in the House of Commons, 'If we had taken a different line from the one we decided to take, we should have acted in the teeth of the advice of the representatives of Canada, Australia, and New Zealand.'[112] Attlee, Noel-Baker, Lord Jowitt, and Secretary to the Cabinet Sir Norman Brook met with MacBride and McGilligan at Chequers to discuss informally the practical aspects of Ireland's secession. Attlee's cabinet thought that 'if they insisted on treating Eire as a foreign state... the practical difficulties would be greater for the United Kingdom than for Eire; and, furthermore, that they would thereby forfeit the sympathy and support of Canada, Australia, and New Zealand.'[113] MacBride informed Attlee that repeal was not a hostile action – it was intended as 'a necessary preliminary to the restoration of friendly relations between Eire and the United Kingdom' because Ireland's difficulty of feeling subordinate to the crown prevented the development of friendly relations with Britain and the Commonwealth. McCabe calls the negotiations 'tortuous,' but that did not seem to be the general perception; both the *Times* and the *Irish Times* noted that negotiations were cordial.[114] After further negotiations in Paris, the basic arrangement of trade, citizenship, and immigration policies remained favourable to Ireland. There was no inconsistency in the British position; as Fanning argues, the abolition of the oath of allegiance, the External Relations Act, the 1937 Constitution, the Republic of Ireland Act show a consistent pattern of the British government choosing to ignore Irish policy, rather than resist.[115]

It also helped that Attlee and MacBride had a good personal relationship; in the summer of 1948, Attlee and his wife went on holiday in the west of Ireland, where MacBride acted as tour guide, playing golf, and going sailing with the Prime Minister and Mrs. Attlee. When the Republic of Ireland Bill passed in the Dáil, MacBride said,

> I should like to pay a special tribute to the assistance which we received from the British Government in this matter. They met us with understanding and goodwill. Mr. Attlee, the British Prime Minister, gave the matter a considerable amount of his personal time and I think I would express the views of my colleague the Minister for Finance, who was present during the discussions we had with him when I say that he impressed us by his high degree of integrity and his understanding approach to our problems.[116]

On 25 November when the Republic of Ireland Bill was announced, Attlee informed Parliament that Irish citizens were not to be regarded as foreigners; the British Nationality Act of 1948 would continue to govern the position of Irish citizens in the United Kingdom, despite the Republic no longer being part of His Majesty's Dominions, and that the status of Irish residents in the United Kingdom would not be adversely affected. This was reassuring to the Irish government, but frustrating to the Conservative opposition, who thought Ireland was securing too many benefits.[117] Noel-Baker believed that choosing Easter Monday to inaugurate the Republic was an insult to Britain and he asked Maffey if a goodwill message should be sent. He replied that good wishes should be conveyed because 'it will show that we are not attaching any great significance to that occasion. To hold back would suggest pique and would give cause to the unrighteous to rejoice at our discomfiture.'[118]

In May 1949, Parliament's Ireland Act recognised Ireland's departure from the Commonwealth and was particularly beneficial to Ireland regarding citizenship and trading rights. The Chief Representative of the Republic of Ireland in Britain and their staff would receive the same privileges and exemptions, excluding income tax, that Commonwealth High Commissioners and staff had, citizens of Ireland living in the United Kingdom would enjoy the same rights as Commonwealth citizens. There would be no change in trading preferences. These measures did not pass without argument - Lord Simon and Serjeant Sullivan inquired as to why Ireland was permitted to keep Commonwealth privileges if she was technically a foreign country. Conservatives were worried that the favourable treatment Ireland was receiving may upset relations with other Commonwealth nations. Despite these protests, the Bill became law and Attlee declared in the House of Commons, 'It is to be hoped that the Bill will be accepted both in the United Kingdom and in Eire as a common sense solution and a further step towards eliminating friction and bitterness.'[119]

But this was not to be due to the Act's reaffirmation of Northern Ireland's status, declaring 'that Northern Ireland remains part of his Majesty's dominions and of the United Kingdom and affirms that in no event will Northern Ireland or any part thereof cease to be part of his Majesty's dominions and of the United Kingdom without the consent of the Parliament of Northern Ireland.' The Act denoted the official end of the 1922 Boundary Commission, which Michael Collins and other Treaty negotiators had hoped would redraw the border in the Free State's favour. Ultimately, the new Republic meant that the Irish question was no longer an issue for the British political elite; the position of Northern Ireland was secure and the rest of Ireland claimed republic status.[120] For the British then, the Irish question had been answered.

Attlee believed that Britain must be firm about maintaining the position in Northern Ireland. Such action would please Conservatives; Churchill commented to Attlee that he 'will have to give some assurances to Northern Ireland.'[121] Attlee was happy to have Churchill's concurrence, particularly after clashes over India, and he readily agreed to placate Stormont. It was also necessary to reassure Northern Ireland, where the reaction was one of fright. Article 2 of Ireland's 1937 Constitution claimed jurisdiction over the entire island which, to Unionists, meant that the declaration of the Republic was merely a prelude to a violent campaign to absorb the North. Unionists were afraid that Britain might waver in its commitment to Northern Ireland and did not see why Ireland was permitted to keep most Commonwealth benefits. Unsurprisingly, Unionists demanded reassurance that they would remain safely in the United Kingdom and made it clear that they would defend their territory from the new Republic if necessary.

Northern Ireland's Prime Minister Sir Basil Brooke responded by pronouncing that repeal had created 'a yawning gap between the North and South which is unbridgeable,' further stating that 'what the Free State is after is the rape of Ulster; it is not marriage... the only solution to this very difficult situation which exists in Ireland as whole, is two Governments.'[122] On 14 December he sent a memorandum to Parliament with Stormont's proposals for inclusion in the bill and pledged to 'fight on all matters which might leave us in the hands of Eire.'[123] Brooke led a delegation to Whitehall in January to address the British government with Unionist concerns. Attlee assured him that 'I shall be prepared to make it clear, if the question is raised in the proceedings on the Ireland Bill, that, should the need arise, Northern Ireland will be defended against aggression in the same way as any other part of the United Kingdom.'[124]

It should have been evident that Britain would not change its position on partition. Attlee's government had never publicly advocated ending partition; on 9 October 1948, Noel-Baker drafted a letter to MP Herbert Morrison warning Labour Party members and candidates not to give pledges to end partition because doing so 'can only be embarrassing to the Party and to individuals concerned.'[125] Attlee reworded this on 13 October to read 'which would, in all probability, be embarrassing to the Party and the individuals concerned.'[126] This revision demonstrates that the Labour Party could not stand by members who advocated ending partition. Attlee recognized the paradox involved, stating that it was 'obvious that the action of the Government of Eire in deciding to leave the Commonwealth would increase the difficulty of arriving at any agreement on partition.'[127] Now Parliament had publicly and formally defined its position on partition.

How did the inter-party government reconcile repeal and the ongoing demand for the removal of partition? Lyons points out that Clann na Poblachta saw no incompatibility between the two, which may indicate that they misjudged the strength and tenacity of both Northern Unionism and the British willingness to protect the connection. MacBride believed that Unionists would eventually concede, writing to the *Irish Times* that 'their attachment to the Crown is more apparent than real' and the feeling that a 32 county Republic would not respect civil liberties was a 'prejudice' which he said, 'I believe, will die with the generation that is now passing out.'[128] Even with the benefit of hindsight, his view of the situation seems remarkably naïve and confirms that MacBride did not recognise the finality in Unionist rhetoric, preferring to see Ulster Unionism through green-coloured glasses. He believed the development of an integrated Europe or the United Nations would provide a forum that a newly independent Republic could use to raise the issue of partition without appeasing the Unionists. Costello argued that neither waiting to declare the Republic nor remaining in the Commonwealth had evoked the slightest response from the North, therefore it was pointless to continue to hope for a reconciliation that would not come.[129] As Costello said in the Dáil, 'Friendly overtures by this Government or any Government in this part of the country to the Northern Ireland Government would still be opposed by the same cascade of scorn and derision as had been directed by the northern ruling classes towards every constructive suggestion from Irish leaders for the ending of Partition.'[130]

The Ireland Act was the first time the Parliament of Northern Ireland was given a veto over the political unification of the country, a high point of Ulster Unionism.[131] Two days after the introduction of the Ireland Act, MacBride met with Attlee, then with Bevin and Noel-Baker, where Bevin explained to MacBride that many in the government were sympathetic to a united Ireland, but that

> we could not ignore the history of the last forty years. Northern Ireland had stood in with us against Hitler when the South was neutral. Without the help of the North, Hitler would unquestionably have won the submarine war and the United Kingdom would have been defeated... as a reward for this loyalty and until the majority in the North decided otherwise the British people would oblige us to give them guarantees that they would not be coerced.[132]

In a report to External Affairs, MacBride's reply to Bevin 'pointed out that what should be obvious to a layman, that Partition was already legally in existence on the British statute book and it was unprecedented to re-enact a law that was already valid.'[133] Also the Irish had consulted with the British and Commonwealth Governments regarding the Republic of Ireland Act, yet 'until the day before the "Ireland" Bill was introduced in the House of Commons no intimation, direct or indirect, was given to the Irish Government that it would contain these provisions.'

The government complained that the British government 'at no stage informed the Irish Government of, or consulted the Irish Government' in regard to the provisions of the Ireland Act involving the North.[134] In response, Bevin exposed the irony of the situation, 'you are complaining of our having given no indication to you of this government of Ireland Bill, why couldn't you have given us even a hint about the Republic of Ireland Act?'[135] The provision safeguarding the North was the only issue that the inter-party government could argue with and they protested vehemently, leading to more anti-partition campaigning. R.F. Foster believes the naïve reaction of Dublin to the Ireland Act showed both Costello's lack of skill and the insularity of post-war Ireland – the official line of Dublin continued to place all the blame for sustaining partition on London.[136] Placing responsibility there was unfair, as Attlee had informed MacBride that there would be no change in the status of Northern Ireland and the Unionists would obviously protest the declaration of the Republic and want reassurance of Britain's commitment to maintaining the connection, 'I have had to conclude that the Government of Eire considered that cutting the last tie which united Eire to the British Commonwealth a more important objective of policy than the ending of partition.'[137] As the *Irish Times* wryly observed after the reading of the Ireland Act, 'the guns of last Easter Monday morning were loaded with blank, but they may prove to have blasted the chief hope of every true nationalist.'[138]

The government did let Attlee and Sir Basil Brooke know how they felt in an *aide memoire* of 7 January 1949, expressing hope that nothing would be 'done by way of legislation or otherwise, which could in any way be construed as prolonging or strengthening the undemocratic anomaly whereby our country has been partitioned against the will of the overwhelming majority of the Irish people.'[139] There was no reply, but perhaps Attlee and his cabinet merely felt that they were restating the obvious in the Ireland Act.

The inter-party government officially protested in the Dáil, with Costello

[placing] on record its indignant protest against the introduction in the British Parliament of legislation purporting to endorse and continue the existing partition of Ireland, and [calling] upon the British Government and people to end the present occupation of our six north-eastern counties, and thereby enable the unity of Ireland to be restored and the age-long differences between the two nations brought to an end.[140]

On 13 May demonstrations were held on O'Connell Street in Dublin, featuring speeches by Costello, de Valera, MacBride, and Norton. Costello later stated that he thought the Ireland Act's reference to the North was an effort to please opposition leader Winston Churchill and the Conservative Party (once again paying little attention to the influence of Ulster Unionists), but that Ireland was successful in securing their main demands, retaining all benefits without losses.[141] Though the Commonwealth countries supported Ireland's departure, they did not want to intervene on Ireland's behalf in this case.

It did not solve ambiguity issues on Britain's part; Ireland was once 'excluded inside the Commonwealth,' now they were 'included outside the Commonwealth.'[142] But Britain allowed Ireland to keep the Commonwealth perks because it benefited Britain as well. Other Commonwealth countries defended Ireland's position, and the Statute of Westminster provided Ireland with the legal right to secede and, as Attlee echoed de Valera, 'Eire was already a Republic in fact.'[143] Because of its close geographic location and tragic history, Ireland occupied a different position than other Commonwealth countries and 'few things in the relationship between the two countries have been logical.'[144]

The British themselves did not seem particularly concerned with the Irish departure. MacBride gave a lecture to the Royal Institute of International Affairs on 24 February stating, 'I would venture to say that very few people in Britain even knew of [the External Relations Act's] existence and that those who did, knew little or nothing of its provisions. Indeed, as a constitutional fiction, it can hardly have been regarded as flattering to the British Crown.'[145]

In April 1949 the British Government announced the London Declaration, mainly as a means to keep India within the Commonwealth. The Declaration stated that Commonwealth countries could become republics, but the British monarch must be recognised as Head of the Commonwealth. Attlee felt that if Ireland had been patient, this may have been a possible solution to combine independence with improved constitutional relations with the UK.[146] This scenario is not likely; the promise of independence was essential to the Irish psyche, and following India's example may have created even further confusion in the relationship with Britain. The Irish were not influenced by India's example; they viewed their own situation within the Commonwealth as unique, ignoring the parallels of religious and cultural oppression. Yet, within thirty years, Ireland would have not have been out of place, as by then there were a majority of republics within the Commonwealth.

Ireland's departure did not fundamentally affect the Commonwealth; although Mansergh believes it would have been valuable to hear Ireland's views on issues like the Suez crisis, South Africa's secession, and the development of the Common Market.[147] Mansergh predicted an obvious disadvantage to secession, Ireland being deprived of an opportunity for a voice in world affairs and Commonwealth countries not being able to exercise great influence on Ireland.[148] Lee takes an opposing view and speculates that Irish diplomats may have made worthy contributions, but it seems doubtful if an Irish absence made much difference to Ireland or to the Commonwealth.[149] The Council of Europe, the United Nations, and the OEEC could provide other avenues of partnership and cooperation and the idea of wanting to pursue these avenues as an independent nation may have been tempting. The emphasis and direction of Irish foreign policy was changing from de Valera's method of working within the Commonwealth to MacBride's strategy of looking towards Western Europe.

However, it might have benefited Ireland to stay within the Commonwealth in order to end partition. In 1936 after the abdication crisis, Seán MacEoin stated in Dáil that de Valera was in a prime bargaining position. If he declared a Republic for the 26 counties, he could then approach the British and inform them that if they wanted Ireland to remain within the Commonwealth and accept the monarch, then Ireland would do so under the condition that it was a monarch of a *united* Ireland.[150] Allegedly, by not attempting this, de Valera missed an opportunity to use the Commonwealth to end partition, though it would probably not have met with success due to Unionist pressure to avoid any link with the proposed Republic. Browne was not unhappy with repeal but also agreed with de Valera's reasoning for keeping external association, the only remaining link in common between the North and the Free State, its retention could help reconciliation between both parts of the country.[151] Yet, as Lee argues, if Northern Ireland Protestants were not convinced to consider unification to persuade Dublin to enter World War II, which in 1940 may have been an option, they would hardly be likely to unite because Dublin chose to remain in the Commonwealth.[152]

If solving the partition problem, seemingly an essential issue, was a possibility while in the Commonwealth, why did Ireland leave? Aside from Commonwealth membership not mattering to the North, Ireland was uncomfortable with dominion status because it came too late and it came as a result of violence. As Costello argued in his Ottawa speech, 'by reason of their seven centuries of struggle with England and because of the fact that the political situations which grew up naturally in Britain and her Dominions... were imposed on Ireland, those could never really be acceptable to Irishmen.' MacBride said in an interview with the *Manchester Guardian* on 21 September 1948 that there was no parallel between the history of Ireland and the other Commonwealth countries because

> descendants of the British pioneers who built the Commonwealth naturally take pride in their common British origin; they feel an affection for their home country and for the crown... Accordingly, the British Crown served as a traditional rallying point for them. But there is no similarity between our history and the history of the Commonwealth countries.

He made a similar point in a lecture to the Royal Institute of International Affairs on 24 February, stating that Ireland had no real attachment to the monarchy based on national sentiment; rather the relationship involved protracted struggle where the Crown was a symbol of oppression.[153] Such a symbol served as a psychological disadvantage and a rallying point for more extreme forms of nationalism. It would have been difficult to raise the issue of partition if Ireland were still a member of the Commonwealth; partition would remain a domestic issue, leaving the Commonwealth could turn it into an international one. As Lyons eloquently wrote, Ireland remained deaf to the lure of the Commonwealth and 'in the end heard only the ghosts of Roger Casement and all those other dead men knocking on the door.'[154]

Conclusion

Twenty years afterward, Costello claimed that the declaration of the Republic was one of the major achievements of the inter-party government.[155] Seán MacEoin agreed and praised both Costello and MacBride: 'we now looked forward to a new dawn in Ireland's history, thanks to the statesmanship of John Costello and Seán MacBride and the unanimous support of the Dáil and Seanad.'[156] This is not an undisputed conclusion; Lee feels that the 'whole performance of the government... seems to have been a shambles from start to finish, perhaps the most inept diplomatic exhibition in the history of the state,'[157] and Foster believes that Dublin's naïve reaction to the Ireland Act highlighted Costello's ineptness.[158] Coogan contends that leaving the Commonwealth had harmful consequences which are still being felt, particularly in the relationship with Northern Ireland, 'as a result of Dublin's severance of its link with the Crown, a far stronger one was forged between Belfast and London.'[159] Both Lee and Foster encompass the revisionist tradition, but mainly in the sense of viewing historical scholarship as an ongoing debate, in which it is preferable to discuss people and movements in a atmosphere of relative detachment without attempting to soften their interpretations in concordance with what is beneficial for the nation. If the establishment of priorities is a fundamental feature of a productive foreign policy, then the events surrounding repeal show a lack of clear design and forethought in Anglo-Irish relations. The inter-party government was indeed 'overwhelmed by the momentum of circumstance'[160] and repeal remains a dubious legacy. Essentially, fortunate timing and the intervention of other Commonwealth countries assured that Ireland did not suffer negative consequences from leaving the Commonwealth.

However, MacBride should be recognised for his contribution to repeal because in the short run his negotiations helped to disguise the reactive rather than active posture of the inter-party government, bolting the barn door after Costello had allowed the horse to escape. In the long term his tactics helped Ireland to become involved in an integrated Europe, demonstrating his 'obsession with Ireland's international position.'[161] He showed an interest in politics of European cooperation and integration, which is not surprising considering MacBride's French background, and more generally, Irish Nationalists' past habit of looking to France and Germany for help in 1798 and 1916 respectively. Despite MacBride's Marshall Plan negotiations, OEEC, and Council of Europe dealings, these did not count as 'real' matters of foreign affairs – the action was in the nature of Ireland's relationship with Britain. Britain was, for a long time, the way Ireland defined herself, and MacBride was attempting in those other examples, to move away from this, to define Ireland without Britain. MacBride's personal assistant Caitriona Lawlor lists repeal among MacBride's prized accomplishments, 'MacBride was happy enough about the achievements of Clann na Poblachta in government - the repeal of the External Relations Act, the fact there were no political prisoners, and the significant increase in the afforestation figures.'[162]

Additionally, repeal was important from a psychological perspective. When asked by the *Irish Times* if repeal would improve relations with Britain, George Bernard Shaw answered 'It will improve relations with everybody. This is not politics, but psychology.'[163] It removed much of the ambiguity and tension of the relationship between Britain and Ireland and gave the Irish a sense of self-determination and would help Ireland to establish an international identity separate from Britain. MacEoin believed that the External Relations Act 'lowered our own dignity as a nation.'[164] MacBride echoed this sentiment, stating that the Act 'was as repugnant to our national sentiment as it was unreal. As a constitutional fiction, it pleased no one.'[165] Furthermore, the move was politically astute for both Fine Gael and Clann na Poblachta.

Otherwise, repeal was not truly a radical move – it did not change much of the day-to-day relationship between Britain and Ireland, 'the country at large... will lose little sleep over this decision,' and other formalities were discarded with little effect.[166] Leaving the Commonwealth had no discernible effect in practice, as Cruise O'Brien points out, de Valera's decision to declare Ireland a neutral country during World War II had established the independence of the Irish state more convincingly than the declaration of the Republic.[167] The boundaries remained the same, as did Ireland's economic relationship to Britain. Repeal was successful due to the benevolent indifference of both Great Britain and the Commonwealth countries. There was little disapproval and no severe retaliatory action; the consensus was that Ireland's withdrawal should not affect friendly relations between Ireland and Commonwealth nations. Leaving the Commonwealth did not provide an answer to the deeper problem of partition; as MacBride commented, 'all obstacles to the creation of a better relationship, with the exception of partition, have now been removed.'[168] Of course, that particular obstacle was immense. Attlee later wrote, 'Much of the old bitterness between the English and Irish had passed away... but the division between the North and South was still a rankling sore.'[169]

What it did provide was a sense of autonomy and independence, fundamental to how Ireland wanted to be perceived both by herself and by other nations. Achievement of sovereignty took precedence over aspiration to unity, which had been the case since 1921[170] and sovereignty was incomplete as long as a formal link existed. In a speech delivered on 8 April 1949, MacEoin declared that 'thirty-three years after Padraig Pearse's historic declaration, we will be able to say, and have it accepted all over the world, that in this part of the country we are an absolutely sovereign Republic.'[171] Other countries were made aware of Irish independence, providing a chance to find forums where Ireland was not seen as a British appendage, which would please MacBride and perhaps provide a way to publicise, if not solve the problem of partition.

3

The Fourth Green Field: Seán Macbride and the Problem of Partition

'We do not see things the way they are. We see things the way we are.'

The Talmud

This chapter examines Seán MacBride and the inter-party government's response to the issue of partition. The desire to end partition had been a major element of Clann na Poblachta's party platform and the anti-partition campaign was a priority of MacBride's while in office. Though it was unsuccessful, the anti-partition movement and the resulting propaganda agencies had an enormous impact on Irish foreign policy and affected Ireland's relationships with both Britain and the United States and demonstrated the reactive policy of the inter-party government, which played a part in propagating tensions in the North.

There were two facets to the anti-partition policy; attempts to bring about cooperation and propaganda at home and abroad. The latter quickly eclipsed the former. MacBride's method consisted of raising the issue in the international arena at every possible opportunity in the hope that publicising the 'unnaturalness' of division and appealing to self-determination would provide the necessary pressure for Britain to rejoin the country. Clann na Poblachta, which attracted republicans disenchanted by the lack of movement on partition, proposed equalling the benefits of the British welfare state in Ireland, establishing concentrated contact with both Northern Nationalists and Catholics, and allaying Unionist fears about 'Rome Rule'. Yet MacBride abandoned these ideas to undertake a propaganda campaign that showed no signs of working. Why did he continue to pursue a fruitless strategy when other options were available? Did MacBride's focus on raising the partition problem sacrifice foreign policy gains in favour of publicising the issue?

Macbride's method did have some positive effects; Ireland's participation in an integrating Europe did much to counter any negative foreign policy effects of their World War II neutrality policy. But he and the inter-party government made the mistake, common in Irish Nationalist politics, of underestimating Unionist tenacity and expended too much energy on publicising partition in the international arena rather than focusing on reconciliation at the national level, discarding opportunities to improve the relationship or at least assuage the Unionist siege mentality.

A great deal has been written about both the origins of partition and how the North and South developed following partition.[1] All seem to agree that the division of the island was an inevitable consequence of Irish demands for independence and Unionist desire to preserve the connection to Britain and that, while partition was not the prominent concern with the 1921 Treaty, all parties in the South spoke vehemently about bringing it to an end.

More recent works by Eithne MacDermott and Ian McCabe highlight both MacBride's political party and Ireland's diplomatic history in the first year of the inter-party government. MacDermott's *Clann na Poblachta* posits that gains made by membership in Council of Europe and the OEEC were wasted because MacBride raised the problem of partition so often. Ireland's concerns were judged to be irrelevant in the wider context; World War II was a recent memory and Britain was viewed as a 'liberator' of Europe from harsher oppression than she imposed upon Ireland, making Irish partition seem minor in comparison.[2] MacBride wisely attempted to broaden the country's perspectives by involving Ireland in pan-European movements, but would then squander these gains by constantly discussing partition. MacDermott correctly points out that he should have raised partition in one area where it counted – the Irish context. Instead, his anti-partition rhetoric 'served... to further cement whatever ties already existed.'[3] She also allows that the political parties in the Republic did not acknowledge or understand the Unionist perspective. *Clann na Poblachta* provides a useful starting point for explaining why MacBride's strategy was ultimately unsuccessful and what may have been done as an alternative but, as the book focuses on the history of the political party, it does not delve very deeply into these issues. McCabe's *A Diplomatic History of Ireland 1948-1949* describes the reasons for refusing to join NATO, but concentrates predominantly on negotiations with the British and Commonwealth ministers regarding repeal. He does not expound on the inter-party government's plan for ending partition or suggest any alternative strategy, but does briefly suggest that since Taoiseach John Costello likely believed that if partition could not be ended, repeal was another option for the inter-party government to prove its republican credentials.[4]

There have been a number of analyses of Ireland's relationship with the United States, concentrating on MacBride's constant attempts to link partition to NATO and the Marshall Plan, and all agree that it had a negative effect on Irish-American relations.[5] Some, notably Ronan Fanning and Seán Cronin, explore how Irish participation in NATO would have affected partition. As Troy Davis writes, the decision to remain outside of NATO due to partition only accentuated the differences between the two parts of Ireland and exposed Irish naïveté about their relationship with America - it sustained partition instead of weakening it.[6]

MacBride's biographer Anthony Jordan does not explore the issue in depth except to make MacBride's basic stance on the matter clear: it was undemocratic and that this view needed to be spread worldwide.[7] Nicholas Mansergh puts the dilemma in a wider Commonwealth context, believing that Ireland overlooked many practical consequences of succession from the Commonwealth - ending partition could only be done by agreement, and if Ireland had kept close to the Commonwealth, reunification may have been a possibility. However, by 1949, all parties had convinced themselves that neither full dominion status nor external association would contribute to the removal of the border. Both Mansergh and David McCullagh in his *A Makeshift Majority* correctly suggest that reunification would never happen without contact and some functional cooperation, for example hydroelectric schemes, transport, and fisheries.[8]

Just as all Irish political parties agreed that partition must end, all writers concur that partition was the central issue in Irish politics. Yet, aside from McCullagh, who ends up taking an excessively pessimistic attitude toward the benefits of cross-border cooperation, the assessments on partition are incomplete because none fully explain why MacBride continued his ineffective propaganda strategy nor do they conceive any detailed methods on how MacBride and the inter-party government could have solved the dilemma.

Background to Partition

It is impossible to pinpoint when the exact division between the North and the South of Ireland took place.[9] Though the idea of partition had been broached during the formulation of the third Home Rule Bill, the beginnings of official partition did not come about until the Government of Ireland Act in 1920. However division between the territory termed 'Ulster' and the rest of the island had existed for centuries and despite Nationalist claims to the whole of Ireland, official partition seemed to be the simplest and least costly way for the British to grant Irish Nationalists some form of self-government. Partition was a way to accommodate rather than resolve historic conflicts. Because Unionism was such a forceful movement, partition was an inevitable political choice; but Nationalists, who underestimated the passion of Unionism, regarded it as a temporary measure.

Yet, in 1912, when Irish Home Rule seemed inevitable, Ulsterman Bonar Law stated, 'Ireland is not a nation; it is two nations. It is two nations separated from each other by lines of cleavage which cut far deeper than those which separate Great Britain from Ireland as a whole.'[10] Unionists saw themselves as a community that enjoyed a contractual relationship with Britain and they did not want to join a more impoverished South and lose the benefits of being British subjects. Moreover, their supremacist attitude toward Catholics coupled with their fear of oppression under a Catholic majority made loyalty to the crown their best option.

In order to pacify Unionists and prevent civil war, the British Government introduced the Government of Ireland Act, which became law on 23 December 1920. It provided for two devolved parliaments; one in Belfast and one in Dublin. The Act also provided for a Council of Ireland to consist of 20 members from each assembly, to promote co-operation and the possibility of a future all-Ireland parliament. A settlement with the South could now be made because the North had been provided for. As R.F. Foster indicates, the Treaty of 1921 did not enable partition to take place; partition actually cleared the way for the Treaty.[11]

Partition was not the major contention with the Treaty; the Oath of Allegiance to the King and dominion rather than republic status were the divisive issues. The debaters in the Dáil left the question of partition aside and focused on questions of sovereignty and alliance instead of what later generations might regard as the more fundamental problem of a divided country. As Lyons points out, of the 338 pages of debate printed in the Dáil report, only 9 pages were devoted to partition.[12] During the 1920s, the belief that economic and other factors would eventually lead to reunification meant that the Cosgrave government did not make an issue of it. Establishing the Free State in the aftermath of civil war and curbing periodic IRA activity meant that reuniting with the North was not the focus. The feeling in the Free State was that partition was fleeting and Ireland would soon be reunited.

Self-determination and 'Unnaturalness'

While campaigning and while in office, MacBride unceasingly affirmed that the removal of partition was inevitable; he believed that a basic bond of love of Ireland united the peoples of the North and South. The difficulty was that they loved different concepts of 'Ireland'. MacBride unwittingly provided an example of this, 'An English friend of mine recently complained bitterly to me because we [Ireland] were celebrating the 150th anniversary of the United Irishmen and of the 1798 Insurrection. He saw in this an overt act of unfriendliness. We, on the other hand, thought it the most natural thing in the world.'[13] Ulstermen may have had more sympathy for 1798 commemorations, but in a country where history and commemoration are so vital, notable historical events like the Siege of Derry, the Battle of the Boyne, and the 1916 Easter Rising have very different meanings across the border. The Unionist view of 1916 demonstrates this divergence; 'when Britain was in deadly danger in the first great struggle against power-hungry Germany, then came the Southern Irish stab in the back which might have dealt world civilization a mortal blow.'[14] How would 'national' events be commemorated if partition ended? It is likely that the Unionist tradition would be subsumed and it is also likely that Unionists realised this. As Clare O'Halloran argues, 'the rhetoric was primarily that of "one nation," [but] there was an implicit exclusion of northern unionists from a nationalism which was wholly gaelic [sic] and Catholic in ethos.'[15]

Parnell's assertion that 'no man has the right to set a boundary to the onward march of a nation,' the frequent use of the word 'unnatural' when referring to partition, and the concept of nationalism that MacBride and the government were trying to invoke put them on uncertain ground. As MacBride stated in the Dáil,

> Our sole claim is that the Irish people should be allowed to determine their own affairs democratically and of their own free will, without interference by Britain. The fact that Britain succeeded, over 25 years ago, in retaining a corner of our island and that she has since occupied it, in no way entitled her to divide the historic Irish nation and to pretend that our island now consists of two separate nations.[16]

But were they pretending? Partition was and is an incredibly emotive issue where each community feels the need to forge an account of the past that vindicates its role in it and offers guidance for the future. Each side also feels need to defend that account in the face of the denials and contrary claims of the other. The problem involves basic definitions of the 'nation'. In his *Nations and States*, Hugh Seton-Watson defines a nation as 'a community of people whose members are bound together by a sense of solidarity, a common culture, a national consciousness.'[17] In the nineteenth century, nationalist theories, particularly in Central Europe, included denying the status of nationhood to others. In contrast to the community in which the definer belonged, some other group was not entitled to be called a nation.[18] Though Seton-Watson does not believe that Northern Ireland fits his definition of a nation,[19] Unionists ultimately defined themselves against Nationalists, possessing a different state power, religion, and language (the official language of Ireland is Irish, though most of the population do not speak it as their first language), thus the sense of solidarity required in Seton-Watson's definition was ironically provided by the Republic. Tom Nairn in his *The Break-up of Britain* also contends that the Republic and the North are two separate 'nationalities' in the sense of two distinct ethno-cultural communities; there are two *potential* national communities and states, but not two corresponding nations.[20]

An argument can be made that the island does indeed consist of two different nations. The examination of national identity continues to be an important way of comprehending the political dynamic of continuity and change in many states. The Irish political culture looked to restore Ireland's Gaelic past, preserving Catholic traditions, and isolating itself from the perceived threat of the colonising, alien culture of Britain.[21] The only favourable post-partition view of the North was as the last Gaelic area, but this image reflects the Nationalist preoccupation with the colonial past rather than any northern reality.[22]

The 'necessity that Ireland be not merely a geographical entity but a single constitutional unit was taken as a matter of faith and, like most fungi and dogmas, it grew best unexamined and in the dark.'[23] The separateness that exists between the North and South is not necessarily a troublesome situation. Partition had some obvious advantages; for the North the standard of living was better and the religious rights of the majority were protected. There were advantages for the Republic as well; partition provided a virtually homogenous society, no political or religious animosity existed as it did in the North, and it provided a political stability that helped the new nation develop without much rancour. The Civil War was injurious enough, but trying to placate Unionist opposition as well may have proved to be impossible. Additionally, after the establishment of the British Welfare State, the gulf between living standards and expectations in Northern Ireland and the rest of the island widened dramatically, Northern Ireland could benefit from the Welfare State and Ireland could not equal this, making Irish unity economically impractical.

Nationhood does not always follow geography and partition and division had been used within the Empire and Commonwealth to solve Nationalist issues. Partition had been employed in India in settling religious and political differences; the division between the Indian National Congress and the Muslim League made a united India unlikely and it was necessary to safeguard minority rights.[24] Division was necessary in Palestine to create a Jewish homeland. Partition was seen as a way to solve post-war problems, one notable example is the division of Germany. Cruise O'Brien feels that the alleged occupation was sustained by the will and votes of the majority living there and this essential fact was ignored in anti-partition propaganda.[25] Partition was merely an institutional recognition of pre-existing and genuine divisions within Ireland. Scholars and politicians have argued over whether Ireland is or is not two nations, but it cannot be denied that there exist two traditions, two aspirations, and two philosophies of life.[26] A letter to the *Freeman's Journal* written by Reverend M. O'Flanagan, the Secretary of Sinn Féin in June 1916 illustrates this:

> Geography has worked to make one nation of Ireland. History has worked against it. The island of Ireland, and the national unity of Ireland, do not coincide... The Unionists of Ulster have never given their allegiance to Ireland. They love the hills of Antrim and Down in the same way we love the plains of Roscommon, but the centre of their patriotic enthusiasm is London... as ours is Dublin. We claim the right to decide what is our nation. We refuse that same right to Orangemen.[27]

Britain and the Partition Problem

Propaganda attempts to end partition targeted Britain as the government believed that the ultimate responsibility for ending partition lay with the British government. They were also confident that Britain could solve the problem with no consequences, such as civil war, and that doing so was in Britain's best interest, 'that a united and free Ireland is as essential to

Britain's welfare as it is to Ireland's.'[28] This view was convenient in some sense; 'by insisting that Britain alone was to blame, Nationalists absolved themselves of any possible guilt for partition and therefore of any obligation to find a solution.'[29] At a lecture to the Royal Institute of International Affairs, MacBride disputed the view that the problem should be settled by the Irish; 'This, I am afraid is a somewhat superficial and evasive viewpoint.' [30] MacBride pointed out that partition was effected by Act of the British Parliament, passed in 1920. British Customs operated the Border, British troops occupied the territory, and British finances were inextricably mixed with those of the Belfast Government. Therefore it was Britain's responsibility to take some action. MacBride again alluded to the right of national self-determination, clearly defined boundaries, and a national history. Despite the amenable relationship Ireland and Great Britain possessed, 'No matter how much one may like one's neighbour, one does not like him to squat in a corner of one's garden. We merely want our garden. It is not really so unreasonable.'[31] Costello called the British denial of responsibility 'Pilate-like' stating that 'the problem was created by the British Government and the British Parliament and it is for them to solve the problem. They cannot wash their hands of it and clear themselves of responsibility for it.'[32]

In a speech after the Ireland Act was passed, MacBride argued, 'Accordingly, this gratuitous guarantee of "territorial integrity" of a portion of our country can only be taken as an attempt to reinforce the unjust partition of our country and to encourage the Belfast Government to persevere in their intransigence.'[33] MacBride had misjudged the chain of command; the Belfast Government was reinforcing partition and the British Government was merely responding to their wishes. Regarding MacBride's Chatham House lecture, H. Duncan Hall observed that 'the audience, while uncertain about his logic, thought he should argue his case with Belfast rather than London.'[34]

As late as 1951, he still considered Britain responsible for partition, which could not continue without Britain's political, economic, and military support. His policy to mobilise opinion as stated at the 1951 Clann party ard-fheis was 'to ensure that Britain will understand clearly that the maintenance of partition constitutes a real inconvenience and is an actual hindrance to her own policies.'[35] At a speech to the Manchester Anti-Partition of Ireland League, Costello stated that

it is our hope that when the British people are fully informed of the facts, when their consciences are awakened to the injustice of what has been done by their Parliament in their name, to the denial of rights to the minority in the North, when they appreciate how deeply and closely their own national interests and security are involved, justice will prevail and that even the cynic and the bigot will be persuaded to see that what expediency once created, expediency now requires that it be destroyed.[36]

However, the British viewpoint was quite different. As opposition leader Winston Churchill said in 1948, 'I shall always hope that someday there will be a united Ireland, but at the same time, that Ulster and Northern counties will never be compelled against their wishes to enter the Dublin Parliament. They should be courted; they should not be raped.' He believed that by declaring Ireland a republic 'Mr. Costello and his colleagues have constituted themselves the authors of permanent partition.'[37]   Public statements by both Churchill and Prime Minister Clement Attlee should have made MacBride and the government realise that the British were not going to change their stance on partition. Northern Ireland Prime Minister Sir Basil Brooke was confident that 'their basic ideas were the same,'[38] highlighted by their past experience of the Second World War and the future security of the United Kingdom. Instead of badgering Britain, it would have been a better plan to work with Belfast.

The 1937 Constitution, Irish Neutrality, and Partition
The Constitution proved to be another barrier to Irish unity. While President of the Executive Council, Éamon de Valera took the opportunity to author a new Constitution in 1937 to divest Ireland of the elements he found abhorrent in the Treaty. The 1922 Constitution was seen as a product of the bargain with Britain, a typical liberal-democratic document suiting a country with any religious complexion; the Catholic Church was not mentioned and religious freedom and equality were guaranteed. The 1937 Constitution was much more marked by Catholic thought. Fianna Fáil tried to build up the image of being the more Catholic party than Cumann na nGaedheal, the party that had passed the 1922 Constitution based on the Treaty's conditions. The preamble to *Bunreacht na hÉireann* contains the passage, 'We, the people of Éire, Humbly acknowledging all our obligations to our Divine Lord, Jesus Christ, Who sustained our fathers through centuries of trial, Gratefully remembering their heroic and unremitting struggle to regain the rightful independence of our Nation.' This phrase leads to several questions of

interpretation; J.H. Whyte correctly asks *whose* fathers were sustained?[39] Also, what *obligations* and which *trials*?

An example of how partition was seen as temporary by the Irish is most famously found in Articles 2 and 3 of the Constitution, which claimed the right of the Dublin government to exercise jurisdiction over the whole of Ireland 'pending the reintegration of the national territory.' Article 2 stated that 'the national territory consists of the whole island of Ireland, its islands and the territorial seas. It is the entitlement and birthright of every person born in the island of Ireland, which includes its islands and seas, to be part of the Irish nation.' This was the first time the claim to the six counties was given legal form and permanence.[40] However, Article 3 allowed temporary recognition of partition by stating that the document only applied to the 26 counties until Ireland was once again united.

Articles 2 and 3 claimed political and territorial control over the entire island while Article 44 claimed religious control or at least partiality: 'The State recognises the special position of the Holy Catholic Apostolic and Roman Church as the guardian of the Faith professed by the great majority of the citizens.' The Catholic Church was singled out and Protestants and other religious denominations were grouped afterwards. During the debates on ratification TD Frank McDermot suggested leaving the phrase out, as it was

the thing in the Constitution which most offended against the idea of the unity of Ireland. It was... a thing that was likely to create misunderstandings and objections in the minds of persons in the North of Ireland... It seems to serve no purpose except to create misunderstandings.[41]

De Valera responded with a justification:

There are 93 per cent of the people in this part of Ireland and 75 per cent of the people of Ireland as a whole who belong to the Catholic Church, who believe in its teachings, and whose whole philosophy of life is the philosophy that comes from its teachings. Consequently it is very important that in our Constitution that fact should be recognised... if we are going to be ruled by the representatives of the people, it is clear their whole philosophy of life is going to affect that, and that has to be borne in mind and the recognition of it is important in that sense.[42]

It can be argued that de Valera added this proviso out of political necessity as well as deference to the Church. De Valera operated within somewhat narrow electoral limitations and 'his proposals had to be acceptable to the largest and potentially most influential pressure group in the country, the Catholic Church.'[43] Yet he did not make the Catholic Church the official or established Church, giving it 'symbolic primacy but no additional authority.'[44]

Despite de Valera's clever political manoeuvring, the clause indicated further proof of 'Rome Rule' to Unionists. In addition, Article 41, which prohibited divorce and encouraged women to remain in the home while raising their families demonstrated a pervasive Catholic influence that could be used to justify Unionist claims that the Free State was a papal state.[45] Article 41, though a social rather than political constraint, demonstrated the close church-state relationship and provided fuel to Unionist fire that, if Ireland were united, they would be forced to live under Catholic ideology.

There was no outright opposition to Articles 2 and 3 in the Dáil and the press saw more controversy in the role of the President, the status of women, and the liberty of the press, which was constrained by Article 40.[46] As the *Irish Times* pointed out, the 'average citizen will be interested far more keenly in the price of cattle and dairy produce than in the abstract platitudes of the new Constitution.'[47] The lack of serious public debate likely reflects the southern Nationalist's familiarity with mere rhetorical gestures and a willingness to accept and support them.[48] Yet de Valera's Constitution made the Irish state appear wholly committed to the maintenance of Catholic values, especially because it led to the repeal of rights enjoyed under previous British law. Unionists could not help but view these Articles as a tyranny of a religious majority that would oblige Protestants to accept constraints that their own religion did not require.[49] Fianna Fáil was returned to office in the 1937 General Election with a minority but the Constitution referendum, held on the same day, passed with a majority vote, 685,000 to 527,000.[50]

While in government, MacBride exhibited a willingness to alter the Constitution to guarantee civil rights, but did not seem to see much difficulty with the existing document:

Under our Constitution, full and adequate safeguards are rigidly imposed to protect the religious and political minorities that may exist, but in so far as it might be suggested that these are inadequate to safeguard the views of any of our fellow-countrymen in the Six

Counties, I think I can say, not merely on my own behalf but on behalf of any Irish Government, that we would be prepared to give them any other additional rights and guarantees that were reasonably required.[51]

Yet the inter-party government did not make any attempt to change the Constitution, possibly choosing to wait for overtures from Britain or the North. The contentious articles were amended, but not until much later.[52] If such amendments had been carried out earlier, it might have led to a more amenable relationship between North and South because it would have demonstrated a willingness on the part of the Irish government to compromise and to mollify Unionists that their civil rights would not be threatened.

Ireland's neutrality policy during World War II also helped to sustain partition. Probably due to exaggerated British intelligence reports of an impending German invasion of Ireland, Dominions Secretary Malcolm MacDonald engaged in secret missions to de Valera in the early summer of 1940, offering Irish unity in exchange for immediate entry into the war. This was the first concrete offer of a united Ireland and the British promised that it would 'at once seek to obtain the assent... of the Government of Northern Ireland' if the Irish accepted the offer.[53] There were six clauses, including 'a declaration to be issued by the United Kingdom Government forthwith accepting the principle of a United Ireland' and promising 'a joint body including representatives of the Government of Eire and the Government of Northern Ireland to be set up at once to work out the constitutional and other practical details of the Union of Ireland.'[54] In exchange, Britain called for Ireland 'to enter the war on the side of the United Kingdom and her allies forthwith' and to 'invite British naval vessels to have the use of the ports in Eire and British troops and aeroplanes to co-operate with the Eire forces' as well as 'to intern all German and Italian aliens in the country and to take any further steps necessary to suppress Fifth Column activities.'[55]

The bargain depended on the Craigavon government in Belfast giving their assent. Robert Fisk argued that can be little doubt that Lord President of the Council Neville Chamberlain would put considerable pressure on Craigavon if he challenged the plan.[56] Yet, British ministers did not believe that the offer would be accepted; as Ronan Fanning points out, de Valera's priority was Irish sovereignty, not Irish unity.[57] Chamberlain told the war cabinet, 'I am bound to say that I hardly anticipate anything but a negative answer.'[58] However, the de Valera government would not take such an offer lightly; as Malcolm MacDonald pointed out, the prospect of securing a united Ireland was better than it ever had been. If de Valera missed the chance, the opportunity may never present itself again.[59] De Valera chose not to accept this offer, believing that there was no guarantee that a united Ireland would transpire and that a joint conference would end in disagreement.[60] MacDonald promised that Irish troops would only be used to defend

Ireland and that the extra equipment provided by Britain would make Germany less likely to invade. De Valera did not see it this way, suggesting that if they did invade or if Britain lost the war, 'the Germans would wish to punish them savagely for presuming to enter the war against them. They would wish to make Eire a lesson from which other powers would learn not to intervene of the side of the United Kingdom.' After meeting with the cabinet, he decided that the British proposals were 'not acceptable.'[61] De Valera wrote to the High Commissioner in London John Dulanty,

The plan would commit us definitely to an immediate abandonment of our neutrality. On the other hand, it gives no guarantee that in the end we would have a united Ireland, unless indeed concessions were made to Lord Craigavon opposed to the sentiments and aspirations of the great majority of the Irish people.[62]

When Craigavon learned of this offer, he was incensed. He fumed that de Valera was blackmailing the British government, who were all too willing to disregard Ulster's loyalty when it suited them.[63] He called the British offer to Ireland 'treachery to loyal Ulster.'[64]

Would the British have reneged on the offer especially in view of Unionist unwillingness to even consider the possibility? De Valera believed so, but he may have been mistaken; Britain would have been grateful for Irish help, especially in 1940 when it was the only European nation openly fighting Nazi Germany. The problem would not be British unwillingness to keep their part of the bargain; the difficulty would be incorporating an unwilling six counties into the Irish state. Attlee later regretted that de Valera missed this opportunity for unification.[65] Despite declaring neutrality and events like De Valera's offer of formal condolences upon Hitler's death and his refusal to close Axis legations or hand over Axis personnel or property, Irish neutrality was hardly strict, rather, as Attlee wrote, it was a 'benevolent neutrality' that favoured the

Allies.[66] During and after the war, Ireland had never been ideologically neutral.[67] Ireland was also heavily dependent on Britain economically and this relationship continued during the war. Ireland cooperated with Britain by supplying volunteers[68] and agreeing to support Britain in the event of a German invasion.[69] However, it made sense to take an official neutral stance; Ireland was militarily weak and in no real danger as long as Britain held out. [70] The policy enjoyed popularity; Ireland united behind it and sustaining the policy in spite of pressure from the old enemy provided a sense of satisfaction.[71] As Mansergh writes in *Problems of War-time Cooperation and Postwar Change*, neutrality was 'the final vindication of independence.'[72]

Though neutrality isolated Ireland from the damaging effects of war and provided a successful test of self-determination and an independent foreign policy, Irish neutrality was a principal factor in influencing the decision of British not to lean on Northern Ireland to unite with the Irish Free State. 'Until 1939 there was a respectable body of opinion in Great Britain, in particularly in the Liberal and Labour Parties, which sympathised with the object of Irish reunion and might conceivably have been stimulated into doing something about it.'[73] However, a united Ireland would in all likelihood remain technically neutral, which would be detrimental to both Britain and America with regard to the Cold War. As the American State Department's Director for European Affairs John Hickerson observed:

> With the United Kingdom in control of Northern Ireland we have, according to the past record, every reason to count on the use of bases in that area in the event of need. I am sure that you will agree that this is a powerful argument for this Government's favoring the continued control of Northern Ireland by the United Kingdom.[74]

It is doubtful that Ireland could have remained neutral if Northern Ireland did not exist. Northern Ireland's connection to the United Kingdom actually made it possible for the Irish to implement a neutrality policy.[75] In addition, Britain felt she owed something to Northern Ireland for participating in the war. As Churchill said in 1943, 'the bonds of affection between Great Britain and the people of Northern Ireland have been tempered by fire and are now, I firmly believe, unbreakable.' In a later victory speech in 1945, he also stated that 'a strong loyal Ulster will always be vital to the security and well-being of our whole empire and commonwealth.' Neutrality, though it provided Ireland with its first independent foreign policy opportunity, made Ireland a 'moral debtor' while strengthening the relationship between Northern Ireland and Great Britain.

The inter-party government would have opportunities to correct these fastenings, with the ability to change the Constitution and to join NATO. Regrettably, they did neither. As the *Irish Times* editorialised in 1947, 'What have we been doing, or what do we intend to do, to persuade our Northern brethren to join us?' De Valera 'ought to talk less about partition… and think more about it.'[76]

The Election of 1948

The partition issue was forced into the background during the war, but as both Inglis and Davis observe, the change of government in February 1948 rekindled partition as a live issue in Irish politics.[77] Partition was not a divisive subject in the 26 counties; all parties agreed that it should be removed as quickly as possible and no physical force should be used. From 1922 on, it was a domestic ritual to refer to partition in almost every political speech. Not surprisingly, during the 1948 general election, MacBride and Clann na Poblachta campaigned for the end of partition and had the newcomer's advantage of being able to chide Fianna Fáil for not solving it. MacBride suggested two noteworthy ideas; improving conditions within Ireland to rival the benefits that the North were receiving under the British Welfare State, and the proposal 'to give the right of audience in the Dáil to the elected representatives of the Six Counties' as well as nominations to the Seanad, an idea similar to the power-sharing government instituted fifty years later, as MacBride said during the campaign, 'In the Constitution, it is claimed that the Dáil is the Parliament of the whole country. Yet Mr. de Valera's government refused to allow elected representatives of Northern Ireland to sit in Leinster House.'[78] Both ideas were far-sighted; at best an improved relationship between North and South could provide an incentive to end partition, at worst a better relationship between the North and South could develop.

The idea of having Northern Ireland in the Dáil met with some approval in the North. Eddie McAteer, a Derry MP elected to Stormont in 1949, expressed enthusiasm, but admitted it would merely be a 'token attendance'; 'I am concerned only with the symbolism of the thing.'[79] Other Nationalist MPs agreed. MacBride's plan was well-intentioned, but Attorney General Cecil Lavery later pointed out some major difficulties; representation would occur without taxation or similar constituent responsibilities which may appear unfair, the difficulties of determining election rules and citizenship requirements could prove arduous, and the proportional representation election system made the prospect difficult. When asked in the Dáil whether these deputies would take their seats, Costello responded,

> Having regard to the constitutional, legal and other difficulties involved, the Government do not intend to make any proposals for the admission to Dáil Éireann of the representatives referred to in the Deputy's question. The Government, however, have been considering whether Seanad Éireann should not be consulted with a view to making provision for giving them a right of audience in the Seanad.[80]

The proposal was put on the agenda for the cabinet meeting of 23 May, then postponed until 4 July, then withdrawn completely.

Lavery also suggested a 'right of audience,' a Council of Ireland where matters of common interest could be discussed, and also concluded that nominating Senators was a possibility.[81] The idea of a Council of Ireland was part of the 1921 Treaty, proposed with the right to vote to create a single parliament for a unitary state. In the Council, representatives from both North and South would cooperate on matters of common interest, like postal services, agriculture, and fisheries, eventually snowballing into an all-Ireland Parliament, but both Dublin and Belfast focused on consolidating power within their individual parliaments and the Council plan was not followed up. If a Council had come into being with Unionists attending as more than a token audience, a closer relationship may have come about.

Fine Gael's 1948 party platform also addressed partition, stating that the final form of the Irish state could not be settled until partition has been ended and the Irish people as a whole could decide what they desired. Fine Gael strategy involved promoting the formation of a 32 county state by a firm and friendly policy towards the North and by increasing national propaganda adapted to changed world conditions, presumably using the Cold War, Ireland's geographic position, and the integration of Europe as leverage. [82]

The Conservatives, normally staunch Unionists, were no longer in power and the new Labour government, which had seemed more amenable to movement on the issue, provided hope that Britain would soften its position on partition. MacBride believed that Attlee was sympathetic to the problem; during his holiday in Ireland in 1948, Attlee 'was very friendly' and would remark on 'how anxious he was to end partition.'[83] However, the position of the British political parties were not so set in stone; Winston Churchill stated in casual conversation in 1948 that 'I still hope for a united Ireland. You must get those fellows from the North in, though you can't do it by force,'[84] and the Labour government proved just as determined to maintain the status quo as the Conservatives. On 14 August 1948, Attlee, MacBride, Secretary for Commonwealth Relations Philip Noel-Baker, and Minister for Health Noël Browne met informally in Mayo where both Attlee and Noel-Baker ruled out any movement on partition.[85] Even when it became obvious that the British initiative was not forthcoming, MacBride told United States Secretary of State Dean Acheson that the British Government was 'over-cautious about partition for fear of eliminating middle-class support.'[86] MacBride held out hope that Attlee's personal feelings would result in a change of government policy.

As a result of the 1948 elections, Fianna Fáil also became more vocal about the issue. As British Ambassador to Ireland John Maffey, later Lord Rugby, observed, 'the platform which won most applause was the one which put out the most violent anti-British ranting.'[87] De Valera embarked on an anti-partition speaking tour of the United States, Canada, and Australia. However, de Valera's tour did not lead to an increase in the anti-partition movement; his audience was largely composed of the converted and his speeches were 'tribal rallies, not political meetings.'[88] John Bowman believes de Valera completed the tour mainly to secure his and Fianna Fáil's ideological territory at home and his speeches were really aimed at the Irish to ensure them of his commitment. This belief is given some credence due to the fact that anti-partition activity in the United States received little active support from the government when de Valera was in power. As Fine Gael candidate Seán MacEoin declared to the *Westmeath Examiner*, 'They [Fianna Fáil] had been 16 years in office, and had done more talk about partition in the few months they had been in opposition that they did during that 16 years.'[89] De Valera astutely placed himself in an area where it was awkward to criticise him, as no individual or party wanted to appear 'soft' on partition. The tour caused more problems for the inter-party government than for Belfast, as the government lost an opportunity to differentiate themselves from de Valera and Fianna Fáil by not relying on propaganda. The inter-party government had to take some action to neutralise Fianna Fáil and repeal of the External Relations Act provided an opportunity to do that.

Leaving the Commonwealth

Many, including Churchill and Attlee, felt that the Irish government had cemented partition by its repeal of the External Relations Act.[90] Repeal and the declaration of an Irish Republic presented a problem. Now that Ireland had removed herself from the Commonwealth, a possible forum for discussion and compromise was also removed. Repeal eliminated the possibility of partition being solved within a Commonwealth context.[91]

The Unionists took advantage of the situation and proved to be quite wily. Brooke met with Attlee at Chequers on 20 November 1948, stating that his 'immediate anxieties would be allayed if he could be given an assurance that the constitutional position of Northern Ireland would not be prejudiced by Eire's ceasing to be a member of the Commonwealth.'[92] Attlee agreed and said that Brooke could publicly state that he obtained such assurance from the British government. Brooke also worried about a 'large influx of Eire citizens who, having acquired some colourful pretext for exercising the franchise, might help to out-vote the loyalists in Northern Ireland on the partition issue.' Attlee had no objection to Northern Ireland tightening voting qualifications. Brooke seemed confident when he reported back to his cabinet, stating they could 'consider and make any recommendations on any matters… affecting Northern Ireland in consequence of the repeal of the External Relations Act.'[93] British and Northern Ireland ministers met on 6 January 1949, where Attlee promised 'an affirmation by parliament that in no event would Northern Ireland cease to be a part of the United Kingdom except with the consent of the parliament of Northern Ireland.'[94] The Unionist position was secure.

While trade and emigration policies remained favourable to the new Republic and there was no more confusing constitutional status in the relationship with Britain and the Commonwealth, Westminster passed the Ireland Act of 1949, stating that partition would remain in effect unless a majority in the North desired otherwise, making it officially clear that Britain was not altering its stance on the partition issue. Clause 1(b) also stated that Britain would not allow areas of Northern Ireland with anti-partition majorities, such as Tyrone, Fermanagh, Foyle, South Down, Derry City, Mourne, and South Armagh to opt for unity with the rest of Ireland. The Ireland Act was the first time that Parliament asserted its position on the North, giving the boundary a sense of permanence. Mansergh sees it as the high point of Ulster Unionism in Anglo-Irish relations.[95] The Act also proved that the British were very familiar with the concept of self-determination. In the longer term, as Tim Pat Coogan points out, the guarantee contained in the Ireland Act 'created a veto on political progress, no matter how ardently this might have been desired by a majority in the two islands, unless the Unionists agreed.'[96] At a special Dáil session protesting the Act, Costello reasserted 'the indefeasible right of the Irish nation to the unity and integrity of the national territory,' and pledged 'the determination of the Irish people to continue the struggle against the unjust and unnatural partition of our country until it is brought to a successful conclusion.'[97]

There may still have been opportunities for unity; the plan seemed to declare the republic first, then solve the partition problem, much like a bear chewing off its leg to get out of a hunter's trap. Was leaving the Commonwealth and declaring the republic inconsistent with solving the problem of partition, what F.S.L. Lyons calls a 'fundamental incompatibility?'[98] Costello seemed to believe that repeal would help solve the partition problem; 'every section of this community in Ireland, every section of the Irish people, can unite with all their energies directed and not distracted towards a solution of this last political problem... We will have removed one of the two remaining causes of friction between this country and Great Britain,'[99] once again leaving Ulster Unionists out of the equation. The Irish government seemed to be playing a chess game but whether the opponent was Fianna Fáil, Unionists, or the British Government was not clear. As in 1921, when the objective was to gain freedom from Britain and then solve Unionist issues, de Valera and other Nationalists may have failed to notice which difficulty was more intractable. It seemed the inter-party government was in a similar situation with repeal.

With Ireland a Republic, ending partition became the last unachieved Nationalist goal. Partition would become the first great test of the inter-party government's foreign policy and ability to think in the long term rather than bow to rhetoric. Irish diplomacy, for better or worse, would centre around the issue of partition and foreign policy would be seen mainly in the light of partition.

NATO and Partition

Choosing not to join the North Atlantic Treaty Organisation seemed to be an exception to the partition strategy rule of entering international organisations to publicise the problem. The North Atlantic Treaty was written and signed in 1949, in response to the growing strength of the Soviet Union after World War II. The Treaty states that if any of the member nations is attacked, all of the signatories will respond together.

The United States encouraged all European nations to join the alliance. A National Security Council report summarises the benefits of Irish participation:

> Strategically located, Ireland affords valuable sites for air bases and naval and anti-submarine operations... Without question Ireland could make a valuable contribution to the collective defense of the North Atlantic community... Despite strong anti-communist sentiments, the Irish government *for domestic political considerations* still adheres strongly to its traditional policy of neutrality which was militarily embarrassing to the Allies in World War II... The United States would welcome use of Ireland's port facilities and the air bases which could be developed there, although they are not considered essential at this time. The advantages to be gained from Irish bases might make their acquisition desirable, *provided this could be accomplished in a manner consonant with our other commitments and without prejudicing collective arrangements.*[100]

Despite the hints that the United States would welcome Ireland into NATO, they refused to take a position on any Irish 'domestic political considerations.' Yet MacBride hoped to link joining with ending partition. He believed that Britain was bound to respond to such a bargain because Ireland's membership in NATO was essential for geographic and strategic reasons. As MacBride said to the *Irish Independent*, 'The last war showed Ireland is a vital link in the chain of North Atlantic defence.'[101] From MacBride's point-of-view, even if Britain remained unwilling to end partition, the United States would eventually intervene because, as TD James Dillon mused, 'Partition is a weapon of international Communism,' as it could be exploited by the Soviets as a contentious issue between Britain and the United States.[102] Such a statement is odd, being that the government denied the existence of communism in Ireland; as J.J. Lee points out, Ireland's 'anti-communist credentials were impeccable. In fact, they were too good.'[103]

MacBride claimed that if Ireland joined a military alliance with Britain while partition existed, revolution would occur in the North with Nationalists accusing the Dublin government of selling them out.[104] He summed up the inter-party government's position:

> In these circumstances, any military alliance with... the state that is responsible for the unnatural division of Ireland, which occupies a portion of our country with its armed forces, and which supports

undemocratic institutions in the north-eastern corner of Ireland, would be entirely repugnant and unacceptable to the Irish people. No Irish Government, whatever its political views, could participate with Britain in a military alliance while this situation continues, without running counter to the national sentiment of the Irish people.[105]

However, no popular vote was ever held to gauge the Irish electorate's reaction to the prospect of joining NATO.[106] De Valera's anti-partition tour and removal from the Commonwealth were taking place at the same time, which may account for the government's desire to 'cleave fast to neutrality if only for domestic political considerations.'[107] The American Ambassador to Ireland George Garrett reported that Church intervention might be able to convince Ireland to join; Archbishop McQuaid assured him 'that the Roman Catholic Church was in favour of Ireland's accepting the invitation to join the North Atlantic group,'[108] but according to MacBride, 'politics always wins over Church.' This statement is Garrett's paraphrase; if MacBride did actually use those words, there is an obvious irony considering the outcome of the Mother and Child scheme two years later.

Costello also believed that Irish participation in NATO was deeply desired by both Britain and the United States. In a Saint Patrick's Day radio broadcast to the United States, Costello said that 'while partition persists... the sympathy of our race in the United States of America cannot be expected to be fully directed towards the task of helping European recovery. While partition persists therefore the defences of Western Civilisation are weakened.'[109] However, Britain was not terribly worried about Ireland's refusal to join - if war broke out, pressure from the Church hierarchy, the Dominions, and the United States would ensure Dublin's participation. Indeed, as MacBride stated in the Dáil, 'we in Ireland are not much troubled by conflicting ideologies. We are firm believers in democracy in its true sense and are firmly attached to the principles of Christianity. Our sympathies, therefore, lie clearly with the nations of Western Europe.'[110]

The United States agreed with Britain's assessment, which made Irish NATO membership a poor bargaining tool. MacBride met with both Acheson and Truman and they affirmed that the United States 'could not helpfully or profitably intervene.'[111] A State Department official succinctly described the American response to the Irish statement that 'they would be delighted to join provided we could get the British to give them back the six Northern counties, we simply replied, in effect, that "it's been nice knowing you" and that was that.'[112]

Irish-American NATO negotiations appear to reflect Lyons' well-known summation of Irish neutrality creating an atmosphere similar to Plato's Cave, where what the prisoners see and hear are shadows and echoes cast by objects that they do not see, mistaking appearance for reality and knowing nothing of the real causes of the shadows.[113] Perhaps neutrality had dulled Irish minds to the nature of the Irish-American relationship as well as the improved Anglo-American relationship and how the war had altered both. America was unlikely to risk alienating Britain, then their most important single ally, for the sake of a country that had remained neutral throughout World War II. As an NSC note indicated, 'Irish participation was by no means essential for NATO's success. Irish military facilities would be merely "complementary" to those already available to North Atlantic forces in this area through the adherence to the North Atlantic treaty of Great Britain and Northern Ireland.'[114] When Dublin argued that partition meant Ireland could not join NATO, Washington concluded that it meant Ireland need not join NATO.

It was *Northern* Ireland that was important to North Atlantic defence – if Britain were a member, Northern Ireland would be as well. A bilateral defence pact was discussed, but the United States felt that such a pact would lead to resentment among other nations and reiterated that the government was still willing 'to welcome Ireland as a member of the North Atlantic Treaty Organisation.'[115]

Joining NATO might have been beneficial to Ireland in the long term and would have been possible to justify. As Minister of Finance Patrick McGilligan remarked, 'the experience would surely help to change ultimately the attitude of the Six Counties and induce at least the reluctant acquiesance which is the minimum necessary for healthy reunion.'[116] In addition, NATO was a good ideological fit and would require minimal exertion; the Irish were hostile toward atheistic communism, NATO was led by the United States, not Britain, and the Soviet Union was not specifically hostile to Ireland, which meant that defence considerations were relatively minor.[117]   Moreover, a CIA report dated April 1949 explains that 'the end of partition is conceivable only in connection with Ireland's adhering to an alliance such as the suggested North Atlantic Pact, in which case bases would presumably be available under the terms of the alliance.'[118] John J. Hearne, Irish High Commissioner to Canada, met with Lester Pearson, the Canadian Secretary of State for External Affairs, on 18

February 1949, where Pearson agreed that the division was 'unnatural and ridiculous,' but there were worse situations and the Irish might ' be getting nearer to unity in Ireland by going into the pact as you are.'[119]

Taking part would have demonstrated that Ireland was willing to cooperate and may have made the United States more amenable to mediation. However, if the inter-party government had proved willing to join, then they left themselves open to criticism from de Valera and Fianna Fáil for selling out the Northern minority and accepting partition.[120] Once again, the undesirability of appearing soft on partition prevented the government from imagining the bigger picture. Regarding defence, Ireland kept to a neutrality policy, but as an expression of anti-partitionism rather than national sovereignty and remained a non-aligned country in a Europe split by NATO and the Warsaw Pact.

The Plan to End Partition

Shortly after the formation of the inter-party government, Costello assured the public that all parties in government were dedicated to Ireland's 'complete territorial unity and absolute freedom. This is a matter upon which there is complete agreement amongst all the members of my government.'[121] The inter-party government's basic formula for ending partition is summed up nicely in Costello's speech at the 1950 Fine Gael party convention:

Having rejected force as a means of ending Partition, we are relying for success on bringing the justice of our cause to the effective attention of our powerful friends in the comity of nations. What we have been doing unceasingly since we assumed office is to raise the Partition question as an international issue at every available opportunity. We have faith in our capacity to persuade other nations of the justice of our cause as well as the harmful effects of Partition in preventing a united Ireland from playing that part in international affairs which our strategic position warrants. In our efforts to rouse world opinion on Partition we are securing the whole-hearted supported and influence of millions of Irishmen and the friends of Ireland   throughout   the   American   continent,   the   British Commonwealth and the world generally.[122]

It is easy to understand why the inter-party government thought this 'sore thumb' strategy might be successful. Attlee himself appeared amenable even if his government did not. Though still not a member of the United Nations, Ireland was becoming more involved in European cooperative bodies, which would allow them to raise the partition question within those bodies. A large emigrant population in America and the British Commonwealth gave Ireland the ability to 'punch above her weight.' As Costello declared in the Dáil, 'Though we are a small nation, we wield an influence in the world far in excess of what our mere physical size and the smallness of our population might warrant.'[123] As the inter-party government believed that partition was unjust and unnatural, surely all they would need to do was expose the injustice to gain sympathy. However, there were several flaws. The inter-party government may have overestimated Ireland's strategic position, counting too much on the United States, who wanted to maintain a close relationship with Britain during the Cold War and who still held negative memories of Irish neutrality during World War II and placing too much blame on Britain for sustaining partition. Constant reference to the issue left the impression within the international community that Ireland had no interest in wider concerns. Perhaps the greatest flaw was that the plan depended too greatly on altering world opinion and not enough on cooperation between the Republic and the North.

In order to coordinate and strengthen the propaganda campaign in Britain and Ireland, the Irish Anti-Partition League was founded in November 1945 in Tyrone by Northern Nationalists. In the beginning the League did emphasise grievances and adversities endured by the Nationalist community in Northern Ireland. MacBride promised cooperation with the Anti-Partition League during Clann na Poblachta's 1948 campaign, especially on publicity and propaganda. The goal was to persuade foreign governments and the public of the moral case for uniting Ireland.[124] Irish exiles in Britain, Australia, and the United States were targeted. The anti-partition campaign received support from Irish-America in its early years. In November 1947 the American League for an Undivided Ireland was formed to coordinate a campaign, collecting 200,000 signatures on a petition asking Truman to try to end partition.[125] The government's response was that the problem was for the British and Irish governments to resolve. The League did have some success in raising the cause in Congress; in March 1950 Congress voted to withhold Marshall Plan funds from Britain as long as partition continued.

The inter-party government's all-party Mansion House Conference began in January 1949 and also emphasised inequities faced by Northern Nationalists, especially political aspects like gerrymandering constituencies, limits of the franchise, and inadequate representation.[126] The *Irish*

Independent commented on the 'splendid beginning' and display of party unity and purpose.[127] Yet the activities of the Mansion House Conference soon turned to propaganda; in their opening statement, they declared,

> we assert once more the right of the Irish people to the ownership and control of all the national territory and we repudiate the right of Britain to carve up the Irish nation or to occupy any portion of it, even though a local majority against unity can be procured in the area which was deliberately selected for that purpose by the British Parliament.[128]

One of the first initiatives taken by the group was to begin a campaign fund for Nationalist candidates in Northern Ireland for election of February 1949. Collections were taken on the steps of Catholic churches after Mass and money was provided from the Department of External Affairs. There were comparatively few attempts to collect outside Protestant churches, which gave the collections, and consequently the initiative, a sectarian air. A few days after the church-gate collections, Brooke observed that the inter-party government 'appear to be holding out to us the hand of friendship and... have... the effrontery to complain that we do not respond.'[129]

Involvement in Northern Ireland elections proved to be counter-productive; the Unionist share of the vote rose from 50% in 1945 to 63%, with a gain of four seats. The interference in the elections of what was a foreign country divided Irish public opinion, some believing that intervention was justified because the elections were an 'unequal fight which the Nationalists of the Six Counties have to wage against the odds set against them. At least they can be given added courage from the assurance that their countrymen south of the Border are with them'[130] while others thought that 'interference with the internal affairs of what is legally – even if not in accordance with the sentiment of a great majority of Irishmen – a separate State can have one consequence... to anger the Northern majority, and reinforce its determination to stand aloof from the South.'[131] The attempt to influence the elections appeared to be pointless political window-dressing and only allowed Unionists to continue their siege mentality rhetoric; Brooke stating that 'the whole constitutional structure of Northern Ireland was being assailed from every angle and it was an elementary duty of the government to answer any attacks which may be made upon its structure.'[132] Irish propaganda in this case failed in its objective and strengthened the resolve of the Northern majority.

Brooke toured the United States in April of 1950. According to the British Ambassador to the United States Sir Oliver Franks, the visit was successful; there were no significant protests and the smoothness of the tour was seen as proof that the anti-partition movement in the United States was diminishing.[133] The American government never wavered from its position that solving the problem was a matter for the Irish and British governments. The Irish public's initial outburst of enthusiasm did not survive the failure of the government to mobilise support from public opinion overseas.

The Irish News Agency

MacBride was anxious to develop a programme of publicising the partition issue. On 13 July 1949, he introduced a bill in the Dáil requesting to begin an Irish News Agency to ensure the case for a reunited Ireland received more attention abroad, an idea that Fianna Fáil had vetoed in 1947. MacBride summarised his reasons for developing such a venture:

> First of all… we have a national objective to achieve. We still have to gain full control of our own country. We still have to assert the rights of the Irish people to determine their own form of Government and their own affairs without outside interference. In the second place, for one reason or another we have to counteract a good deal of hostile propaganda… that is published constantly in the Press of the world. From the third point of view, we need news channels of our own in order to encourage the development of our industrial life, of our foreign trade, of our tourist traffic, to make known our cultural developments and also to make known our viewpoints in the field of international affairs as the need arises.[134]

At the time, all Irish newspapers belonged to London-based Press Association, a holdover from when Ireland was part of the United Kingdom. This link was oddly overlooked after Ireland became a Free State. The Irish media received a great portion of their information from Britain, and MacBride believed 'undoubtedly, the viewpoint of a country must become distorted if it is presented through a channel other than a national channel.' Therefore major news and features about Ireland should originate from Ireland to avoid any bias. The proposed Irish News Agency was 'not intended to be a propaganda machine,' it would break through the 'paper wall' of English-owned newspapers and news agencies and 'place Ireland on the map and that to that extent then it will be serving a propaganda service by making Ireland known throughout the world in different spheres.'[135] As Agency journalist Brian Inglis recalls, the Agency was established with the idea that if what was happening in Ireland could be more frequently, accurately, and fairly presented, the anti-partition campaign would have a better chance of success.[136] MacBride requested appointments of additional staff for the Irish News Agency as well as additions to External Affairs based in the United States in cities with substantial Irish populations like Boston, Chicago, and New York.

The Dáil passed the final bill to fund the Agency on 24 November 1949. MacBride had once worked as a journalist for the Havas agency in Paris, for London's *Morning Post*, and as a sub-editor of the *Irish Press* and knew something about how the newspaper business worked. His first choice for head of the Agency was Clann na Poblachta member Noel Hartnett, whom Conor Cruise O'Brien called a 'dedicated republican propagandist.'[137] After a party-related argument between Hartnett and MacBride, MacBride then asked Cruise O'Brien to run the Irish News Agency.[138] Cruise O'Brien refused the appointment at first but realised that fighting with MacBride would have a detrimental effect on his career in External Affairs.[139] He also hoped the public assurances would be true and ignored what he suspected MacBride's intentions really were. Cruise O'Brien wanted to develop a bona fide news agency and chairman Roger Greene agreed to this. Hartnett also agreed not to indulge in propaganda; Cruise O'Brien thinks that if Hartnett were on good terms with MacBride, he would have run it as a propaganda unit, but as they were quarrelling, Hartnett was 'devoting himself heart and soul to thwarting and tormenting Seán MacBride.'[140] MacBride made no effort to change the direction of the Agency; both internal party conflicts and duties as Minister were diverting his attentions and he did not make any attempt to influence Agency decisions.

The goal of the Agency was to counter-balance 'incorrect' interpretations of the partition issue, and was organised into news, photo, and features departments. Talented people became involved, O'Dowd Gallagher, a well-travelled Fleet Street foreign correspondent was in charge of the news division, as well as Peadar O'Curry, Noel Hartnett (who ended up taking a position on the board), former Irish ambassador to the United States Robert Brennan, and journalist and historian Brian Inglis and many went on to become major figures within Irish journalism. Yet Cruise O'Brien's biographer Donald Akenson calls the Agency an 'all star cast putting on a pantomime.'[141] It was difficult to maintain the public belief that the Agency was not a propaganda machine. In addition, the

Agency did not possess all the technology necessary, as one staff member commented, 'we were just marginally faster than Reuter's original pigeon post, one hundred years before.'[142]

The Agency did not formally begin operations until the summer of 1950 and did not get off to a promising start. Agency representatives were sent to cover the first major meeting of the Council of Europe Assembly in Strasbourg. It was Ireland's turn to provide the chairman of the Council of Ministers and they sent MacBride. Held up by trying to install a teleprinter, the Agency representatives decided not to meet the Irish delegation. Instead, the Associated Press, the chief rival of the Agency, arrived to meet the delegates, who did not realise that their representative was a journalist and spoke freely in front of him. Thus, the Agency was scooped. On the other hand, the reporting regarding the debate on European defence went well, at least in Inglis' opinion.[143] The *Irish Times* published the Agency's report in full on its front page. The story was a straightforward account of the debate, but it made Irish intervention seem unpopular and unwise, as the Irish delegates had raised the issue of partition and this seemed to make the other delegates impatient. MacBride and de Valera were present and de Valera's plea for an end to partition met with silence, not because the other delegates were necessarily unsympathetic, but because the overwhelming desire of those present, including Churchill, Ernest Bevin, Robert Schuman, Georges Bidault, and Paul-Henri Spaak, was to set up a structure for bringing about improved European cooperation. The prevalent feeling was that the Irish issue was not relevant.[144] The Irish delegates were not happy with the Agency's report; in their view, bringing up partition may have been unpopular but they attracted attention by inflicting the issue on both elder and up-and-coming statesmen, who might have been irritated at the time but surely would begin to take notice of the problem. Therefore, the debate should have been reported as a strategic advance.[145] The Agency argued back that it was not their duty to slant stories and the news must be presented as it appears – if word got out that the Agency was a propaganda outfit, it would become impossible to sell stories. The delegates, especially MacBride, did not agree.

Despite the talent involved and the potential for such a venture, the Irish News Agency did not meet expectations. MacBride failed to sell the idea to even the Irish press, who did not oppose it, but did not actively promote it either.[146] Despite assertions to the contrary, the Agency gained a reputation abroad as a propaganda machine, and foreign newspapers, with the exception of Irish-American ones, were reluctant to purchase articles. In Britain, the National Union of Journalists was against the Agency because it could prove to be a rival. Moreover, there were financial problems; the Agency was set up with £5,000 from the government and never broke even. Eventually under the direction of Brendan Malin, the Agency broadened its scope beyond events relating to Northern Ireland and began covering European developments and Irish life through its news and features divisions. The Agency began a deal with United Press International, but the controversy of the Mother and Child scheme and the fall of the inter-party government led to Agency business being placed on the back burner.[147]

De Valera allowed it to carry on, hoping it would eventually pay its way, but since it was Government-funded, it could not issue the kind of story which would lead to angry questions being asked in the Dáil.[148] Features putting Ireland in a favourable light were sent to editors and a great majority came back with rejection slips. The Agency's weakness was that it could only report what happened in a straightforward manner, while others could be more salacious and more critical. In June 1959, a Fianna Fáil government under Seán Lemass took over and decided to close it. The Irish News Agency was associated with the anti-partition policy of MacBride and the politics of the inter-party government, which were no longer popular.[149] Ten or twelve years later it would have been of value not just to Ireland, but also to the world press when Northern Ireland became major news. As Douglas Gageby laments, 'it died, not without honour, but with so much unfulfilled.'[150] Another opportunity to prove that Ireland was not obsessed with the partition issue appeared to be lost.

Other Options

MacBride may have been more successful in gaining publicity for his cause, as the Anti-Partition League did at the start, by concentrating more on the denial of rights to the Catholic minority in the North. There were legitimate human rights complaints; dubious electoral practices, discrimination in public and private employment and public housing, regional policy and policing as well as local electoral boundaries being blatantly manipulated to ensure Unionist power. If partition could be seen as a human rights issue rather than one of self-determination and geo-political unnaturalness, the government may have had more luck with their propaganda campaign. The international post-war climate may have been more favourable toward correcting problems such as religious intolerance. At a speech on human rights in Strasbourg on 19 August 1949, MacBride tried to link partition with human rights abuses, stating that partition is a problem 'which is so pertinent to the establishment of peace and concord in Western Europe.' This point is hard to argue; the relationship between Britain and Ireland was good despite Ireland's departure from the Commonwealth and more significant issues such as Soviet violation of human rights and threats of military infringement into Western Europe appeared more menacing that the Irish dispute.

In the first month of the inter-party government, MacBride stated that

we should have closer contact with our brothers and sisters in the North, whether Protestant or Catholic, Unionist or Nationalists. There should be as much economic and cultural relations as possible. This would be helpful and make them appreciate that we are all human beings; that we are prepared to recognise their rights, and expect that they will be prepared to recognise ours.[151]

MacBride suggested beginning with a customs or economic union and declared in the Dáil that he would be

glad to take steps that would in any way bring about a closer relationship between our people and those of the partitioned counties. Rather than the exchange of representatives, I feel that a much more useful purpose would be served by the establishment of direct contact on matters of mutual concern between the two Governments. Accordingly, I should be willing, at any time, to meet representatives of the Belfast Government for the purpose of discussing matters of economic co-operation which might be of benefit to Ireland as a whole.[152]

David Mitrany, founder of the functionalist theory of politics, posits that 'there are many such needs which cut across national boundaries and an effective beginning could be made by providing joint government for them.'[153] The functionalist argument states that through a natural, gradual process whereby citizens came to share functions and develop contacts, state boundaries would be diminished. Such cooperation may have been helpful in cultivating a closer relationship between Ireland and the North, especially with regard to the functionalist de-emphasis of political aspects. The aim would be to find areas of common concern and build from there. Mitrany has argued that such developments must not be imposed by elites because the fear of losing sovereignty would entrench borders and deepen opposition; the practical activities of citizens must be the focus; cooperation would not be 'a matter of surrendering sovereignty, but merely of pooling so much of it as may be needed for the joint performance of the particular task... Eventually, this web of joint relationships and joint administrations will blur political lines.'[154]

There were many opportunities for such cooperation in late 1940s Ireland. MacBride said that 'in so far as cooperation on economic matters may be of assistance in minimising the effects of Partition and in bringing about a better understanding between those in defacto control of the Six Counties and ourselves, I should welcome it.'[155] Though not the best turn of phrase, it did demonstrate willingness to begin cooperating with the North, which had not been attempted since the Boundary Commission. Brooke was willing to collaborate on issues of security and trade. The Great Northern Railway (GNR), Erne hydroelectric scheme, and River Foyle fishing rights were non-political in nature and showed that cooperation was possible.

The Great Northern Railway linked the North and the Republic and operated an extensive rail network on both sides of the border. Based in the Republic, the GNR was a privately owned company in an era of state-owned transportation. In 1946, the Ulster Transportation Authority, set up by Stormont, took over Great Northern Railway's road services in the North. GNR chairman Lord Glenavy warned the Northern Ireland Minister for Commerce Brian Maginess of probable company losses that year, warning that something must be done if services were to be maintained. GNR also approached the Dublin government. Maginess became worried that Dublin would use the crisis for political purposes, believing that Dublin could afford to buy out the company.[156] The Córas Iompair Éireann-UTA joint report was presented to Dublin and Belfast in April 1950; rather than have two commerce ministers discuss the situation, the permanent secretaries of the departments met in Dublin. Yet, by mid-August Brooke had changed his mind and William McCleery, the new Minister for Commerce met Dublin's Minister for Industry and Commerce Daniel Morrissey in Dublin. The meeting went well and McCleery reported back that 'the Republican government are just as unwilling to have to buy out the railway... no likelihood of Dublin trying any "quick ones" and that none of the unpleasant possibilities which were recently under consideration is likely to arise.'[157] A later meeting between Acting Minister of Commerce Liam Cosgrave and McCleery ended in disagreement; Cosgrave suggested subsidies or establishing an all-Ireland Transport Board while McCleery advocated purchasing GNR. A purchase was finally agreed upon at £3.9 million, but it was not finalised because Dublin wanted to run it as a joint venture and Belfast wanted the UTA to take over in the North, only allowing the cross-border services to be jointly run, feeling that a joint venture was 'wholly undesirable from a political point of view.'[158] The disagreement was left for the next Fianna Fáil government to settle.

At the same time, a major agreement to drain the lands around and develop Lough Erne began. A proposal was brought forth by Dublin's Electricity Supply Board to establish a hydroelectric scheme that would also allow Stormont to control flooding on Lough Erne. Brooke was enthusiastic, primarily because it would make his constituents in Fermanagh happy. The Erne Drainage and Development Bill, published on 8 May 1950, came before the Dáil and Stormont the following day, stating that 'any works necessary in Fermanagh shall be carried out by the Northern Ministry, but to the satisfaction of the Electricity Supply Board.'[159] It was technically an agreement between the Northern Ireland Ministry of Finance and the ESB rather than the two governments, but it laid the foundations for further partnerships. An *Irish Times* editorial praised the scheme, asking, 'Is there any good reason why the example of the Erne should not be followed in other directions?'[160]

Fishing rights to the River Foyle, located in Donegal, Derry and Tyrone were held by the London-based Honourable Irish Society, who once held the charter for Derry city though the area they claimed the right to was located entirely in Donegal. This was challenged by 80 Donegal fishermen in Dublin High Court, who won their case, the judge deciding that the fishery was public, not private property. The Society appealed the decision to the Supreme Court. In 1949 Northern Attorney General Major Lance Curran wrote to Cecil Lavery suggesting a 'get together with a view to the adequate regulation of the fishing in the River Foyle,' with the caveat, 'I hope that you and those concerned in your Government will regard this in its true light, namely as an attempt to arrive at a practical solution of the problem in a friendly spirit. You will appreciate that my approach to you is informal.'[161] The two governments agreed to buy the fishing rights and set up a joint authority to manage them. This was the first such initiative between Dublin and Belfast. At the February 1951 Fine Gael ard-fheis, Costello stated that the North 'have given some grounds for the belief that friendly relations can do much to achieve eventual unity more certainly than threats of bloody warfare.'[162] Liam Cosgrave commented in the Dáil:

For some time, I believe, the whole approach to Partition has been based too much on showmanship and not enough on statesmanship, and that a great deal of reckless talk on both sides of the Border has prevented practical steps or, on some occasions, has hindered certain practical steps, that might be taken towards achieving a united Ireland...I think that the proper approach to this problem lies along the lines that have been adopted in relation to the Erne hydro-electric scheme and the Foyle fisheries agreement, and, although there may be some temporary divergence of view, the discussions that took place in connection with the Great Northern Railway.[163]

All of these were practical circumstances, not political concerns, which forced cooperation, as Mitrany suggested. North-South cooperation was acceptable to Belfast as long as it did not encourage Dublin to hope for unity.[164] Seán Lemass would later institute North-South relations and practical cooperation after becoming Taoiseach in 1959 and developments may occur as a result of greater unity with the European Union; in a few years time 'one can expect the border between the North and South to mean less in practical terms than it does now.'[165] MacBride, Costello and Cosgrave recognised the benefits of cross-border cooperation, yet this indirect but pragmatic approach may not have solved the problem quickly enough for the government and they may have felt that indulging in too many cross-border initiatives would be equal to recognising the North and the permanency of partition. If cooperation had continued without strident propaganda, then behaviour and policies may have gradually become more compatible. Like the Good Friday Agreement of 1998, it was not a resolution of difference, but a structure within which difference might possibly be managed.

Conclusion

MacBride contended 'that Ireland is one nation is beyond the realm of argument.'[166] He made the mistake of underestimating the strength and tenacity of Unionism and did not make allowances for their viewpoint. As Basil Chubb proposes, 'because the nationalist frame of reference included a woefully inadequate concept of Ulster Unionism, people simply did not take realistic account of the views of the million and more Northern Protestants, let alone accord them value.'[167] Partition was not merely a rock in the road, it was as Brooke said, a 'barrier of race, history, and outlook' and the Irish government needed more inventive plans for linking the two sides.[168] The inter-party government's error was not to consider developing and strengthening links to Northern Catholics and not trying real grass-roots initiatives to court Unionists. The Republic should have put more effort into publicising unfair discriminatory treatment instead of ideals like self-determination and geography, and developed practical rather than elevated concepts. Instead they put propaganda in place of real policy initiatives and looked like they were merely posturing. Was the government trying to prove its commitment to the issue without actually doing anything about it? The concept of unity seemed to be of minor importance in practical politics, but fundamental in terms of ideology.

In his address to the Anti-Partition League in Manchester, Costello, in keeping with government policy, referred to the north as an 'artificially created political structure' and urged the audience to inform, educate, and condition public opinion about partition and need for settlement. He did show some insight as he spoke about cultivating an appreciation of the Northern Irish point-of-view, but such insight was hard to sustain in light of the Mother and Child controversy, which was brilliantly exploited by Unionists as further proof of a theocracy where individual liberties are sacrificed to religion.[169]

Though the inter-party government's anti-partition strategy did lead to an expansion of the Foreign Service, a united Irish people within the Republic, and the end of diplomatic isolation, the strategy also demonstrated the reactive nature of the government as they did not seem to fully examine alternative methods to solve the problem. The strategies they adopted at first, such as creating an Irish News Agency, establishing friendly relations with the North, and revamping the Council of Ireland, dwindled in favour of more anti-Unionist rhetoric and anti-partition propaganda. Equalling the benefits of the British Welfare State in Ireland may not have been economically possible, but concentrated contact with both Northern Nationalists and Catholics, and allaying Unionist fears about 'Rome Rule' were feasible and would have been the best course of action for ending partition, or at least improving the relationship between the North and the Republic. Yet such actions may have proven too slow to suit, and the inter-party government demonstrated an unwillingness to think long-term toward a better relationship with Belfast. As McCabe writes of the repeal of the External Relations Act, the government seemed 'overwhelmed by momentum of circumstance,' responding to events rather than directing them.[170] This appears to be true in the circumstance of partition as well.

4

Rattling the Sabre: Seán Macbride, Ireland, and the United States

'All politics is local.'[1]

Thomas P. O'Neill

Ireland and the United States have historically had a significant yet complex relationship. In his time in office, Seán MacBride was involved in negotiations with President Harry Truman's government regarding Marshall Plan aid and proposed entry into the North Atlantic Treaty Organisation. The combination of Irish neutrality during World War II, the escalating Cold War, and MacBride's fixation on the partition issue would greatly affect the relationship between Ireland and the United States during his time in government. His attempts to make Irish Marshall Plan cooperation as well as Irish NATO membership conditional to the ending of partition were unsuccessful. MacBride made a tactical error by believing that the United States would be willing to mediate in respect to partition. Did this mistake show an incomplete understanding of both the Irish-American relationship in the recent past and current power politics? Was he really unable to recognise that the American political climate was the most important issue, that the Cold War was not the best time to try such an approach, or were other factors at work? It seems likely that the inter-party government knew enlisting American help would not work; rather, it was done to please home constituents rather than solve the problem.

MacBride may have misread American willingness to help on the partition issue but there were some benefits deriving from this policy. For example, his virtual dominance in Marshall aid negotiations, despite such negotiations being within the domain of the Department of Finance, gave the Department of External Relations a more prominent profile.

There have been a number of analyses of Ireland's relationship with the United States during this period.[2] Wartime issues, such as Ireland's neutrality and American opposition to this policy, are also well documented.[3] All commentators conclude that Ireland gave more cooperation to the Allies than a technically 'neutral' nation would. Brief attention has been paid to Ireland's involvement in both the Marshall Plan and NATO, but mostly in the context of wider studies, with the exception of Bernadette Whelan's *Ireland and the Marshall Plan* and Ian McCabe's *A Diplomatic History of Ireland 1948-1949*. Recent writings mentioning MacBride's attempts to link partition to NATO and the Marshall Plan agree that it had a negative effect on Irish-American relations.[4] Works concerning the dimension and character of the partition issue and its effects on Irish politics include John Bowman's *De Valera and the Ulster Question* and Clare O'Halloran's *Partition and the Limits of Irish Nationalism*.

This chapter differs from the studies above as it examines in greater detail why MacBride decided to follow the strategy he did, why the strategy was flawed, and what Marshall Plan and NATO negotiations and the attempt to use the 'sore thumb' strategy reveal about the Irish-American relationship and the myths about that relationship.

The Historical Relationship Between Ireland and America

The United States and Ireland possessed 'a common revolutionary-republican tradition of resistance to Britain.'[5] Both Ireland and the United States were former colonies of Britain, but the United States was much more heterogeneous ethnically and religiously, better off economically, and won decisively in their struggle with the British. Unlike Ireland, America was not a close neighbour of Britain and was not economically dependent on them.

The Irish government thought that America would be sympathetic to ending partition. This belief is not surprising considering the amount of political clout that the Irish-American community possesses. The claim that Ireland has a special relationship with the United States is an enduring feature of Irish foreign relations. In a 1922 memorandum that explained why Ireland would be well suited to begin a career on the international stage, Irish Minister of Foreign Affairs Charles Gavan Duffy stated that 'we are supposed to have great influence upon American politics and policy.'[6] However, that supposition is not as straightforward as it first appears; Irish-American politicians did not use their clout to the advantage of Ireland itself. As TD Donal O'Callaghan admitted in 1921, 'it was all a myth talking about 20 millions of [the Irish] in America. There never was more than half a million in the Irish movement in America.'[7]

There was a mass exodus of Irish to America after the Famine in late 1840s. From 1846 to 1891, it is estimated that three million Irish came to the United States.[8] Many also emigrated after smaller crop failures in 1863-66 and 1880-83. The newly arrived ethnic and urban-centred Irish clashed with nativist society, and American suspicion of Catholicism reinforced the Irish immigrant's cohesiveness.[9] The Irish in America tended to remain in self-contained communities and tended to marry 'within the tribe'.

The White Anglo-Saxon Protestant establishment in the United States seemed to parallel British domination of Ireland. Irish emigrants and the succeeding generations took an interest in events in Ireland mainly because 'many of the American Irish continued to feel that they lacked the respect that other Americans enjoyed, and they came to pin their hopes for greater prestige and acceptance among their fellow citizens on events in Ireland itself.'[10] 'The Irish nationalist effort in the United States was very much a part of the impulse to improve the standing of immigrants from Ireland, for a conquered homeland offered living proof of the inferiority of her people.'[11] The Fenians were founded in the United States in 1858 and Clan na Gael in 1867. It would appear that the combination of Irish nationalism and the Irish-American talent for gaining political power might work in Ireland's favour.

Yet after assimilation, the descendants of emigrants had other concerns. The idea that the Irish were 'America's political class' is quite true, but they used political power for local concerns, not wider Irish ones. Gradually 'the story of the Irish in America had become the story of Americans of Irish descent.'[12] An example of this mindset was that a majority of Irish-Americans voted for Woodrow Wilson in 1916, despite his attack on Irish-American 'hyphenism'.[13] Such activity shows American interests prevailing over Irish ones.

Irish-Americans of this era were less interested in politics in Ireland than a generation earlier. Rather their interests lay in American perceptions; the ethnic solidarity of Irish-American communities, a result of nativist Protestant discrimination, helped form political machines in New York, Boston, Chicago, and Philadelphia. Gradually the descendants of Irish immigrants became less conscious about Ireland and more with local concerns. American isolationism after World War I encouraged this outlook.

Although the reference to Germany as 'our gallant allies in Europe' in the 1916 Easter Rising Proclamation did not go over well, America was the most important target for Sinn Féin propaganda in 1919 and the party also did a lot of fundraising in Irish-American communities. The Irish Nationalists put faith in American support. After the end of World War I, Sean T. O'Kelly was dispatched to Paris in 1919 to try to win international recognition for Ireland at the Paris Peace Conference in the hopes of taking advantage of President Wilson's desire for 'self-determination' for small nations. However, Wilson himself was Anglophile of Ulster Protestant descent and had no sympathy with the Irish case for self-government.[14] The Irish delegation was unsuccessful.

Ireland, then, would not benefit from the Irish-American talent for politics; 'by 1916 Irish nationalism in America had little to do with Ireland.'[15] Even before then, Irish-American organisations did not focus on Ireland; 'essentially they were pressure groups designed to defend and advance the American interests of the immigrant.'[16] Even when a descendant of Irish-Catholic immigrants became President in 1960, John F. Kennedy's administration concentrated on Cold War politics rather than policy regarding Ireland and had a cordial relationship with Britain's Macmillan government.

Some argue that the Irish gift for politics is misunderstood. Lawrence McCaffery points out that the Irish have had no trouble gaining political power, but 'once in office Irish politicians have either abused power or failed to direct it constructively.'[17] Daniel Patrick Moynihan, a well-respected Irish-American Senator, concluded that the Irish are skilled at acquiring political power, yet inadequate at its application; 'in a sense the Irish did not know what to do with power once they got it.'[18]

Moreover, the British could also claim a special relationship with the United States; legal and linguistic likenesses existed and at least one-third of Americans could claim British descent.[19] England and America had been drawing closer together and American administrations consistently favoured Britain whenever Anglo-Irish issues came up. American foreign policy, motivated by self-interest, required cooperation with Britain.

Seen in this context, Ireland's relationship with the United States was more complex than is sometimes assumed. The Second World War would further the divisions between Irish-America and Ireland.

Irish Neutrality and the United States

One of the reasons for declaring neutrality at the start of World War II had been partition; then-Taoiseach Éamon de Valera believed that civil strife would occur if Ireland allied with Britain. Declaring neutrality was also an opportunity for Ireland to show independence from Britain: 'the right to pursue a policy of neutrality in wartime has generally come to be considered in the twentieth century as the ultimate yardstick of national sovereignty.'[20]

The policy also affected Ireland's rapport with the United States, who did not respond well to Ireland's decision. The Irish position during the war 'placed a strain on traditional Irish-American friendship.'[21] As John Hickerson, the head of the State Department's Division of European Affairs, wrote to the American Representative in Dublin David Gray in January 1945, 'the people of the United States, I believe, will not soon forget that the one time in history when Ireland had an opportunity to do something to assist this country the Irish Government turned a deaf ear.'[22] A communiqué from the British Embassy in Washington in March 1949 explained that 'whilst there has, of course always been a measure of sympathy in this country for Ireland, it has been markedly strained by Eire's strict neutrality during the war... [including] her refusal of United States' requests for naval and/or air facilities in the anti-submarine campaign.'[23]

To add to the tension, Gray, an Anglophile and uncle by marriage to Eleanor Roosevelt, did not get along with de Valera and did much to malign him and Irish policy to the American government. According to T. Ryle Dwyer, Gray's machinations to discredit de Valera and the Irish neutrality policy led to a freezing of relations between the two nations.[24] His campaign to discredit the Irish government during and after the war worked and 'Irish-American relations at the end of the conflict were altogether poisoned and the strain between the two nations seemed set to continue for some time to come.'[25]

The point has been made that Irish neutrality was not 'strict' at all, rather a 'benevolent neutrality' that favoured the Allies. As Nathan Becker of the State Department remembered, 'of course, the Irish were very good as neutrals, they let us do most anything that was reasonable.'[26] This included supplying volunteers, allowing the Office of Strategic Services to establish an official liaison in Ireland, and agreeing to support Britain in the event of a German invasion.

Despite this, many in the American Government continued to see Irish neutrality as traitorous. Hickerson vented to Gray's replacement George Garrett, 'The British were our allies in the last war when Ireland's neutrality operated to the advantage of Germany.'[27] Myron C. Taylor, the Representative of the President to the Holy See, informed President

Truman that he had once suggested to Truman's predecessor Franklin Roosevelt in 1941

that he ignore De Valera, grant him no favors, and treat him with contempt... De Valera's vanity had grown out of all proportion to the importance of his area of Ireland and its relatively small population. His defeat in the recent elections [1948] is indicative that in his case at least a bit of patience, backed by a few pointed words, and ignoring the too-ambitious leader, was effective.[28]

Taylor also informed Roosevelt that 'there can be little doubt that the I.R.A. is being financed and in part directed by German agencies in Eire.'[29] The Irish refused to hand over the treaty ports to the British during the war and would not close the Axis legations. These were proper actions for a neutral nation but were not appreciated by the United States, who thought that the ports were vital to the British war effort and the legations 'centers of espionage.'[30] After denial of the ports, 'Ireland was off America's conscience for good, if indeed she'd ever been on it.'[31]

On 2 May 1945 de Valera paid a visit to the German legation to offer condolences upon Adolf Hitler's death. While this was proper diplomatic protocol for a non-belligerent state, de Valera's visit was widely criticised. The *New York Times* commented that 'considering the character and record of the man for whose death he was expressing grief, there is obviously something wrong with the protocol, the neutrality, or Mr. de Valera.'[32] Why did de Valera behave in such a manner, in what Maffey called a 'conspicuous act of neutrality'?[33] De Valera's behaviour at Roosevelt's death a few weeks earlier had been far more effusive; he adjourned the Dáil as a mark of respect, stating that 'personally I regard his death as a loss to the world.'[34] He made no favourable comments and did not dismiss the Dáil after Hitler's death. Perhaps he was irritated with Gray and wanted to stress Irish sovereignty. On the other hand, as Dwyer surmised, de Valera may have been 'tweaking the tail of the British Lion; but a more correct analogy would probably have been that he was ruffling the feathers of the American Eagle.'[35] De Valera also respected Dr. Edouard Hempel, the German Minister in Dublin, 'for whom he had a much higher regard than he had for Gray.'[36]

Neutrality had not only coloured how the American Government viewed Ireland; it also dulled Irish minds to the nature of the Irish-American relationship as well as the improved Anglo-American relationship and how the war had altered both. As Lewis Douglas wrote to

British Foreign Secretary Ernest Bevin in 1948, referring to the Anglo-American relationship cemented by the war, 'Unity among our two peoples can and will, I believe, lead us through the troubled times of the present to a long period of tranquillity. Division between us can only mean a catastrophe for us both.'[37] America was unlikely to risk alienating Britain, then their most important single ally, for the sake of a country that had remained neutral throughout World War II; 'Americans were less ready to offend the British than to offend the Irish.'[38]

In addition, for many Americans, World War II altered the way they perceived their nation's place in world affairs. The isolationism of the inter-war years was firmly in the past. This change can be seen in the enthusiasm for membership in the United Nations, which contrasts to the American attitude in joining the League of Nations. The burgeoning Cold War meant that the United States needed to be a strong presence in world affairs. This outlook also strengthened the relationship with Britain, who vigorously supported the containment of communism.

Ireland, America, and Anti-partitionism

In 1945, the position of the American government toward the partition of Ireland was very clear; it was a problem for the United Kingdom and Ireland to solve and 'the partition question is one in which the United States cannot become involved.'[39] In the years between 1945 and the formation of the inter-party government in 1948, there were no signs that this position would change. Yet, the government continued to try to use the Americans to bring about an end to the problem. In a letter to Seán Nunan, the Irish representative in Washington, MacBride supposed that 'the attitude of the State Department has always been opposed to giving any assistance to the solution of the Irish question. But I feel now that an opportunity really offers to do it.'[40]

MacBride had some reason for believing this. One of the issues during the 1948 general election campaign was the lack of movement on partition. Here was an opportunity to best Fianna Fáil. MacBride believed that the British Labour government would be more sympathetic than the normally Unionist Conservatives. George Garrett succeeded Gray as United States Minister to Ireland in the summer 1947 and he had a much more cordial relationship with the Irish government and appeared prepared to examine the partition question on its merits.[41] Perhaps the new government thought that more propaganda would reawaken the commitment of Irish-Americans.

The large numbers of Irish-Americans and their apparent political clout probably influenced MacBride's thinking. One of the goals of the inter-party government's anti-partition propaganda campaign was to marshal the support of Irish-Americans to petition their government to intervene. As has already been mentioned, MacBride created an Irish News Agency to provide a favourable impression to American newspapers. Putting Ireland in a positive light could influence more Americans to support the cause.

In a later interview, MacBride recalled that 'As far as policy-making, I was conscious I was dealing with a very hostile State Department and my only leverage was the Irish-American members of Congress.'[42] He may have overestimated how much help Congress could provide. From 1948 to 1951, 16 anti-partition resolutions were proposed in Congress; three in the Senate, 13 in the House of Representatives. Only one resolution came out of committee and the vote on whether the House should consider it was defeated 206 to 139. In 1949 four Congressmen, John Fogarty (Rhode Island), Thomas Lane (Massachusetts), Enda Kelly (New York), and Mike Mansfield (Montana) and one Senator, Everett Dirksen (Illinois), moved unsuccessful resolutions against partition and on 29 March 1950 Fogarty announced an amendment to a Foreign Aid bill, suspending Marshall aid to Britain until partition ended. His amendment did not mention Britain by name, stating that the United States would withhold

> any assistance under this act, where it appears that any participating country is impairing in whole or in part its economic recovery by reason of the expenditure of any portion of its funds, commodities or services in the maintenance or subsidization of any dependant country, which naturally is or should be, an integral part of some other participating country, until such time as such participating country shall sever its control of, and refrain further from maintaining or subsidizing such dependant country.[43]

However, he followed that statement up with 'in plain English it means that all funds that shall be appropriated through the authorization of this bill will be withheld from the United Kingdom as long as partition exists in Ireland.' The bill passed 99 to 66. [44]

At first glance, this would appear to be a victory for the Irish-American lobby in Congress. However, there were only a small number of members in the House of Representatives at the time and many who were there were well-known supporters of the previous resolutions. Perhaps

Fogarty, a representative with a large Irish-American constituency, was looking for a symbolic victory. Mid-term elections were coming up in November so the amendment could be viewed as a bid for Irish-American support. Also, as the relationship between President Truman and Congress was tense at the time, the Republicans in the House were willing to support the bill because it provided an opportunity to embarrass Truman.[45] Under the House rules, changes in bills were tentative and depended on a formal role call vote at the end of the debate. Thus prior arguments could be reversed. The *New York Times* headline of 30 March 1950 read 'House cuts off aid until Britain ends Ireland partition' with the subhead 'Action likely to be reversed.'[46] The article pointed out that the vote followed assurances by the sponsors that 'there would be ample opportunity to reconsider the action.' The *Washington Post* hinted that the Representatives were 'in a playful mood' and 'nobody seemed to take the vote very seriously.'[47]

The Irish government's assessment was quite different; Costello called the amendment 'a justification for putting the question of partition on the international plane.'[48] MacBride remained silent about Congress' action, merely stating that 'Britain was violating the fundamental principals of democracy by keeping Ireland divided.'[49] There does not appear to be any direct connection between MacBride's lobbying and the bill; there is no correspondence in the Department of Foreign Affairs files between MacBride and any of the Congressmen who spoke in support of the amendment, though the Irish Embassy did send Senators and Congressmen copies of MacBride's anti-partition speeches.[50] The Irish government did not provide the impetus for the amendment. Bill Peer, a Brooklyn Irish-American who had recently been made a director of publicity for the American League for an Undivided Ireland, apparently suggested the idea to Fogarty while on a trip to Washington.[51]

The leading American press considered the action irresponsible on the part of the House. A *New York Times* editorial surmised that the amendment was 'intended merely as a demonstration' and further felt that the 'European Recovery Program is being made a football of domestic politics.'[52] The *Washington Post* called the vote an 'outrageous and schoolboyish exhibition.'[53] Even the *Irish Times* remarked that 'we could wish that the Congressional friends of our sundered country had chosen a more tactful, and less perilous, means to make their sentiments felt.'[54] Moreover, the amendment ignored both the practical side of denying Britain Marshall Plan aid and that denial's potential economic effect on Ireland.

The amendment was rejected in committee on 31 March and the Foreign Aid Bill passed 266 to 60. Further evidence that the Amendment was a symbolic stance was that all the Congressmen who spoke in favour of the Amendment voted for the final version of the bill.[55]

MacBride was probably correct about the State Department; a likely reason that most of the resolutions died in committee was because Congress often asked the Department for advice in matters of foreign relations. The State Department's memo to Tom Connally, Chair of the Senate Foreign Relations Committee affirmed that partition was 'not a matter in which the United States could properly or usefully intervene.'[56] There is no doubt that sympathy for the cause of Irish unity existed; several state legislatures and Congress passed resolutions opposing partition, but this had little practical effect other than to sustain the hopes of the Northern nationalists.[57]

This does not mean that the American government ignored anti-partition activity. In November 1947 the American League for an Undivided Ireland was established. The group gathered 300,000 signatures for a petition, which they sent to Secretary of State George Marshall on 12 May 1948 with the demand that 'European Recovery funds should be withheld from Great Britain in order that the growing source of irritation be eliminated in Ireland.'[58] The petition gained attention, but not the kind that the League was looking for. Threats to Marshall Plan aid irritated the State Department; Hickerson wrote to Matthew Connelly, President Truman's Secretary, on 28 May 1948 that

> this Department has been receiving a number of communications from Irish societies and individuals expressing the view that economic aid should not be given to Britain as long as the northern counties remain separated from Eire... this Department would prefer that publicity regarding this petition [from American League for Undivided Ireland] be kept at a minimum.[59]

The insistence that this was a serious issue to world peace was similar to crying wolf; 'this last named policy [American non-involvement] is imminently sound and the U.S. can do nothing but lose by meddling into a matter which is not nearly as serious as the [Irish-American] extremists would have us believe.'[60]

Yet it was necessary to appear strong on partition to satisfy the electorate in Ireland. After his defeat, de Valera embarked upon an anti-partition tour to the United States, Australia, New Zealand, and Britain.

Thus the new government could not be outdone in expressing their nationalist zeal; de Valera was manoeuvring in a field where it was almost impossible to attack him, so 'MacBride duly banged the anti-partition drum.'[61] He and Taoiseach John Costello also made trips to the United States. From 8 April to 2 May 1949, MacBride travelled to Chicago, San Francisco, Boston, New York, and Washington DC; where he gave speeches, all of which were well-covered in Irish newspapers, about avoiding world conflict, the benefits of European integration, the Irish position on NATO, and the injustice of partition, missing the official Irish Republic celebrations in Dublin on 18 April. The American Government recognised the dilemma of Irish political parties in respect to partition; the CIA explaining that 'if political parties keep the issue before the people, it is because they cannot do otherwise and continue to exist.'[62]

Yet de Valera's tour largely preached to the converted and the British were not very concerned. The British Representative in Ireland John Maffey, later Lord Rugby, reported to the Dominions Office that Irish-Americans were 'slightly less frenzied' than they had been about the problem.[63] Troy Davis indicates that policy makers within the Foreign Office were simply not worried, for the most part, about the Irish and their compatriots in America having an adverse effect on Britain's relationship with the United States.[64]

It was unwise to add the United States to the 'sore thumb' strategy if ending partition was the Irish government's aim. It got to the point that whenever MacBride visited government officials, prior warnings would be issued. One such brief for President Truman read:

It is anticipated that Mr. MacBride's appointment will be in the nature of a courtesy call. In the course of the conversation, however, Mr. MacBride may refer to the Irish partition issue, Irish defense requirements, ECA aid to Ireland, and the civil aviation issue. It might prove highly embarrassing to our relations with the United Kingdom if announcement were made that the Partition Issue had been discussed. Therefore it is suggested that this subject be avoided if possible.

If MacBride did introduce the subject, the response should be that the United States 'cannot intervene in this issue between two friendly Governments.'[65]

The meeting between MacBride and Truman took place on 23 March 1951. MacBride did mention partition in an oblique fashion, referring to the 'political difficulties' involved if Ireland were to join NATO.[66] Truman kept to his brief and replied that he hoped Ireland would join but that the matter was between two friendly nations and the United States could not intervene. MacBride then mentioned the possibility of military assistance to Ireland, but not a specific bilateral defence pact. Truman said that the 'strain now being placed upon the United States to provide arms for both itself and for the most urgent need of allies who are more exposed than was Ireland' may prohibit this request, but promised to consider the possibility.

The American government had little sympathy with Irish-American posturing despite the fact that there were vocal efforts to address the partition question in America. Many Ancient Order of Hibernians chapters requested to Truman several times that partition be ended and sent copies of the pamphlet 'Ireland's Right to Unity' from the Dublin Mansion House Conference. Irish-America managed to keep the partition issue alive, but did not influence the government to change it.

The United States also maintained a cordial relationship with Northern Ireland. Truman wrote to Sir Basil Brooke that 'the interests and attachments binding us to our friends in Northern Ireland are deep seated and esteemed. To you and the people in Northern Ireland may I express the good wishes and hope for continued happiness and well-being.'[67] Brooke replied on 9 August 1949 that 'we in Northern Ireland are proud to know that so many Presidents of the United States have been men of Ulster descent and that large numbers of Ulster men and women are playing an important part in the life of your country today.'[68]   He reminded Truman of Northern Ireland's role during the war: 'this bond of kinship and friendship between the United States and ourselves was immeasurably strengthened during the world war when 300,000 members of the United States Forces came to Ulster for the completion of their training and found an abiding place in the hearts of our people.'

If they had chosen to involve themselves, could the United States have succeeded in making the British end partition? And did an 'unsympathetic' attitude ensure its permanence? Would the British have even responded if the American government put pressure on them? Britain had already made her stance on partition clear; the Ireland Act of 1949 stated that partition would remain unless a majority in the Northern Ireland Parliament agreed to its removal. The British government would not have allowed mediation without Northern Ireland's consent and it is highly unlikely that Unionists would have willingly participated. Seán Cronin argues that the United States, by allowing Britain to unduly influence their policy toward Ireland, was 'taking sides against a united Ireland.'[69] While Cronin's point that the

United States and Britain had a close post-war relationship is correct, Davis convincingly counter-argues that there is nothing to suggest that the United States would have opposed any solution to partition agreed on by Britain and Ireland.[70] The American decision not to involve itself in the partition issue did not mean that they took any positive action against Irish unification.

The motives of Irish-American politicians taking a vocal anti-partition stance seemed to mirror Irish politicians - such a stance was necessary to impress their constituents. Gaining votes was the goal rather than achieving unity. The use of partition as a political weapon rather than a genuine problem to be solved continued. This may have helped politicians within a domestic political context, but it jeopardised a cordial relationship between Ireland and the United States.

After the General Election in May 1951 the American anti-partition campaign ebbed upon de Valera's return to power and his Fianna Fáil government maintained a policy of 'silence and discretion' regarding unity.[71] When asked in the Dáil what he thought about the partition movement, de Valera answered, 'If I am asked: "Have you a solution for it?" in the sense: "Is there a line of policy which you propose to pursue, which you think can, within a reasonable time, be effective?" I have to say that I have not and neither has anybody else.'[72]

Ireland and the Marshall Plan

The basis of the Marshall Plan lay in Secretary of State George Marshall's Harvard University commencement speech of 5 June 1947, where he pledged American help to restore 'the confidence of the European people in the economic future of their own countries and of Europe as a whole... to assist in the return of normal economic health in the world, without which there can be no political stability and no assured peace.'[73]

The Marshall Plan, also known as the European Recovery Programme (ERP), was open to allies, former allies, enemies, former enemies, and neutrals during the war. Thus Ireland was permitted to participate. American motivation could be viewed as 'an attempt by the United States to create a bloc of states centred around itself. In addition, each European state was considered valuable in terms of promoting key United States foreign policy interests,'[74] the paramount one being anti-communism.[75] Like participation in the Council of Europe, this may have signalled a violation of neutrality. In his introduction to *Ireland, Europe and the Marshall Plan*, Till Geiger points out that involvement could be viewed as a threat to Irish sovereignty and the desire to conduct affairs free of outside interference.[76] However, the financial benefit made it worth participating and Ireland had already expressed its views on communism. In addition, Whelan argues that Ireland was drawn into the Marshall Plan due to demands of British and United States economic, political, strategic diplomatic policies and Irish economy- Ireland had 'little or no control over its own destiny on this matter.'[77]

The case for Ireland to be offered aid was very strong. Neutrality may have put a strain on Ireland's rapport with the United States, but her geographical location made a good relationship important to both British and United States security.[78] Marshall aid would also provide some relief to Britain's strained dollar reserves and improve Irish agriculture to help alleviate the post-war food shortage. The Irish economy was suffering from stagnating production, inflation, and balance of payments in deficit with every country except Britain. Raymond J. Raymond correctly argues that the United States extended the offer in order to reduce Ireland's drawing on the dollar pool of the sterling area so the United Kingdom would be financially viable.[79] Spain, in a similar post-war position to Ireland, did not receive Marshall Plan help.[80]

The lack of a potent communist threat may have prejudiced any aid. The CIA had determined that 'Communism has little appeal to the Irish, whose views on political, social, and economic matters are conditioned by religious beliefs' and the ideology was an 'almost insignificant force, and internally at least offers no conceivable threat to the State.'[81] The Irish government did not hesitate to declare its aversion to communism. MacBride had declared in the Dáil that 'I am not aware that there can be the slightest doubt as to where Ireland stands in regard to the general world conflict.'[82] Despite a lack of a threatening communist presence, Ireland's immediate economic difficulties were similar to those of most Western European countries and there were political, diplomatic, and security arguments for inclusion.[83] There was no real public opposition in Ireland itself and the state of the Irish economy meant that Ireland did not have much choice but to investigate.

On 4 July 1947, Ireland received an invitation to attend a meeting in Paris on 12 July to 'take part in the drawing up of a programme covering both the resources and needs of Europe for the following four years.'[84] Representatives of sixteen Western European Countries met in Paris to frame a joint response to the American offer. On 16 April 1948 the Committee of European Economic Cooperation (CEEC) met in Paris and adopted a convention, established a permanent organisation of sixteen participating countries, thus officially forming the Organisation of

European Economic Cooperation (OEEC). An *Irish Independent* editorial supported the idea, stating that there was 'good ground for hoping that the agreement signed yesterday in Paris will endure and be of lasting value to the world.'[85]

After the General Election of 1948, organising Irish participation in the ERP and meeting the steps to qualify for aid fell to MacBride and his department, as did how the money should be spent. MacBride would distinguish himself in the OEEC but he was not quite as successful in dealing with America itself.[86]

The first controversy involved loan versus grant status. In May 1948, Ireland was offered a $10 million dollar loan to be dispersed during the period of June through October from Marshall aid funds. It was decided to give Ireland loans rather than grants because there were 'no over-riding political considerations which would warrant preferential treatment for the Irish... the decision [loan or grant] should be made on an economic basis in comparison with the other CEEC countries.'[87] The aim of the ERP was to restore the Western European economy as a whole, thus making the area less vulnerable to communism and Ireland was peripheral to this aim. The country 'didn't have a relatively high rate of priority on our program at that time.'[88] Plus, Ireland was of comparatively minor economic importance and not badly damaged by the war, not suffering to the same extent as other countries. Raymond argues that political reasons, specifically lingering American annoyance at Irish neutrality, were also factors.[89]

On 18 May, MacBride led a delegation to Washington to argue for a grant. At a 20 May he met with Hickerson. His main argument was that 'we have, as a nation, a fundamental objection to undertaking obligations we see no prospect of meeting.'[90] MacBride tried to emphasise the need for a grant, stating that, as an agricultural nation, Ireland suffered war damage due to a lack of fertilisers and feeding stuffs and Irish agriculture had suffered 'as effectively as if it had been ravaged by war.'[91] He also pointed out that Northern Ireland benefited from the Marshall Plan through London largely in grant form.[92] Despite Raymond's conclusion that MacBride made a good case, it was unwise to use these arguments, as Britain was far more war damaged than Ireland and it only emphasised Northern Ireland's participation in the war effort.

Hickerson replied that increasing Irish aid was an unnecessary burden to American taxpayers and partition was a problem for the Irish and British to work out. The favourable terms of the loans ensured that the Irish would find repayment fairly easy; there were four separate loan agreements and the repayment of the $128 million total was not to commence until 30 June 1956 with 27 years to remunerate at an interest rate of 2.5% beginning 31 December 1952.[93] The economic recovery that would result from the loans would make repayment possible, as J.J. Lee recapped, 'Ireland would have no difficulty meeting the repayments out of the increased output which the delegation confidently predicted would result from Marshall Aid!'[94]

In May of 1948, the Executive still needed full Congressional approval for allocation of Marshall aid funds. The State Department wanted to ensure that nothing would go wrong.[95] Any attempt by MacBride to enlist the Irish lobby could weaken support for the entire aid package. The House of Representatives Appropriations Committee questioned why Ireland was receiving aid while other wartime neutrals such as Sweden, Switzerland, and Portugal were not in line to receive any. The response was that Ireland needed ERP funding due to their close relationship with the sterling area. Congress had also insisted that some proportion of aid be given as loans; thus the United States had to make choices. Ireland was seen as able to handle loans. Paul Hoffman, the Administrator of the Economic Cooperation Administration (ECA), was clearly irritated by Ireland's behaviour; if Ireland rejected a loan, that may be the end of ERP offers to Ireland. Moreover, if the Irish could contemplate rejecting the loan, perhaps they did not really need it.

The discussion brought out the second issue, tying ERP aid to partition. This was alluded to when MacBride brought up the funding that the North would be receiving, hinting that the United States was encouraging partition by 'increasing the disparity between the economies on both sides of the border.'[96] MacBride mused to Hickerson that it was difficult to comprehend why the United States would not want to help cure a 'sore spot' in Europe. Hickerson replied,

I then explained that, frankly, as they knew, during the last war bases in Northern Ireland had been of great assistance in the anti-submarine campaign and had undoubtedly saved many American and Allied lives. At present we and the British [sic] were working together on the closest possible terms… If Ireland had taken over the Six Northern Counties, where would this leave us if Ireland remained neutral the way she had in the last war? I finished by expressing the hope that Ireland would one day be a member of the Brussels group [the forerunner of NATO].[97]

MacBride returned to Dublin and asked the cabinet what to do. The Secretary of the Department of Finance J.J. McElligott believed the loan would be advantageous; $10 million for June-October would benefit the sterling pool and the British Treasury were also in favour. Yet, the Irish government voted to reject Marshall aid for the time being at a cabinet meeting on 11 June.

However, the situation would soon change. The British dollar reserve was so depleted that Sir Stafford Cripps, the Chancellor of the Exchequer, announced in June that Ireland would not be able to withdraw dollars from the sterling pool after 30 June. The Irish could have restricted access if Ireland agreed to participate in the ERP. Geiger has posited that this was not entirely the Exchequer's decision; that 'indirect American pressure on the British government forced the Irish government to accept ERP loans after Irish ministers had decided to refuse any assistance except in the form of grants.'[98] Daniel Davies further argues that America asked the British to remove Ireland from the sterling pool.[99] Whatever, the impetus, on 25 June the cabinet agreed to accept the initial offer of a loan and on 1 July, the Dáil voted to accept Marshall Aid.

MacBride may have misjudged American willingness to intervene, but he did manage to boost his authority within the inter-party government. His early pre-eminence in the cabinet enabled him to ensure that ERP concerns, OEEC business, applications for Marshall Aid, and plans for spending the money were handled by the Department of External Affairs rather than Finance. MacBride was put in charge rather than the Minister of Finance because the European Economic Cooperation Agreement stated that the Administer of the ECA would negotiate directly with the OEEC and the OEEC must approve each country's national programme. MacBride was Vice-President of the Council of Ministers of the OEEC and was given the task of negotiating with the ECA on behalf of the sixteen countries involved.

His friendships with Garrett and European Ambassador At Large for the ECA W. Averill Harriman certainly helped increase his influence. He was well-thought of in United States government circles; a CIA assessment of MacBride called him

the outstanding personality of the present Government... MacBride has an impeccable revolutionary pedigree... Like Costello, a brilliant and successful barrister, he is noted for his forceful advocacy and remarkable talent for cross-examination. He is probably the best debater in the Dáil. He is definitely of Prime Ministerial caliber. He is charming, affable, and intelligent, an excellent diplomat.[100]

The CIA believed that MacBride was 'likely to remain a powerful force in Irish politics.'[101] Despite his near-constant harps on partition every time they met, Secretary of State Dean Acheson seemed to enjoy MacBride's company. When Nunan's replacement John Hearne realised that he had scheduled Acheson to be at two separate dinners for MacBride and provided him a potential excuse for missing one, Acheson replied that 'I saw no reason why I should not dine twice with Mr. MacBride.'[102] The OEEC also provided another European forum for Ireland. With the ERP, MacBride managed to extend his influence beyond diplomacy into foreign and domestic economic policy.

Despite the popular support and MacBride's enthusiasm, the response of Department of Finance to the Marshall Plan was sceptical. McElligott believed that 'we cannot expect any measure of salvation from the so-called Marshall Plan' in a review submitted on 1 August 1948.[103] The Department of Finance did not see the benefits of long-term economic planning. As T.K. Whitaker later remarked, 'no one who took part in preparing the recovery programme (and that includes myself) ever looked on it as a development programme, but rather as an exercise that had to be undertaken to persuade the Americans to give us Marshall Aid.'[104] In addition, Marshall aid proposals could threaten the Department's close relationship with the British Treasury; after 1922 the Department had been modelled on the British Treasury, and collaborated closely with them; the Irish and British economies were linked and close personal ties and friendships existed between Finance and Treasury officials - many Finance officers were on a first-name basis with their Treasury counterparts but not with their colleagues in Irish Departments. Finance was afraid Ireland would be unable to pay back any loans. They also thought more conservatively; increased heavy borrowing might provide 'a standing temptation to governments to incur expenditure without regard to the economic consequences.'[105] Cabinet hegemony was at stake; as External Affairs had assumed the leading role in negotiations and planning, their Department could be strengthened at Finance's expense. If they did accept a loan, Finance would have also preferred to use the money to repay the national debt.[106]

In the end, MacBride won out. The cabinet approved his plans in December 1948. Most of the Marshall aid loan went toward long term projects such as public investment to stimulate industrial development, land rehabilitation, rural electrification, telephones, and improvements in fishery and harbour facilities, and afforestation – projects with little immediate return, though viable in the long run, and strikingly similar to Clann na Poblachta's economic policy presented during the 1948 general election.

As a condition for participating, an economic programme had to be submitted to the OEEC. The *Long-Term Recovery Programme*, published as a white paper in January 1949, a scheme 'liberally laced with imaginative projections,'[107] was the responsibility of MacBride and Frederick Boland, Secretary of the Department of External Affairs. This nascent attempt may have demonstrated a lack of imagination toward development possibilities; but it proved useful for future economic planning. As John Murphy accurately states, the beginnings of economic planning were found in the first inter-party government rather than Whitaker's better-known memo in November of 1958.[108] Despite the improvised nature of the document and the dependence on projects with little immediate return, the white paper was the first attempt at an overall economic plan since the establishment of the state. As MacBride remarked in a speech to the National Press Club on 14 March 1951, the ECA was 'constructive and helpful' and the 'direct financial aid which we received was valuable but far more important in my view was the economic planning which we had to undertake in conjunction with the E.C.A.'[109]

In subsequent years, Ireland did not qualify for as large a share of aid; America believed that the Irish economy had shown signs of recovery. In late 1951, the American government announced that economic assistance was to be considered solely in terms of strengthening NATO and promoting European political unity. Ireland did not want to participate in a mutual assistance pact and in January 1952 her involvement ended.

As Whelan has contended, Marshall aid had no dramatic economic impact and Ireland did not share in the Western European recovery of the 1950s. Economic growth and prosperity did not result and the balance of payment situation worsened and led to a period of economic depression. Yet Marshall Plan participation did have some tangible benefits; it accounted for fifty percent of the total inter-party government's investment, it improved Ireland's standard of living, and it gave the government economic planning experience and a modernised planning system. Involvement also offered Ireland a chance to re-enter the mainstream of European diplomatic life, to consider their position on European cooperation, to rehabilitate the national image, and to establish a harmonious working relationship with both the United States and the

United Kingdom.[110] As Fanning indicates, the Marshall Plan was the 'first great milestone in the path leading tortuously but inexorably to increased Irish involvement in European affairs.'[111]

MacBride's Department also benefited from Marshall Plan involvement. As Michael Kennedy maintains, the ERP helped the Department of External Affairs expand from a small operation not always taken seriously by its peers in Irish administration to an influential department ranking alongside Finance as one of the senior departments in Irish civil service.[112] Participation not only provided the motivation for a restructuring of the Department; it allowed External Affairs to expand its brief into foreign economic policy and multilateral diplomacy; the ERP section developed into the Economic Section, which would handle relations with the EEC.

In the case of the Marshall Plan, the Irish government could not afford to put principle above practical concerns. By the end of Ireland's participation in the plan, they received $128 million in loans, $18 million in grant aid, and $1.25 million in technical assistance. Most agree that the Irish government did not demonstrate good political judgement, both in the way they responded to getting a loan rather than a grant and by attempting to raise the issue of partition. The meeting between MacBride and Hickerson about the Irish receiving loans rather than grants should have made the American position on partition clear to the Irish government. However, MacBride either chose to ignore or downplay the American position.

The North Atlantic Treaty Organisation

MacBride's approach to the Marshall Plan overestimated Ireland's bargaining position with the current American administration. Their response to the invitation to join the North Atlantic Treaty Organisation also demonstrates an incorrect appraisal of current power politics, but this time with more dire consequences.

On 7 January 1949, the United States informally approached the Irish government through their embassy in Washington about issuing an official invite to consider being a NATO founding nation. The United States was still miffed about Irish wartime neutrality, but, as with the Marshall Plan, Ireland's strategic location and close connections to Britain meant that they could not be completely ignored. A CIA situation report determined that Irish participation would be useful because of its strategic location athwart the chief seaways and airways to and from Western Europe. Its terrain and topography lend themselves to rapid construction of airfields which would be invaluable as bases for strategic bomber attacks as far east as the Ural Mountains... because hostile forces in Ireland would outflank the main defences of Great Britain, and because it could be used as a base for bombing North America, the denial of Ireland to an enemy is an unavoidable principle of United States security.[113]

The government responded to the American invitation in an aide-mémoire handed in on 8 February 1949 stating that the Irish government agreed 'with the general aim of the proposed treaty' however,

any military alliance with or commitment involving military action jointly with, the state that is responsible for the unnatural division of Ireland, which occupies a portion of our country with its armed forces, and which supports undemocratic institutions in the north-eastern corner of Ireland, would be entirely repugnant and unacceptable to the Irish people.[114]

The aide-mémoire suggested finding a solution to partition for the reason that 'any detached or impartial survey of the strategic and political position must lead to the conclusion that a friendly and united Ireland on Britain's western approaches is not merely in the interest of Britain but in the interest of all countries concerned with the security of the Atlantic area.'

When asked in the Dáil later that month to summarise the government's policy on NATO, MacBride responded

Ireland, as an essentially democratic and freedom-loving country, is anxious to play her full part in protecting and preserving Christian civilisation and the democratic way of life. With the general aim of the proposed Atlantic Pact in this regard, therefore, we are in agreement. In the matter of military measures, however, we are faced with an insuperable difficulty, from the strategic and political points of view, by reason of the fact that six of our north-eastern counties are occupied by British forces against the will of the overwhelming majority of the Irish people. Partition is naturally and bitterly resented by the people of this country as a violation of Ireland's territorial integrity and as a denial in her case of the elementary democratic right of national self determination. As long as Partition lasts, any military alliance or commitment involving joint military action with the State responsible for Partition must be quite out of the question so far as Ireland is concerned. Any such commitment, if undertaken, would involve the prospect of civil conflict in this country in the event of a crisis.[115]

MacBride surmised that Ireland was of vital geographic and strategic importance, so the United States would at least acknowledge the grievance, if not aid in its removal, in order to secure Ireland's presence in NATO. He was not aware that the invitation to join was actually at the suggestion of the British Foreign Office. A note from Ernest Bevin to the State Department the day before Ireland received the official invitation warned that, 'if the Irish raised partition as a barrier to joining the pact' the response should be that the issue was 'beyond their competence' to discuss.[116] The State Department was not as anxious to secure Ireland's membership as MacBride thought, and the American government's response to the aide-mémoire was that the partition issue was 'entirely the concern of the governments of Ireland and the UK' and the situation was not relevant to membership of NATO.[117]

MacBride then made 'tentative overtures' about abandoning neutrality and joining NATO in exchange for American support for ending partition.[118] In his view, neutrality would not prevent Ireland from participating in NATO; Ireland joined the OEEC and the Council of Europe and only the Soviet veto kept Ireland out of the United Nations. A CIA report stated that MacBride 'considers it politically impossible for Ireland to join a military alliance while Partition continues,'[119] but that political impossibility referred to partition, not Irish neutrality. MacBride was much more preoccupied with partition than with neutrality. Noël Browne confirms this, writing that MacBride wanted to abandon neutrality and join NATO, which went against Clann na Poblachta party policy; Browne cites the example of MacBride's 'strange nomination' of Denis Ireland, a NATO supporter, to the Seanad.[120] The Catholic Church was also keen to join; according to Garrett, Archbishop John Charles McQuaid 'assured me that the Roman Catholic Church was in favor of Ireland's accepting the invitation to join the North Atlantic group.'[121] MacBride himself stated that 'my overall attitude was if a choice came of ending partition by joining NATO, I would say let's join NATO... anything destabilizing partition was worth doing.'[122]

On 4 April 1949, the North Atlantic Treaty (NAT) was signed in Washington. Seven days later, MacBride met with Acheson. They discussed the present state of Europe and partition and NATO membership. Once again Acheson reiterated the American unwillingness to become involved.[123]

MacBride suggested that Ireland would be happy to join if partition did not exist. He expressed the hope that North Atlantic Treaty signatories could try to create a situation where the problem could be discussed. MacBride may have been hoping that Article 4 of the North Atlantic Treaty, which stated that 'the Parties will consult together whenever, in the opinion of any of them, the territorial integrity, political independence or security of any of the Parties is threatened' could be utilised in this regard. Of course, MacBride would have to make sure that this tactic, similar to the 'sore thumb' strategy being employed by the Irish in intra-European groups like the OEEC and the Council of Europe, would be feasible before committing Ireland to the Atlantic Pact.

This approach was also unsuccessful. On 3 June 1949, the State Department informed Nunan that

the North Atlantic Treaty has been concluded by the participating nations for their collective defense against aggression and for the preservation of their common Christian and democratic heritage. It was not intended to settle long standing territorial disputes or similar matters which might be at issue between the parties or between a party and any other state.[124]

A year later, the Irish government was still peddling this idea. The National Security Council (NSC) reported that

the United States replied to the Irish Government to the effect that NAT was not a suitable framework within which to discuss a problem solely the concern of the United Kingdom and Ireland, and that we failed to see any connection between partition and NAT, which was not intended to provide a new forum for the settlement or discussion of long-standing territorial disputes. All other signatories took similar positions.[125]

This willingness to bargain contrasts with de Valera's stance on neutrality during World War II. De Valera's response to the proposed exchange of Irish unity for participation on the side of the Allies was that he would not abandon neutrality.

MacBride's overtures were refused by the United States for four reasons. First, MacBride misjudged Ireland's necessity to the pact. An NSC note indicated that 'in the early development of NATO, the United States Government made a study of [Irish ports and airbases] and concluded that although Ireland's military potential was by no means an element essential to the success of NAT, Ireland should be given an opportunity to join the organization.'[126] Irish participation was not necessary for NATO's success and the ultimate conclusion was that there was no military reason to pursue Ireland. As Britain was a member, Northern Ireland's bases and ports would be available for NATO's use. Irish military facilities would be merely complementary to those already available to North Atlantic forces in this area through the adherence to the North Atlantic treaty of Great Britain and Northern Ireland.[127] Therefore partition was not a problem in the context of Western European defence.

Additionally, despite official neutrality, Ireland was ideologically aligned with the West and the 'power of the pulpit' ensured that Ireland would remain so. An example was Irish intervention in the Italian election of 1948, where it seemed that the Italian Communist Party might win a majority. If there were conflict, it was easy to see where their loyalties would lie. An NSC report surmised that

despite strong anti-communist sentiments, the Irish Government for domestic political considerations still adheres strongly to its traditional policy of neutrality which was militarily embarrassing to the Allies in World War II. In a war against communism, a policy of Irish neutrality undoubtedly would be more benevolent to the Western Allies than in World War II and less useful to the Soviet Union, which has no diplomatic representatives in Ireland, than Irish neutrality was to the Axis.[128]

Third, MacBride misjudged the friendship between Britain and the United States. After World War II and in a Cold War context, they were close allies. The United Kingdom was the most responsible for getting America involved in Europe and was an original signatory of the Brussels Pact. The British were undisturbed about Ireland's absence; they were not surprised by the Irish response to the offer and they were certain that Ireland would be an ally in any war with the Soviets. Furthermore, the Ireland Act of 1949 had guaranteed that Britain would not abandon partition unless a majority in the Northern Ireland Parliament consented. Acheson, Cronin argues, was an 'Anglophile,' the son of an Anglican bishop with 'little sympathy or patience with Irish nationalism or its advocates.'[129] This is not a fair assessment of Acheson; he proved willing to listen to Irish concerns and he should not be singled out as the only Anglophile in the State Department.

Fourth, MacBride was blind to the realities of Cold War power politics. MacBride did put the issue in a global framework; rather he placed partition in terms of an Anglo-Irish framework. A Foreign Office report correctly pointed out that 'Anglo Irish politics influence Éire's approach to every problem.'[130] Of course, the United States had other concerns. The nation was moving from a period of non-involvement in European affairs to becoming more involved in a tense atmosphere. Despite James Dillon's comment that sustaining partition was in 'the prime interests of Communism in the world to-day' by fomenting division between the United States and the British Commonwealth, the United States did not take that idea seriously.[131] As NATO's basic purpose was to 'keep the Soviets out, get the Americans in, and hold the Germans down,' a comparatively minor political squabble between two friendly nations was not a major concern.[132]

Domestic political concerns provide some explanation of the government's behaviour. MacBride thought that joining NATO might lead to Northern nationalists accusing the government of selling them out which could bring about the fall of his government. In a speech to the National Press Club on 14 March 1951, MacBride declared that 'Partition is the cause of such feeling in Ireland that no Irish Government could attempt, without immediately being driven from office, to enter into a military alliance with the power which is responsible for it.'[133] Of course this was based on the assumption that Northern Ireland would join the Republic if permitted: an assumption that was a miscalculation. If the inter-party government had proved willing to join, then they left themselves open to criticism from de Valera and Fianna Fáil for selling out the Northern minority and accepting partition. MacBride told Garrett that 'anti-partitionists would feel that Eire was giving something to Western Europe and America without getting anything in return and it would be considered foolish to have thrown away such a promising opportunity to bargain.'[134] Once again, the undesirability of appearing soft on partition prevented the government from imagining the bigger picture.

De Valera and Fianna Fáil backed the policy; which is not surprising as they upheld neutrality in the last world war. MacBride revealed later that there was no one in the government who wanted to join NATO. I didn't have to fight for it in the Cabinet. Each member had his own set of reasons, I'm sure. Some objected because of partition, others because it was a military alliance. We had emerged from a war in which we had been successfully neutral and this was a bipartisan policy.[135]

This was not entirely accurate; some in government were pro-NATO, like Minister of Finance Patrick McGilligan and Dillon, who had advocated abandoning neutrality to aid the Allies during World War II. Yet, they did not protest too much because they did not want to appear soft on partition. The *Irish Times* criticised the government, pointing out that partition 'will not be ended by a childish refusal to help the British, Canadians, Americans, and the rest to insure themselves against the dire hazards of a possible war.'[136] The paper called not joining 'a serious mistake' and stated that the Irish government's position did not reflect the true attitude of the people.[137]

Archbishop McQuaid had expressed a favourable opinion toward joining NATO. But Garrett pointed out that 'the Church's opinion on the issue would cut very little ice, as whenever in recent Irish history politics and the church have clashed, politics have always come out on top.'[138] This, of course, is only true in the context of civil war and partition, in domestic politics, the Church had much more say.

From 1949 to 1950 MacBride tried to negotiate a bilateral defence treaty between the United States and Ireland, maintaining that in event of an invasion Ireland would be defenceless. Garrett thought a defence treaty was a good idea:

It is unfortunate all around that political considerations make it impossible for any Irish Government to accept membership in the North Atlantic Council until the question of Partition has been resolved. Military aid, I feel convinced, would furnish the impetus that could lead to a bilateral treaty, which, although in the nature of a side-door entrance, would, nevertheless, bring Ireland into the defense picture against any aggression on the part of the U.S.S.R.[139]

The final decision on that matter was that 'United States-Irish bilateral arrangements would create friction and resentment among the NAT signatories who have assumed collective mutual assistance obligations.'[140] A bilateral treaty would probably be unnecessary; the Truman administration's containment policy, shown in response to increasing communist influence in Greece and Turkey, demonstrated an American willingness to protect countries under communist threat.

As late as 13 March 1951 with the inter-party government's days dwindling, MacBride paid a courtesy call on Acheson. They spoke about the struggle against communism and MacBride once again brought up ending partition. Acheson noted that

he [MacBride] thought there was an increase in the realization of this point of view even in London but that he did not think that, by itself, the United Kingdom would do anything about it. He expressed the view that if the United States were to encourage the United Kingdom to do something result would flow from such a step.

Acheson replied that, 'I had always regarded the problem as one which should be decided by his Government, the United Kingdom and the people of the northern counties.'[141] Neither side had altered their perspective.

The unwavering position of the United States is encapsulated in an NSC Statement of Policy written on 17 October 1950, 'the United States should... Continue its present policy of maintaining an attitude of readiness to welcome Ireland as a member of the North Atlantic Treaty Organization, at this time leaving the initiative to Ireland... Avoid discussion of bilateral arrangements for a military assistance program outside NATO.'[142]

The government would later try to package not participating in NATO as a foreign policy success, one that protected neutrality and kept the Irish people from revolting. Cronin agrees with that evaluation, arguing that in 1949, Ireland successfully avoided being drawn into a military alliance that would have limited its sovereignty at home and independence in foreign affairs.[143] Yet, that 'success' was not intentional; it was not the goal of the policy. As Boland wrote to Ambassador to the Holy See Joseph Walshe, 'the major objective of our present efforts is to get the United States or Canada, or both to act.'[144] Cronin further argues that 'if partition was a good enough reason to stay out of the second world war, then it was sufficient reason to stay out of the cold war.'[145] Yet, although partition was a decisive factor, it was not the only reason Ireland stayed out of World War II. De Valera claimed that the principal reason was that a small country would only be damaged in a conflict involving major states.[146] When offered the opportunity to end partition in exchange for Irish participation in the war, de Valera refused.

Ultimately, if the government was serious about not joining NATO due to neutrality, they should not have shown themselves willing to bargain. If they sincerely wanted to solve the partition problem, then they should have joined. As Dermot Keogh observed, MacBride and the government's 'posturing on NATO was as gauche as it was naive. It introduced a note of crude horse-trading into high diplomacy.'[147] The argument that 'the Alliance itself would be an ideal means by which Ireland could emerge from isolation, play an active part in international affairs, and contribute to the containment of communism' is correct, as well as erasing some of the stigma of World War II neutrality.[148]

Joining NATO would have been beneficial to Ireland in the long term and would have been possible to justify to public opinion. Taking part would have provided another opportunity for functional cooperation between the North and South. It might have also influenced Britain; 'the United Kingdom are in no way opposed to North and South coming together when they can agree to do so and… co-operation on Western European affairs would seem to point in this direction.'[149] As McCabe correctly surmised, 'Eire's acceptance of participation in NATO would have presented Britain with the major difficulty of justifying her continued support for the Unionists' position on the partition of Ireland.'[150] Taking part would have demonstrated that Ireland was willing to cooperate and may have made the United States more amenable to mediation. As a CIA report dated April 1949 explained, 'the end of partition is conceivable only in connection with Ireland's adhering to an alliance such as the suggested North Atlantic Pact, in which case bases would presumably be available under the terms of the alliance.'[151]

In addition, NATO was a good ideological fit; the Irish were hostile toward atheistic communism; the *Irish Times* editorialised that non-participation was 'a direct contradiction of the Irish people's natural instincts.'[152] NATO was led by the United States, not Britain. The treaty was strictly defensive, which would have suited a neutral nation, where it is permissible to respond when threatened. On the other hand, the Soviet Union was not specifically hostile to Ireland, which meant that defence considerations were minor.[153]

Also, participating would have helped increase their influence in European politics, where the Irish were trying to make an impact. Bevin and Paul-Henri Spaak were the chief European proponents of the Atlantic Pact. Bevin and Anthony Eden were disappointed that Ireland did not join.[154] Apparently 'Spaak was indignant over the Irish position,' the

United States Ambassador in Brussels reported and, 'thought their contingent proposition was absurd and typical.'[155]

After de Valera's return to power, he followed the inter-party government's policy, declaring that 'we accept the line taken by the previous Government. It would be extremely difficult for any Government to take any other line, the circumstances being what they are. So long as partition exists it would not be possible for any Irish Government to enter into the Atlantic Pact.'[156]

Ireland never became a NATO member and MacBride's own attitude toward the organisation had altered as he became more involved in human rights causes and less obsessed with partition. In 1983 he was

much more hostile. He grew totally opposed to membership, even by a united Ireland, citing three main reasons: NATO's commitment to nuclear weapons; its support of undemocratic and colonialist regimes, notably in South Africa; and his belief that the division of the world into power blocs accelerates the arms race and increases the likelihood of a world war.[157]

Conclusion

The United States would later play a major part in the Good Friday Agreement, but involvement came only when violence had intensified in the North and after the Cold War had ended, at a time when the British, Irish, and Northern Irish were willing to talk together. The United States was also more comfortable with a peacemaker role, as Richard Bourke observed, 'since the end of 1980s, conflict resolution has been a minor growth industry.'[158]

MacBride may have appeared over-optimistic and naïve, especially if he expected the United States to respond to the partition issue and, like the larger campaign to end partition, MacBride and the inter-party government persisted in a policy that was not working. However, they did this largely for the benefit of domestic political concerns so that the government would not appear weak on partition. Irish-American politician and former Speaker of the House of Representatives Thomas P. 'Tip' O'Neill's assertion that 'all politics is local' was true in two senses: the Irish at home determined foreign policy in respect to partition, and the Irish abroad were more focused on America than on Ireland. Both Irish and Irish-American politicians were perhaps also more concerned with their constituency's response than practical solutions to the partition situation. Hickerson wrote to Garrett in May 1948 that 'as a result of Mr.

De Valera's use of the American public as a sounding board to demonstrate his firm position against partition, the Costello government has been required to demonstrate to the Irish electorate that it is equally zealous.'[159]

The policy toward the United States cannot be considered a triumph in terms of ending partition, yet it might be seen as successful if the goal was to appear firm on the partition issue. It can be argued that the Irish government was fully aware that America would be unwilling to help solve the problem, that it would be impossible to 'press a great power into the services of a small nation.'[160] Thus they saw no harm in beating a dead horse, even though it might jeopardise a good relationship with the United States.

5

Coming out of the Cave: Ireland's Role within European and International Organisations

'If we do not attend to whatever foreign affairs we have, though they be relatively small, they will be attended to all the same, but not by us.'[1]

Desmond FitzGerald

In *Irish Foreign Policy 1919-1966*, Michael Kennedy and Joseph Morrison Skelly indicate that the years between 1946 to 1955 are often seen as 'wilderness years' in the area of Irish foreign policy.[2] They maintain that this opinion is inaccurate and recent research has borne them out; the restructuring of the Department of External Affairs, Irish participation in the Marshall Plan, and involvement in the Council of Europe and other multilateral organisations prove otherwise. As Minister for External Affairs, Seán MacBride was directly responsible for Ireland's growing role in European politics. By expanding Ireland's international presence, he was attempting to forge an independent identity for the country. Institutions like the Council of Europe allowed MacBride an international forum to seek support for ending partition and his apparent obsession with the topic sometimes led to the impression that partition was all Ireland was concerned with. Yet, despite the shadow of partition, Ireland made many positive contributions to European integration and events taking place during his tenure led to the expansion of the Department of External Affairs and long-term economic planning. MacBride's attempt to internationalise Irish politics would also play an influential part in shaping his later career.

After the repeal of the External Relations Act and the departure from the Commonwealth, Ireland played a more significant role in international relations than is sometimes credited. Scholars of modern Irish history have tended to focus more on Ireland's relationship with Britain and the situation in the North than with other foreign policy issues.[3] However, relatively recent works exist detailing the Irish relationship with Europe, including books by Miriam Hederman, Michael Kennedy, Dermot Keogh, and Bernadette Whelan.[4] The ongoing revisionist controversy may stimulate even more research on Ireland's role in Europe, as revisionist historians have tended to be less sentimental and less 'colonial', developing a more European interpretation of Irish history rather than an anti-British one.[5] More study of Irish foreign policy would be beneficial, because as yet, the 'mapping of the landscape of Irish foreign policy since 1919 is far from complete.'[6]

As well as comparatively little being written on Ireland and Europe during this period, there are a few misconceptions about Irish foreign policy. Such errors include overestimating the Irish obsession with partition and describing the period as stagnant. In their respective studies of Clann na Poblachta, both Eithne MacDermott and Kevin Rafter briefly mention MacBride's role in European integration, but conclude that positive gains were squandered by the 'sore thumb' policy of publicising partition.[7] David McCullagh writes in his *A Makeshift Majority* that 'although MacBride played a largely constructive role in the Organisation for European Economic Cooperation, the overall impression left by Irish foreign policy during the period is of a spoiled adolescent, with an inflated idea of its own importance and no understandings of the realities of power politics.'[8] In *Ireland 1798-1998*, Alvin Jackson suggests that 'in the realm of foreign affairs the Inter-Party government ventured little from the paths of righteousness explored by Fianna Fáil'[9] which is also an incomplete assumption because the inter-party government did attempt to veer away from Fianna Fáil policy, both by leaving the Commonwealth and escalating the anti-partition campaign to prove themselves more republican than the republicans. D.J. Maher claims that from 1948 to 1960, Ireland 'exhibited a considerable degree of reserve' and only after 1961 did any real movement occur.[10] R.F. Foster's *Modern Ireland* gives no mention of the inter-party government's achievements in the realm of European relations, instead pointing out the 'insularity' of post-war politics.[11] Yet, F.S.L. Lyons, in *Ireland Since the Famine*, allows that the inter-party government 'did achieve in that direction [the development of modern Ireland] more than posterity has been inclined to give it credit for.'[12]

None, with the exception of biographer Anthony Jordan, focus on MacBride's specific influence and his role within groups like the OEEC and the Council of Europe or the fundamental part he played in the expansion of his department, but Jordan merely touches on these matters without providing much detail. This situation is unfortunate because the burgeoning Irish presence in international relations may be the one notable area where MacBride and the inter-party government demonstrated an active, rather than reactive policy. Daniel Davies has argued that MacBride expressed enthusiasm for a greater degree of European integration in order to improve Ireland's standing in the Economic Cooperation Administration (ECA).[13] This theory has a few defects, for one, he had shown an interest in integration before his dealings with the ECA began. He also continued enthusiastic participation in European movements long after Marshall aid had been allocated. The supposition also overlooks MacBride's desire to find a place for Ireland within Europe.

MacBride's contribution has also been overshadowed somewhat by later politicians and advocates of European cooperation such as Frank Aiken and Seán Lemass. As Patrick Keatinge, from a political science perspective, correctly concludes, MacBride 'can be said to have grasped firmly the few opportunities open to Ireland in those years for pursuing an active foreign policy.'[14] Therefore, a more detailed examination of his influence is definitely due.

Irish Neutrality?

As Ireland was part of the United Kingdom until 1921, Britain insulated the island and prevented it from developing a distinct foreign policy. [15] The important exception was the 'England's difficulty is Ireland's opportunity' mindset. Hence, Ireland did not involve itself in Europe, except to ask for help in battling the British, establishing ties to the French in 1798 and the Germans in 1916, for, as Seán T. O'Ceallaigh colourfully put it, 'whipping John Bull'. There were no feelings of attachment or antagonism toward any other European country; Ireland's main gripe was with Britain, which coloured her relationship with other countries. Furthermore, the tradition of emigration was limited mainly to Britain and her dominions and the United States. Ireland shared no borders with another foreign power, so they had no close contact with neighbouring countries and their only property dispute was with Britain.

With the important exception of the six counties, Ireland was a Free State within the British Commonwealth after 1921. Not surprisingly, the Irish were more concerned with the formation of statehood than with foreign policy issues; 'new states, in their formative years, need first to establish their sense of national and international identity before entering into international organisations where they may have to dilute their sovereignty for the greater good.'[16] However, the country was not completely insular; Ireland was a member of the League of Nations and Michael Kennedy concluded that the League provided Ireland with 'an international identity, purpose and sense of place' in the crucial years of consolidation.[17]

Ireland adopted an official neutrality policy during World War II and managed somewhat successfully to keep to this policy. However, many argue that the country was not truly neutral, what Norman MacQueen calls a 'peculiar neutrality.'[18] If Ireland was not truly neutral during the war, it was even less so afterward, 'neutrality had been a wartime expedient but was not necessarily a peacetime preference.'[19] De Valera's primary concern was sovereignty, not neutrality. Despite the successful show of independence, for geographic, economic, and historical reasons, Ireland maintained a close relationship with Britain and the increasing post-war bipolarisation of Europe also put Ireland and Britain on the same side. By 1949, even MacBride admitted that, in the future, Irish security 'would be bound up with Britain's security.'[20]

The Cold War also affected Irish neutrality. A staunchly Catholic country, Ireland's ideology was firmly anti-communist. As future Taoiseach John Costello declared in the Dáil, 'whether or not we were neutral in the last war, there can never be any question again of this country being neutral in any future war.'[21] Ireland was not on the fence between the Eastern and Western blocs; partition, not neutrality, had kept Ireland out of NATO, providing 'the *sole* obstacle to Ireland's participation in the Atlantic Pact.'[22] As MacBride stated in the Dáil while discussing the idea of a federal Europe, 'we in Ireland are not much troubled by conflicting ideologies... Our sympathies, therefore, lie clearly with the nations of Western Europe.'[23] A notable example of the lack of ideological neutrality was Ireland's intervention in the Italian election of 1948, where the Communist-led Popular Democratic Front seemed capable of winning a majority in the Italian Parliament. Irish interference, consisting mainly of soliciting contributions to generate anti-communist campaign materials, can hardly be described as the act of a neutral nation.[24] Conor Cruise O'Brien observed that the

> tendency to associate the national interests with those of Britain, anti-Communism, sympathy with Catholic parties and statesmen in Western Europe, traditional respect for the political views of the Irish

Catholic hierarchy... all these attractions pulled in the same way; towards involvement on the Western side in the Cold War.[25]

Despite Ireland's official non-participation in World War II, there were many similarities between the European countries that had been involved in the war and Ireland in the late 1940s: they all experienced stagnant economies, reshuffling of political parties and groupings, developing Cold War loyalties, and a general 'mood of disenchantment.'[26] Yet immediately following the war, European activists virtually ignored Ireland because, as Hederman points out, it was a relatively poor country, it was not a particular threat to be mollified or challenged, there was little pre-war political or economic upheaval, the major Irish political parties were not involved in any international political movements,[27] and the younger generation of Irish politicians were unknown to their European counterparts.[28] Moreover, Irish politics could be rather parochial; Irish TDs 'tended to be primarily local... representatives, responsible for advocating and advancing of affairs for his constituents and his locality.'[29] Foreign policy, if a concern at all, was definitely a secondary one. Keatinge points out that a typical TD was unlikely to be well informed about foreign affairs.[30]

MacBride was an exception. As Keogh indicates, 'MacBride was a Christian Democrat and it was quite fashionable to speak of European unity in 1948 within those circles. MacBride saw himself in the fashionable company of Alcide de Gasperi in Italy, Robert Schuman in France, Konrad Adenauer in Germany and Pius XII.'[31] He was well suited to a diplomatic life; French was his first language, he had lived in Paris until he was 15, he was enthusiastic about European unity, and as a lawyer and founder of a political party, he was familiar with constitutional and international issues.

Another advantage was timing - MacBride arrived in government at a propitious period. Though Ireland remained bound to Britain in some ways, she was looking to distinguish herself in others. She did not want to be seen as an appendage; the psychological importance of separating from the mother country, especially after repeal, must be taken into consideration. The inter-party government's self-perception situated Ireland as a 'link between the Old World and the New World.'[32] Such assessments may have been grandiose and misguided; as Keogh concludes, MacBride 'suffered from having spent too long in Plato's Cave.'[33] Yet, this perception does provide a cogent reason, other than publicising partition, for favouring closer contact with Europe. Senator James Douglas, one of the first delegates to the Council of Europe, summarised the country's changing mood during a Seanad debate on proposals for a united Europe:

> For years our people were insular in their outlook and only a small minority took a real interest in international affairs. During the war we were prevented by the censorship from reading any news which the powers that be thought might interfere with our neutrality, and, generally speaking, the Government during that period discouraged too much interest or curiosity on the part of the man in the street in what was taking place in Europe. A change took place after the end of the war, and I think I am correct in stating that there is now much more interest in European affairs than there has been for a long time.[34]

Involvement in European movements allowed Ireland to escape the confines of Anglo-Irish preoccupations and a relationship that had become stifling.[35] For the Republic, to be European was a way to be acceptably 'not British.' As Frederick Boland observed, the difference between MacBride and Éamon de Valera, the previous Minister of External Affairs, was that MacBride believed in Western European cooperation while de Valera looked to Commonwealth cooperation.[36] The inter-party government marked a change of direction. Neutrality had been de Valera and Fianna Fáil's policy; the new government looked to formulate a unique course of action.

De Valera believed that the External Relations Act, though ambiguous, could provide a bridge that might end partition; he told his biographer Frank Gallagher, repeal of the act was the 'height of folly' which 'troubled' him.[37] He also told Nicholas Mansergh in February of 1952 that he had wanted Ireland to remain associated with the Commonwealth.[38] Whereas de Valera would have preferred to remain just inside the Commonwealth, the inter-party government took Ireland out in 1949, and as Mansergh points out, a distinctive voice within the Commonwealth was lost.[39]

The counterpoint then to secession was membership in the European Recovery Programme and the Council of Europe, a return to the cultural area to which she was a part. As Ireland chose not to join NATO and was not yet a member of the United Nations, participation in European integration provided her with an opportunity to make herself known. The relationship with Britain, the United States, and the Commonwealth may have been the focus in the immediate post-war period, as emigration made Britain and America the two foreign countries Ireland was most familiar with, yet she also took an interest in fellow Catholic states like Italy, Spain, Portugal, and France, especially due to the perceived threat of atheistic communism.[40] MacBride proved willing to support Spain and Portugal's entry into the Council of Europe despite their fascist regimes. In late 1948, the Director of the Political Division of the Spanish Foreign Office Señor Juan Sebastián de Erice suggested that a neutral bloc consisting of Spain, Portugal, Argentina, and Ireland be formed to defend Catholicism, especially in regard to access and defence of the Holy Places in Palestine and resistance to Communism.[41] Nothing came of the proposal, as Ireland preferred to consult with the Vatican regarding Catholic associations, and Ambassador to the Holy See Joseph Walshe believed that the Vatican 'would prefer to see us maintain our extremely strong position in the English speaking Catholic world, as a defender of Catholic principles... rather than as an ally of countries where the use [is] made by politicians, of the Catholic religion to uphold essentially undemocratic regimes.'[42] The discussion shows that an alliance had at least been contemplated.

Post-war plans for integration 'offered Ireland an opportunity to develop beyond the confines of Commonwealth and diaspora.'[43] Yet, there were also pragmatic reasons for encouraging relationships with other European countries; Ireland was tied to Britain economically – 90 percent of Irish food exports went to the UK, and Ireland wanted to improve the stagnant post-war economy with other agricultural markets and trading partners.[44] MacBride believed that increased foreign trade was necessary for economic development and the improvement of living standards.[45]

Similar to neutrality, the idea of a closer relationship with Europe provided cohesion within the Republic. Wider involvement in European affairs would help decrease any leftover preoccupation with civil war politics; 'a new generation is rising, which, I trust, will approach the problems of Ireland's reconstruction objectively and with a mind free from past dissensions.'[46] MacBride accurately surmised that no major disagreements existed in the foreign policy of the Irish political parties; 'Fundamentally, there is no difference of policy between the Parties in the House in relation to our external policy. My function, therefore, is to give effect to the best of my ability, to the general policy upon which the Government and all Parties in the House are agreed.'[47] Participation would also provide the opportunity to show sovereignty and independent decision-making power. Britain and Ireland were equal in terms of international law and would later possess the same status in the European Community.

Ireland and the Council of Europe

The Council of Europe was the result of attempts at international cooperation after the end of the war. The idea to form a 'United States of Europe' was first proposed by Winston Churchill in his address in Zurich on 19 September 1946. Other concepts regarding the tightening of cooperation among European countries emerged almost simultaneously. The goal was to create some form of closer association to recover and reassert influence in the post-war world.[48] Founded in 1949, it was the first European post-war political organisation. Its aim was to create a common democratic and legal area structured around the European Convention on Human Rights and to develop ways of cooperation on a wide range of issues. The basic structure has remained unchanged since its founding.

As Ireland did not join the European Economic Community until 1973, from 1945 to 1973 the Council of Europe provided the most important link to Western Europe and, until Ireland was permitted to join the United Nations in 1955, the only international forum where Ireland could participate as an equal, and learn how international organisations operated.

In addition, with the notable exceptions of Churchill and Ernest Bevin,[49] Britain did not appear enthused; 'the official attitude of Great Britain toward the young Council of Europe was cold and disinterested, and even in some cases almost hostile.'[50] When Churchill asked for Prime Minister Clement Attlee's support before the Hague Conference, Attlee replied that 'it would be undesirable for the Government to take any official action in regard to this Conference.'[51] The Irish sensed this ambivalence; a 1950 External Affairs memo indicated that 'British policy seems to have been directed, in the main, to the task of slowing up or side-tracking any proposals for a greater degree of European cooperation.'[52] British aloofness could provide a chance for the Irish to distinguish themselves as well as providing an opportunity to prove that military neutrality did not mean political isolationism.

An International Committee of Movements for European Unity convened a meeting to demonstrate support for the cause of European unity and to make recommendations for its execution, believing that 'only a genuine European federation would be able to ensure the permanent peace of the continent.'[53] Ireland sent a delegation to The Hague for the Congress of Europe which began on 7 May 1948. The delegation consisted of Senator James Douglas, President of University College Dublin Michael Tierney, and Labour Senator Eleanor Butler. The *Irish*

Independent called the Hague Congress 'one of the most remarkable gatherings of our time.'[54] Professor Tierney reported that he was 'greatly impressed by the representative character of the Congress and by the sincerity and extent of the movement for a united Europe.'[55]

The delegates reported back to MacBride, stressing the atmosphere of Christian Democracy present at the assembly.[56] This attitude encouraged MacBride, who 'combined enthusiasm for aspects of European cooperation and convergence – particularly in respect of individual rights, democratic values and the defence of Christianity.'[57] He believed that a united Europe would be safe from communism, which he felt was 'an ideology that takes little or no cognisance of the elementary principles of democracy and personal liberty.'[58] The Church also supported the idea; Archbishop of Dublin John Charles McQuaid was 'very interested in, and favourable to' European unity and Church-State relations were important to MacBride.[59]

Aside from MacBride, few other politicians in Ireland were excited about closer ties with the continent. The Irish delegates at The Hague found themselves among Prime Ministers, elected parliamentary representatives, and distinguished national figures, which may say something about the official level of commitment, as Ireland sent Senators rather than the Taoiseach or cabinet ministers.[60] While reporting to the Seanad regarding The Hague conference, MacBride was quick to point out that 'I am speaking on my own, without the authority of the Government and without in any way committing the Government to any proposals contained in this resolution or to the proposal for the formation of a united states of Europe put forward at The Hague.'[61] Ireland did not send delegates to the Interlaken meeting beginning on 1 September, believing 'it was not of sufficient importance.'[62] Only one Irish delegate was sent to the Paris meeting to draw up the Statute and Agenda for the Consultative Assembly in Strasbourg.

Like the British, Irish political parties seemed to prefer traditional, intergovernmental organisations like the OEEC to the Assembly of the Council of Europe, a new concept, which can explain this lack of participation.[63] A recent Anglo-Irish trade agreement had shown the importance of the British market, and during his tenure in office, de Valera had tried to maintain good relations with Britain and was wary of pooling sovereignty in a federal Europe, as he argued in the Dáil regarding free trade agreements, 'Only the powerful States can, in any sense, regard themselves as completely sovereign and, you deprive yourself of the means of doing as you please the moment you sign any international

delegates to the Council of Europe seemed to devote their time to making speeches about partition; speeches which were designed to be read at home, but which unfortunately had to be listened to abroad.'[72] He later admitted that MacBride was 'well fitted to play a useful and acceptable role in the major international organs to which Ireland then belonged,' but was hamstrung because the government, who could not appear less than vigilant regarding the topic, obliged him to administer 'pin pricks to Great Britain in the councils of these institutions.'[73]

This may have been an effective strategy for drumming up support at home, but it did not win Ireland friends in the Council. The Council's reaction to the partition speeches tended to be 'boredom mingled with bewilderment' at best, frustration at worst.[74] At the second session of the Council, in response to MacEntee's speech linking partition with human rights abuses, President Spaak replied, 'We must not allow every Debate to become the object of a dispute between the Representatives of Ireland and Great Britain... I beg you to keep to the matter at hand.'[75] At a meeting to discuss a potential European Army, Spaak became so exasperated that he beat furiously on his desk with a ruler to stop the partition conversation.[76]

The division of Ireland was a comparatively small dilemma and was not seen as a sufficient reason for offending Britain, whom many European politicians felt grateful to in the aftermath of World War II. During the opening address of the Consultative Assembly of Council of Europe given by Edouard Herriot, he thanked Churchill 'for in many moments of deep tragedy he bore upon his shoulders the whole weight of the world crying out for help. From his mind sprang the movement which has brought us together here.'[77] Irish public opinion understood the situation; *The Leader* pointed out 'while it is well that our statesmen should draw attention to the end of partition, it must be quite obvious that no western European governments or non-communist politicians are prepared to seriously embarrass Great Britain under existing conditions.'[78] It was not only a matter of obliging Britain, the *Irish Times* editorial of 13 August 1949 pointed out that 'most of the delegates at Strasbourg have lived at one time under the rule of real dictatorships' and references to a six county 'police state' left them cold.[79] Larger issues than an Irish domestic dispute were in question; Churchill himself at a speech at The Hague stated that 'territorial ambitions must be set aside and national rivalries must be resigned to the question of who can render the most distinguished service to the common cause.'[80]

MacBride defended the anti-partition strategy in the Dáil:

Obviously, if close co-operation is to be achieved between European nations, the first essential is to discuss and, if possible, remove the causes of friction that may exist between the nations that compose the Council of Europe. Partition is certainly one of the outstanding causes of friction in Western Europe to-day. As Irishmen, we make no apology for desiring the territorial unity of our nation... As Europeans, we make no apology for seeking to remove one of the causes of disunity in Europe.[81]

He also accurately pointed out that

our representatives, however, did not confine themselves to matters of purely national interest. On the broader plane, of international co-operation, they were to the fore with their contributions to the discussions on the many complex problems that arose; these included such matters as the future political structure of Europe, economic co-operation, human rights, cultural co-operation and co-operation in the field of social security. They made important contributions to the work of the various Assembly Committees, as well as to the debates in the Assembly itself.[82]

Speeches on partition were not just political posturing for the Irish; their delegates did sincerely consider partition to be unjust. Furthermore, Irish initiatives went wider than the rhetorical focus on partition might suggest.[83] Once anti-partition fever died down, Ireland became a model member of the Council, the first country to accept the jurisdiction of the European Court of Human Rights. Delegates of the Council commented that 'Ireland had an individual approach to many questions, that their suggestions were made with cogency and that they were constructive.'[84] The widespread portrayal of Irish delegates bringing up the issue at every possible opportunity is inaccurate – the transcript of the August 1950 sessions show that they were focused on the issues at hand.[85] MacBride involved himself in improving the structure and function of the group, making efforts to achieve closer unity between the Committee of Ministers and the Consultative Assembly. 'Mr. MacBride already has managed to keep on excellent terms with all his European colleagues.'[86] He worked well with others and proved to be dynamic, or at least this is how the world press perceived him – 'a trio of "little ministers" – Belgium's Spaak, Austria's Gruber and Ireland's MacBride – have been giving the hot-foot to the slower-moving Ministers of the larger Western

European countries.'[87] The Belgian pictorial *Le Face à Main* reported that 'avec Churchill et Spaak, dont la popularité est énorme, c'est Sean MacBride, le brilliant ministre des Affaires étrangères d'Irlande, qui a le plus de succès.'[88]

Ireland's initial involvement in the Council concerned the spheres of democratic values and human rights. MacBride insisted that human rights be at the top of Council of Europe's priorities, which was the realm where Council excelled and he played a significant part in its development.[89] He was partly responsible for the negotiation and ratification of the European Convention on Human Rights, the greatest accomplishment of the Council of Europe, as Bevin wrote to MacBride 'a positive achievement of the first importance.'[90] Jordan believes that the document was one of the successes that MacBride was most pleased with.[91] Ratification of the document, which guarantees the right to life, liberty, security, fair trial, freedom of thought, conscience, religion, and speech, became a condition of membership of the Council. MacBride hoped that it could help bring about a federal union of Ireland; at least it would protect the rights of the Nationalist minority in the North.[92] In addition, he sponsored and signed the Convention for European Economic Cooperation in 1948, the Statute of the Council of Europe in 1949, and the Geneva Convention for the Protection of War Victims in 1949. He also utilised the Council to emphasise the importance of civil liberties, and highlight plight of political prisoners, which were long-standing concerns of his.

Ireland also benefited from the fact that it possessed an equal say within the Assembly. When asked about the allocation of delegates within the Council, MacBride replied, 'I am glad to say that the number of delegates allocated was not based on population or national income figures. It was intended... to give adequate representation to small countries irrespective of their size, population or wealth. To that extent, I think that the small nations of Europe have benefited.'[93] Thus, sovereignty was not compromised and Ireland had just as much of a say as larger, more populous countries. The Council did not rely on military measures, a detail which differentiated it from NATO. As de Valera compared, 'membership of the Council of Europe imposes on us no obligation which is inconsistent with our national rights. Membership of NATO, on the other hand, implies acceptance by each member of the territorial integrity of each of the several states comprising it.'[94]

In the beginning, there was confusion about protocol, procedure, and points of order during the first session due to the newness of the assembly and the different parliamentary traditions of members. Seán MacEntee remarked that 'it has been somewhat difficult for those of us who have not attended a conference of this sort before to know exactly what facilities we have at our disposal.'[95] After the General Election on 30 May 1951, de Valera and Fianna Fáil were returned to power and were not as enthusiastic about the Council, becoming the 'most articulate group of Cassandras in the early days of the Council of Europe.'[96] Discussion on European topics diminished until Seán Lemass became Taoiseach in 1959. Yet Ireland's successful participation in the Council of Europe provided the fundamental springboard for moving into European mainstream. Such experience would serve Ireland well after entry into the United Nations and the European Union.

The Organisation for European Economic Cooperation

The Organisation for European Economic Co-operation (OEEC) was formed to administer American aid under the Marshall Plan for the reconstruction of Europe after World War II. It developed into the Organisation for Economic Co-operation and Development (OECD) in 1961. Conference negotiations led to the creation of the OEEC in order to meet Secretary of State George Marshall's request for 'some agreement among the countries of Europe as to the requirements of the situation and the part those countries themselves will take.'[97]

By 1947, Ireland's international reputation had faltered due to neutrality, the memory of de Valera's visit to the German legation to offer condolences upon Hitler's death, and the veto of Ireland's application to join the United Nations. Neutrality had also put strain on Ireland's rapport with the United States. However her geographical location made a good relationship important to both British and United States security.[98] The case for Ireland to be offered aid was very strong despite her lack of a threatening communist presence; Ireland's immediate economic difficulties were similar to those of most Western European countries, and there were political, diplomatic, and security arguments for inclusion.[99] There was no real public opposition in Ireland itself and the state of the Irish economy meant Ireland would seriously consider the American offer.

Ireland received an invitation on 4 July 1947 to attend a meeting in Paris on 12 July to 'take part in the drawing up of a programme covering both the resources and needs of Europe for the following four years.'[100] Here was the 'the first time that Ireland has had an opportunity of cooperating in an international organisation in which the members of the British Commonwealth of Nations were not also participating.'[101] Representatives of sixteen Western European Countries gathered in Paris to frame a joint response to the American offer. On 16 April 1948 the CEEC met and adopted a convention, established a permanent organisation of sixteen participating countries, thus officially forming the OEEC. An *Irish Independent* editorial supported the idea, stating that there was 'good ground for hoping that the agreement signed yesterday in Paris will endure and be of lasting value to the world.'[102]

Organising Irish participation in the ERP and meeting the steps to qualify for aid fell to MacBride, as did how the money should be spent.[103] Participation in the OEEC was not only useful for receiving Marshall Aid, but it was more beneficial because it forced the government to consider their position on European cooperation as well as formulate an economic programme, not something previous governments had done. MacBride saw the value in this, 'one of the most essential and urgent steps to give effect to economic planning... is to be in a position to plan for and integrate the economy as a whole.'[104] He was enthusiastic, stating that 'the task of the OEEC is not merely to divide the aid which the US have so generously provided, but it is to provide an impetus and a plan for the development of economic co-operation in Europe.'[105] He saw the organisation in broader terms, as he wrote to Spaak, 'the OEEC could fulfil a valuable function if it could formulate a long distance policy for the development and the integration of the participating countries... the council of the OEEC could become, in effect, an economic government for Western Europe.'[106] He then wrote that 'I think that it is necessary that the Ministers of all participating countries should meet at frequent intervals and discuss informally current problems as well as long range policy. Such meeting would ensure greater interest and greater co-operation on the part of the Governments and nations concerned.'[107] During their time in the OEEC, MacBride and Spaak corresponded often; Spaak addressing MacBride as 'Mon cher Ministre et Ami,' while MacBride addressed him as 'Mon cher Président et Ami.' The two ministers had much in common; both came from prominent political families, both lied about their ages to enter the military, MacBride joining the IRA in 1918 and Spaak enlisting in the Belgian Army during World War I. Both spent time in prison, MacBride during the Civil War and Spaak in a German prisoner of war camp. Both studied law and became Foreign Ministers of small nations that chose neutrality during World War II (although Belgium's situation was very different), and both shared an interest in European unity. MacBride and Spaak may have believed that the OEEC should be strengthened and expanded, but the British and the Scandinavian countries preferred limited economic cooperation.[108]

In February of 1949, a committee of nine ministers of the OEEC met in Paris, on MacBride's initiative, to figure out how the OEEC could become more effective to hasten European recovery and encourage economic cooperation. MacBride received 'unstinted praise' from member nations and the Economic Cooperation Administration for his resourcefulness.[109] American diplomat Vinton Chapin wrote of MacBride on 4 March 1949,

> Ireland has participated in the Paris meetings of the OEEC wherein MacBride's special abilities and temperament have filled him to perform useful services among the most important nations as a 'leg man', who had no special interest in European power politics. This ability conforms to the Irish contention that it is a nation with a long tradition of resistance to religious and political oppression and therefore in a position to find friends among other nations.[110]

As the OEEC was an international body, it too was subjected to the 'sore thumb' strategy of publicising partition. Fianna Fáil TD Dr. J.P. Brennan asked MacBride if he would give an assurance that on his proposed visit to Paris on March 14th next to attend the Committee on European Economic Cooperation 'he will not discuss thereat any political—other than economic— matter, until the partition of the country will have been solved to the complete satisfaction of the people of Ireland.' MacBride responded by stating that 'the matters to be discussed at the resumed meeting of the C.E.E.C. on March 14th appertain primarily to the economic sphere,' but, when pressed, promised that 'in any question of importance that may arise in the relationship of this country with Great Britain… the question of Partition will be considered and discussed.'[111] Despite this, MacBride remained sincere about making the organisation work; in a speech to the OEEC Council, he suggested meeting more often and not being afraid of making unpopular decisions;

> the work should not be left merely at an official level, otherwise this organisation runs the risk of many other such international organisations that we have had over the last quarter of a century or more. It will just become an organisation for the compilation of statistics, but it will mean nothing to the people of Europe.[112]

Ireland received Marshall aid and the OEEC's main task involved removing obstacles to intra-regional commerce after 1951. Ireland remains a member of the OECD, which grew from the OEEC to discuss, develop and refine economic and social policies, advocating a commitment to a market economy and pluralistic democracy. While membership in the OEEC and the Council of Europe did not remove the border, it did raise the country's profile and Ireland enjoyed a renowned reputation in European circles 'thanks to the activities of its peripatetic French-speaking foreign minister'[113] whose 'contributions to the work of the OEEC have done much to enhance [Ireland's] national prestige abroad.'[114]

Expansion of the Department of External Affairs

MacBride gave External Affairs the prominent profile it had previously lacked as well as providing a sense of direction and undertaking needed administrative reforms. During his tenure, External Affairs was responsible for the administration of the ERP, the creation of an Irish News Agency, the extension of the American embassy and Washington DC office as well as increased contact with European embassies and missions, also a separate trade section, a second assistant secretary in 1948, in 1949 a third assistant secretary and two new sections; political affairs and information as well as establishing a Cultural Relations Advisory Committee, a Public Relations office at the Consulate General in New York, and increasing international distribution of the department's *Weekly Bulletin* from 2,000 copies in November 1949 to 4,300 copies in March 1951.[115]

With these expansions and new responsibilities came an increase of staff and requests for more money. As MacBride pointed out,

> Some of our most important missions abroad were so understaffed that their members were unable to get away from their desks to maintain essential contacts with the outside world. The headquarters of the Department itself was in the same position. The staff were overwhelmed with the mass of work arising in the ordinary course of Departmental duties, and there was little or no provision for the steady systematic work which must be done if our major objectives in the political field are to be achieved.[116]

MacBride highlighted the contributions of the Department and its staff in its first year of operations in the Dáil:

> From the point of view of the Department of External Affairs, this year has been one of tremendous importance in many fields. Events of

paramount importance have occurred in the course of the year, both in our relationship with Britain and in the international field generally; the passage of the Republic of Ireland Act, the Atlantic Pact; the passage of the Ireland Act in the British Parliament; the launching of the Council of Europe; the increasing importance of the Organisation for European Economic Co-operation; the making of trade agreements and the development of cultural relations. These were all events that cast tremendous work and responsibility on our small Department of External Affairs. Before proceeding further, I should like to pay special tribute to the staff of the Department for the manner in which they responded to the extra calls which are being constantly made upon them by the pressure of events and by the resulting additional burdens... I cannot praise their self-sacrificing enthusiasm and devotion to their work too highly; many times I have been reminded of the spirit and enthusiasm that prevailed in the national movement. It is, of course, this type of spirit that should prevail in a small foreign service such as ours at times of crisis.[117]

His request was necessary; due to the frenetic pace of the last year and MacBride's future plans, the Department had an increased workload and certainly needed more personnel and more funding. He continued by predicting that

in present circumstances I see no hope of the work of the Department becoming lighter. On the contrary, if we are to perform our functions effectively in regard to the Council of Europe, the Organisation for European Economic Co-operation and Partition, as well as the many other functions which fall on the Department, the work is bound to increase. In these circumstances, additional staffs are essential.[118]

He then asked the government

to provide for an expenditure on external affairs higher by £74,025 than that provided last year. I should say quite frankly that I do not feel called upon to make any apology for this increase. We cannot expect to make political headway abroad and attain our national aims unless we are prepared to tackle the task of putting our point of view across much more actively and vigorously than we have done in the past.[119]

The increased volume of correspondence between Dublin and other nations abroad demonstrates the growth of the department and MacBride's efforts to expand its profile. Also, by actively promoting his Department, MacBride encouraged young and talented people like Conor Cruise O'Brien to work at Iveagh House and take an interest in foreign affairs. Such contact and recruitment would benefit the Department when Ireland was admitted into the United Nations; able, experienced people were already on hand to provide support. In the post-war years, External Affairs developed in stature to reduce Finance's dominance in the administration and become one of the primary departments of state. MacBride's ability to see the bigger picture at least in the realm of European unity made him 'a pioneer in the sense that he articulated long-term national objectives in a Dáil which all too frequently succumbed to the temptations of short-term partisan advantages.'[120]

Ireland and the United Nations

Ireland's official application for membership was submitted in August 1946. There was domestic and international interest in the application; the *Irish Times* commented on the 'considerable array' of foreign representatives gathered in the Dáil Gallery to hear the debate.[121] There was a very full attendance of members as well. Though de Valera saw Irish membership in the United Nations as incompatible with absolute sovereignty, he felt that joining was the better alternative because, 'it is natural that small States should strive to bring about an international organisation which would guarantee their independence and general freedom. The trouble is that no such organisation can come into being without very great sacrifices on the part of all its members.'[122] No note of opposition existed, though very few TDs were overly enthused, feeling that 'we must play our modest part in international affairs.'[123] The *Irish Times* was confident, believing that no 'serious opposition will be raised against Eire's application.'[124]

The prediction proved to be untrue. The Soviet Union vetoed the application's entry ostensibly on the grounds that Ireland had no diplomatic presence in the Soviet Union and that during the war, Ireland did not help the Allies, instead offering support to the Axis powers and Franco's Spain. Ireland's anti-communist stance was probably more responsible; the membership of the General Assembly was weighted toward the Western bloc and the Soviet Union did not want its position in the Assembly weakened.[125] This argument is confirmed by the fact that, when Ireland was finally admitted into the United Nations, it still had no diplomatic relations with the Soviet Union. Before official admission, Ireland was involved in specialised United Nations agencies like the World Meteorological Organisation, and the Food and Agricultural Organisation, as membership in the General Assembly was not necessary for participation.

The decision to apply for membership was unanimous and MacBride was enthusiastic at first. He recounted in the Dáil:

The decision to apply for membership of the United Nations Organisation was taken by this House on the 25th July, 1946... Ireland possesses the qualifications for membership laid down by Article 4 of the United Nations Charter[126] and should, therefore, be admitted to membership; it further requested the Security Council to reconsider Ireland's application in the light of that determination.[127]

Unlike participation in other international organisations, MacBride did not associate UN membership with the removal of partition; Commonwealth Secretary Philip Noel-Baker remarked on MacBride's mature outlook toward the United Nations and the lack of an attempt to link partition to Irish participation.[128] While he conceded that neutrality in theory might be affected, he did not foresee any future problems in practice due to the ideological differences among the permanent members of the Security Council:

Membership of the organisation involves acceptance of the obligations contained in the charter of the United Nations... The most far-reaching of these obligations are those obliging members to carry out the decisions of the Security Council with respect to threats to, or breaches of, the international peace which have not been settled by peaceful methods. It is important to note, however, that such decisions require the concurrence of all the permanent members of the Security Council, namely, the United States, Great Britain, Russia, France and China. In this connection, I should point out that lack of unanimity amongst the permanent members has, so far, prevented the implementation of Article 43 of the charter, that is, the article requiring each member to conclude an agreement with the council specifying the armed forces and other facilities to be made available to the council for the purpose of maintaining international peace and security... there is no obligation, by virtue of Ireland's application for membership of the United Nations Organisation, to take any sides...

The question of what Ireland's attitude would be in the event of a war would be a matter for this House to decide.[129]

However, the veto remained in place and a few months later, MacBride seemed to have doubts, both about Ireland's future role in the UN and the efficacy of the organisation itself:

The fact... that we have been excluded from it [the United Nations] demonstrates that its mechanism is open to abuse. In this connection I should mention that, at some time in the near future, it may become necessary that the Government should consider whether our application for membership of the United Nations Organisation should not be withdrawn...[130]

In a letter to Vinton Chapin of the American Legation, MacBride mentioned the 'natural resentment created by the rejection of our application,' and 'a growing scepticism with regard to the effectiveness of the United Nations as at present constituted.'[131] The Irish people also may have also been wary of joining, feeling disenchanted with the organisation. *The Leader* editorial of 13 March 1948 commented, 'The Palestine problem, at least, is valuable in showing that UNO [United Nations Organisation] as an international force against aggression and war is virtually powerless when prompt action is necessary.'[132] Not only did the government have doubts about the organisation of the United Nations, but the experience with the League of Nations, a loss of face at being eager to join, then being forced to wait, and the aversion to be seen striking a bargain with Soviet Union to lift their veto, also led to apprehension about becoming a UN member.

Yet MacBride's faith in organisational assemblies themselves remained undiminished:

I have delayed in bringing this matter formally before the Government and the Dáil as I did not wish, in the present situation, to take any steps that would indicate a lack of faith in any attempt that was being made to discuss world problems at a conference table. No matter how abortive or fruitless such conferences may prove, it is still the only way of avoiding conflict. The more representatives of different nations meet to discuss their problems, the greater the possibility of reaching understanding and peaceful solutions.[133]

Nearly a year afterwards, MacBride was asked in the Dáil if the government would continue to seek admission. He replied that the application was still pending and that 'the Government is not called upon to take any further action in the matter.' Independent TD Patrick Cogan then asked, 'is the Minister aware that Ireland's application for membership of the United Nations Organisation has been twice rejected, on the veto of Russia? Would it not be exposing this country to unnecessary humiliation to repeat the application?'[134] Cogan later suggested that Ireland withdraw her application, calling it 'a more dignified course' because any change of attitude by the Soviet Union toward Ireland

> might be interpreted by freedom-loving nations as a change of our policy towards Russia, which is a thing we would not like to have happen. On the other hand, I do not think we would like to have our admission ticket into the United Nations Organisation peddled about in exchange for the admission of some countries under Communist rule.[135]

MacBride seemed nonchalant about the waiting game, citing that his Department was quite busy without UN membership:

> In the midst of all the work that has had to be performed by the Department in the course of the year, I have been very thankful indeed that the Russian veto on our admission to the United Nations Organisation has been maintained. Frankly, the prospect of having to provide representatives at another international body such as the United Nations Organisation and to have to attend yet another series of international conferences, was frightening in existing circumstances.[136]

Ireland's application was vetoed again in September of 1949 along with the applications of Portugal, Italy, Austria, Finland, Jordan and Greece. Eventually Ireland was admitted to the United Nations in exactly the type of situation Cogan predicted, as part of a package deal with Soviet-bloc countries.

Conclusion

The United Nations became an arena where Ireland could further some of its political aims, strengthen long-standing contacts throughout Europe and North America, establish relationships with Africa and Asia, and help to preserve the international order.[137] From the mid 1950s until the mid 1960s, the Irish delegation 'led by an extraordinary team of talented, dedicated diplomats, occupied a prominent place in the General Assembly.'[138] Ireland was one of ten non-permanent members elected by the General Assembly of the United Nations to serve on the Security Council in 1962, 1981-1982, and 2001-2002. The United Nations became a vital focal point of Irish foreign policy, both for making diplomatic contact with other nations as well as a forum to state opinions on international issues. The Irish delegates never formally raised the issue of partition in the General Assembly but did argue against it as a way of solving political conflicts.[139] Ireland defended the rights of minorities in Tibet and South Tyrol and supported resolutions on decolonisation. Ironically the United Nations, which MacBride once, in a moment of frustration, said he was happy not to be in for the time being, would shape his later career to a large extent.

Cruise O'Brien once lampooned MacBride as living in a 'dream world in which he is a brilliantly successful statesman, elegant, eloquent, strolling with the leaders of Europe; what he is doing is not very clear, but with what distinction he does it!'[140] Such a characterisation is unfair, as MacBride did much to raise Ireland's profile within Europe. Cruise O'Brien later wrote in 1969 that 'Ireland has acquired an adequate measure of international respect. Her spokesmen find a hearing, when they have something to say. They can exercise a small, but not insignificant influence, on the great movements which help to shape world politics.'[141] Though Cruise O'Brien does not mention it, MacBride can take credit for establishing such respect.

Michael Gallagher surmised that the decisions of inter-party government 'had considerable long-term significance, even though they made little contemporary impact.'[142] This is especially true of foreign policy. Many believe that serious foreign policy pursuits began with admission to the United Nations, as they believe economic planning began with Whitaker's memo, but both had their roots during the inter-party government. Choosing not to participate in NATO and the repeal of the External Relations Act may have shown a lack of purpose and foresight in foreign policy, but European integration demonstrated that the inter-party government was indeed forward thinking in some respects. MacBride gave some of his best, most articulate and well-thought out speeches in the Dáil on foreign policy issues and travelled more than any previous Minister for External Affairs. Unfortunately domestic problems, like the Mother and

Child controversy, would overshadow both the government's foreign policy gains and MacBride's contribution to them.

MacBride's focus on foreign affairs meant he was out of the country much of the time, 'promenading on the world stage…[and] must have felt culture shock on returning to the provincial mundanities of Dublin.'[143] His absences led to his influence in the cabinet waning and the Clann, as a relatively recent party, did not receive the attention it needed. Yet MacBride's attempts to break with the past and look toward broader horizons for the future ultimately benefited him personally as well as Ireland. As then-President Mary Robinson explained in 1991,

I myself feel that because we were so uncertain of ourselves when we were first of all ruled by Britain, and then in this century when we achieved the Free State and then the independent republican status from 1937,[144] we still lacked self-confidence as a nation. We still were defensive, ambivalent, self-deprecating. And I believe that it has been an enriching experience to have become part of a wider European continent; that's partly psychological. I think that there has been an awareness that we have ourselves as a strong culture, that in many areas we can stand on equal terms. That has been good for the national psyche and for the sense of our identity.[145]

What the *Irish Independent* wrote regarding the OEEC could also be applied to this period of Irish international relations; 'the preliminaries have concluded. The edifice has been built and the work is about to begin.'[146]

6

Catholic First, Irishman Second: The Fall of the Inter-party Government and the End of Clann na Poblachta

'In this country a man must have upon his side the Church or the Fenians.'[1]

John O'Leary

The first inter-party government is chiefly remembered for two events, the declaration of the Republic and the Mother and Child controversy. While declaring the Republic benefited Seán MacBride and Clann na Poblachta, his role in the Mother and Child controversy split his party and led to the end of his career in Irish politics. The handling of the issue sheds light on Irish Church-State relations, MacBride and the Irish Catholic Church hierarchy's attitude toward women, and ultimately provides another example of the reactive nature of the inter-party government.

Many of MacBride's contemporaries have written about the Mother and Child conflict and its aftermath.[2] There are also engaging secondary works detailing the origins and outcomes of the crisis.[3] However, these can be difficult to sift through due to the diverse theories and differing interpretations that the various authors propose. Both Eithne MacDermott and Kevin Rafter's respective books on Clann na Poblachta describe the end of the inter-party government and the end of the Clann itself. The Dáil debates and the Irish press help illuminate both government's actions and public opinion.[4] John Horgan's recent *Noël Browne: Passionate Outsider* provides a more balanced view than Browne's own memoir *Against the Tide*. Yet aside from Anthony Jordan in his *Seán MacBride: A Biography*, who takes the debatable position that MacBride acted honourably and reasonably during the controversy 'given the prevailing culture,'5 there is little analysis of either MacBride's role in the controversy or what his response indicates about both his personality, his abilities as a party leader, and the atmosphere in the country, particularly regarding the nature of the Church and State relationship

The Fall of the Inter-party Government

MacBride possessed a high profile as Minister for External Affairs, but by 1951 his reputation was 'effectively in tatters.'6 As Noël Browne remembers,

> He would scan the cabinet agenda, and on those subjects in which he had a special interest, would submit a treatise to the Taoiseach. In the early days, this memorandum was carefully unfolded and conscientiously read out by the Taoiseach to a politely attentive Cabinet. It was treated with some respect... As the memoranda proliferated, it became obvious that all was not well in Clann na Poblachta; they were now treated with a tolerant amusement, and the epistles filed somewhere.7

There are several reasons for this decline in influence. The increase in Taoiseach John Costello's confidence and authority meant that MacBride had less leverage within the cabinet. He was also losing influence within his party; the decision to enter a coalition government had already alienated some of the party's Republican sector, minor government scandals and the response to the Mother and Child controversy helped further divide opinion within Clann na Poblachta. As MacDermott correctly proposes, the Mother and Child controversy split the Clann rather than the government.8 In addition, MacBride's ability to control his party was further weakened because he travelled more than any previous occupant of his office and his frequent absences led to his power diminishing in both the party and the government. For example, he spent much of March 1951, the lead-up to the Mother and Child controversy, in France and the United States. As Sir Gilbert Laithwaite, Lord Rugby's replacement as British Ambassador to Ireland wrote, MacBride 'is thought by some to pay less attention to holding his little Clann na Poblachta party together than is wise.'9 C.S. Andrews, a fellow IRA member in the 1920s, commented that MacBride was 'industrious in whatever interested him but sustained effort did not appear to be one of his characteristics... He worked best in an organisation when he was the leader.'10 Personality conflicts, which seemed a common feature of his political career, were also a factor. By 1951, MacBride had fallen out with Clann member Peadar Cowan, expelling him from the party, and the Secretary of his Department Frederick Boland and was soon to fall out with Noel Hartnett and Noël Browne.

Recollections and explanations both at the time of the controversy and later on are conflicting.[11] The phrase 'widely differing reports' is frequently used whenever the scheme is discussed. Browne did publish the correspondence between himself, MacBride, Costello, and the hierarchy, but certain unrecorded face-to-face meetings and discussions are still open to interpretation.[12] What can be accurately determined is that Browne, as Minister of Health, was given the task of improving and implementing a programme for mother and child health care. Mother and child health care was a concern of his as Ireland had the highest infant mortality rates in Europe. The 1947 Ryan Act, passed by the previous Fianna Fáil government, made provision for free medical treatment of expectant mothers and children up to age 16. As Coogan states, 'no one in the Dáil, or the hierarchy, either objected or waved a crozier as the Bill passed into law.'[13] The hierarchy expressed objections privately to then-Taoiseach Eamon de Valera after the bill had passed, claiming that the plan was 'entirely and directly contrary to Catholic teachings, the rights of the family, the rights of the Church in education, the rights of the medical profession and of voluntary institutions.'[14] De Valera replied to these concerns on 16 February 1948, two days before his government fell, what Coogan describes as 'an outburst of instantaneous procrastination.'[15] He wrote that because the Act had been referred to the Supreme Court to test its constitutionality, 'I think it better to make no personal comment on the matter at this stage.'[16]

A health service for mothers and children was first mentioned by the inter-party government in the Dáil on 6 July 1948 when Browne requested money for the Ministry, stating that 'I have not made up my mind as to the exact method of providing the mother and child service and am awaiting the outcome of the deliberations of the council which I have recently established to advise me on matters relating to child health.'[17] The Church was not mentioned in any context at this time and in the next day's session, TD Honor Mary Crowley stated that 'I think the section of the Health Act dealing with mother and child welfare is the most important section of the whole Act and I hope that the Minister will put it into force as soon as possible.'[18] Seán MacEntee chided Browne for taking so long to implement a scheme that the previous government had already put in place:

If the Minister were not there at all, everything that has been done so far would have been done almost automatically. It would have been done because his predecessors had prepared the plans and put the machine in motion to give effect to those plans, and those projects would have come along in due and regular course, like motor cars from the assembly line... What, for instance, has the Minister done to bring into operation the provisions of the Health Act, 1947—the Fianna Fáil Health Act—in relation to mother and child welfare?[19]

Dr. Ryan, the previous Fianna Fáil Minister of Health and the architect of the 1947 Act, was also anxious for it to be implemented.[20]

Browne had already asked for and received cabinet approval to redraft the Act.[21]

At this time, no one objected to the lack of a means test. In the first years of his Ministry, Browne focused on eradicating tuberculosis; several members of his family had died from the disease and he proved committed to that venture, both in increasing the amount of sanatoria and providing access to medicines. By July 1950 2,000 new beds had been provided for tuberculosis patients and the death rate dropped from 123 out of 100,000 in 1947 to 73 out of 100,000 in 1951.[22] In 1950 he began formulating the mother and child welfare scheme in earnest. By June 1950, the draft proposals were completed and details of the plan appeared in the 10 September 1950 issue of the *Sunday Independent*. The scheme would involve free, but voluntary care for mothers as well as children under 16 with no means test.

He first encountered problems from the Irish medical profession, who would have to staff and run the scheme. Doctors opposed the plan because they feared a reduction in their incomes and argued that the plan resembled 'socialised medicine'. However, some doctors recognised the merits of the scheme. Surgeon Betty O'Shea wrote to the *Irish Times* that 'I cannot understand why Dr. Browne's proposals, the most enlightened and far-reaching ever put before the people by any Irish cabinet Minister, should not be welcomed by any doctor who puts the people's health before the sectarian interests of his profession.'[23]

Because the struggle with the bishops became more public, the role of the Irish Medical Association (IMA) is often underestimated. The *Irish Times* of 9 April 1951 remarked on the front page that 'most of the controversy which has raged around the Mother and Child scheme for the last nine months has been conducted by the Irish Medical Association.'[24] In his article 'Church-state relations and the development of Irish health policy: the mother-and-child scheme, 1944-53,' Eamonn McKee concludes that 'it was Browne's commitment to taking on the doctors in the name of a free-for-all service which set him against the Irish Medical Association and thus against a large section of the cabinet and hierarchy.'[25]

J.H. Whyte believes that Browne, as a radical who wanted social change, deliberately behaved in a contentious manner during the mother and child crisis because he was hoping for a showdown between the Irish state and the IMA.[26] He also indicates that Browne 'appeared to develop a pathological hatred of the doctors' in private practice.[27] His experiences as a house officer in Newcastle Sanatorium in County Wicklow may have contributed to an unsympathetic attitude for the medical establishment and he seemed to 'have set out deliberately to provoke the profession, in particular, the Dublin consultants, by criticising in public their manner of practice and preoccupation with money.'[28] MacBride confirmed this view when he stated in the Dáil that 'little or no attempt was made by my late colleague to avoid the clash, and I am not even certain that he [Browne] did not provoke it.'[29]

Whyte further posits that he was so preoccupied with his battle with the IMA that he never anticipated problems with the Catholic hierarchy. Furthermore, Browne had been unaware of the previous correspondence between de Valera and the bishops. Barrington agrees, stating that Browne treated the hierarchy's objections 'in a somewhat cavalier manner and considered that the doctors were the chief opponents to be beaten.'[30] However, the earlier difficulties with the IMA and cabinet colleagues, especially MacBride, would make his problems with the Church hierarchy much more difficult to solve.

The 1937 Constitution granted the Church a 'special position' within Ireland, and although no accord between Church and State officially existed, the Church had an immensely powerful position in Irish public life and in law, particularly in matters involving social welfare and education. The leading hospitals and most secondary schools were run by religious orders, the clergy held a number of university chairs, and, as James Deeny points out, taught most of the leading people in government.[31] In his memoir *Against the Tide*, Browne pointed out the huge measure of control the Church possessed in the operation of health services and observed that not only did the Church have such power but, 'the Church had for so long not been subjected to any serious criticism or examination in her administration of the health services.'[32] The hierarchy feared that education of women for motherhood that would be provided under the plan would include instruction on 'sex relations, chastity, and marriage,' which, in their view, was not the state's job.[33] The scheme might also result in Catholic women being treated by non-Catholic doctors and 'education' could someday lead to contraception and abortion, although both were illegal at the time. As Barrington indicates, there existed growing acceptance of both birth control and the idea of abortion in Britain.[34]

The bishops also sympathised with the Irish Medical Association's worries about socialised medicine; the Archbishop of Dublin John Charles McQuaid's father and uncle were doctors. He also belonged to the Knights of Saint Columbanus, an organisation that included many doctors and provided contact between the IMA, the hierarchy, and the cabinet.[35] In addition, McQuaid was fervently anti-communist and examples in Eastern Europe of the state taking over from the Church made him vigilant about the government superseding the authority of the Church. The hierarchy also felt threatened by the establishment of the National Health Service in Northern Ireland, which they accepted, despite being far more radical than Browne's scheme. McQuaid biographer John Cooney concludes that 'Browne, a democratically elected politician with a social vision, was a pawn in McQuaid's Cold War struggle against Communism and its milder but no less insidious from of "socialised medicine", which had spread to Britain and Northern Ireland in the guise of the Welfare State.'[36]

After Browne presented the plan to the cabinet, Costello submitted the scheme to the bishops for their advice. In their reply to Costello dated 10 October 1950, they declared that

> In their opinion the powers taken by the State in the proposed Mother and Child Health Service are in direct opposition to the rights of the family and of the individual and are liable to very great abuse... If adopted in law they would constitute a ready made instrument for future totalitarian aggression.[37]

Browne did agree to make concessions, but remained firm on the no-means test principle. He submitted a revised memo for the hierarchy's review and gave it to Costello to send on. Costello did not deliver it immediately and there was a delay of several months before the hierarchy received it. Browne heard no more after the meeting with bishops in October 1950 and assumed all was well until he a received a letter dated 9 March 1951 that showed that the bishops were intent on preventing implementation.[38] As F.S.L. Lyons reflected, 'Through a series of misunderstandings that would have been farcical were not the consequences so tragic, Dr. Browne believed he had satisfied the Hierarchy when in fact he had done nothing of the sort.'[39]

Browne had never secured cabinet approval for details of the proposal – leaving himself in an exposed position when the cabinet later rejected the scheme, proof of Browne's lack of political instinct.[40] As he later said, 'I had no reason to believe that there would be opposition from the Hierarchy. Even if I had known I would still have expected the Cabinet to implement the law.'[41] Browne was on good terms with McQuaid; their early correspondence, mainly concerning hospital chaplaincies, appeared to be gracious.[42] There had been no criticism from the Irish hierarchy regarding the more comprehensive National Health Service in Northern Ireland, which is odd because the possibility of Catholic women being treated by Protestant doctors was much greater. When Stormont announced in August 1947 that the NHS would expand into Northern Ireland, the only contention involved voluntary hospitals being replaced by a government-appointed Hospitals Authority. Archbishop John Francis D'Alton of Armagh protested and in November Stormont allowed the one Catholic voluntary hospital to opt out of the service. The Catholic Church did not have a special position in the United Kingdom and their extent of hegemony in medicine and education were not as great. Furthermore Costello had asked the bishops for their advice; as Whyte points out, the hierarchy did not have the time to review every piece of legislation on the chance that it might challenge Catholic teaching; sometimes outsiders needed to draw attention to it.[43]

Browne had consulted independently with a theologian who could see no problem with the scheme and assured him that nothing in the plan went against Catholic faith and moral teaching.[44] Browne did not reveal his identity at the time or later in his memoirs, but John Horgan discovered that it was Monsignor P.F. Cremin, Professor of Theology at Maynooth.[45] Cremin reasoned that if a more radical scheme was tolerable for co-religionists on the other side of the border, then no problem should exist for implementing Browne's scheme in the Republic. The bishops, however, replied that the scheme did go against Catholic *social* teaching. In April 1951, the cabinet decided to drop the scheme after continued protest from the IMA and extensive correspondence from the hierarchy.

At a special seven-hour long meeting of the Clann na Poblachta National Executive, the party decided to give MacBride permission to ask for Browne's resignation. On 10 April, he delivered a letter demanding Browne resign as Minister for Health backed by Costello.[46] Browne replied to MacBride and Costello, then arranged for the correspondence to be published in 12 April's *Irish Times*. Browne had been the first Minister to use the media to publicise his policies, broadcasting regularly on the radio and managing a publicity section in the Department producing pamphlets in Irish and English. He made not have been politically astute, but he was media savvy. This action was sensational; at the time such correspondence was kept out of the public domain. Costello was shocked at the disclosure, proclaiming that 'all this matter was intended to be private and to be adjusted behind closed doors and was never intended to be the subject of public controversy.'[47] Browne's action also put both the government and Clann na Poblachta in the position of having to defend themselves. After his resignation, he received immense public support; letters to the major Irish papers praised Browne and noted that 'he can gain satisfaction from the thought that he has the sympathy of the vast majority of the people of Ireland, and that the way he was coerced to bring his scheme to a conclusion and resign his Ministry has disgusted one and all.'[48]

Browne was young, only 32 and an unknown in politics, when he became minister and the Health portfolio was also fairly recent, only a year old. Colleagues' assessments of Browne vary, but most agree that he was hard working and 'a person of passionate social concern.'[49] While researching his *Church and State in Modern Ireland*, J.H. Whyte discovered that for the 'first two years or so in office, Dr. Browne's ministerial career was generally applauded' and he had 'won a generally respected opinion for himself among the officials with who he had to deal.'[50] Even MacBride later admitted that 'Noël Browne was a first-class Minister for Health. He did a first-class job of work on the eradication of TB.'[51] Some TDs preferred him to MacBride; as Independent Oliver Flanagan declared, if given the choice, he would rather have Browne in government than MacBride because 'the Minister for External Affairs has his heart in Paris, his notebook in Strasbourg, his ambitions in Washington and his intentions in the United States, but Deputy Dr. Browne's body and soul and ambitions lie in the sick beds of the poor of this country, and that cannot be forgotten.'[52]

However, Browne did have his critics. While James Deeny, the Chief Medical Advisor in the Ministry of Health, admitted that he was compassionate and 'had a lot going for him,' he ultimately found Browne 'intolerant, and begrudging of other's efforts and, while a magnificent destructive critic… he had few constructive or practical ideas.'[53] MacEntee, known for his acid tongue, called him 'the strangest piece of flotsam the stormy sea of Irish politics has thrown up in three generations,'[54] largely due to his liberal outlook and his education in England and at Protestant Trinity College Dublin.[55] He resented that Browne was taking credit for projects begun under the previous Fianna Fáil administration, remarking in the Dáil that 'Instead of building the hospitals which are so urgently required, the Minister now wants no less than £6,000 to buy a bugle of his own - or should it be a megaphone? - in order to tell the people of Ireland what a wonderful Minister for Health has been miraculously given to them.'[56]   After Browne's resignation, Costello declared that

I had formed in my own mind, having regard to my experience over the last six months and the history of the affairs I have given in the barest outline, the firm conviction that Deputy Dr. Browne was not competent or capable to fulfil the duties of the Department of Health. He was incapable of negotiation; he was obstinate at times and vacillating at other times. He was quite incapable of knowing what his decision would be to-day or, if he made a decision to-day, it would remain until to-morrow.[57]

Clann member and TD Con Lehane stayed true to the Clann's party line and agreed with Costello:

My experience of the ex-Minister for Health has been that he is constitutionally incapable of listening to criticism. Perhaps that is not anything for which he should be particularly blamed; but I have had the experience of seeing him walk out over a fairly long period, a period of a year or more, from five, if not six, different committee meetings.[58]

Browne later defended himself by disclosing that 'in my opinion it hardly mattered whether I attended meetings or not' as they were ultimately a waste of his time.[59] While this attitude is admirable in the sense that he wanted to get back to what he viewed as important work, it provides further proof of his political naïveté. McQuaid's Secretary, Father Mangan, described Browne arriving at Archbishop's House to meet with McQuaid wearing a Trinity College scarf.[60] In addition, Browne did not bring anyone with him to take notes at the meeting with McQuaid.

Was Browne well respected and dedicated? Or was he inconsistent and unwilling to compromise? His competence is not in doubt; it is only questioned after the scheme fell apart and the cabinet seemed pleased with his performance up to then. As Deeny concluded, the government gave Browne the post, allowed him free rein, and then withdrew support and reneged on their stated policy when trouble started.[61] As for his inability to compromise, in the Dáil at the start of his Ministry, Browne asserted that

I am always at the disposal of Deputies on either side of the House if there is any suggestion they have to make which they feel may lead to the improvement or betterment of our health services. I am very glad to have the assistance of the medical members of the House and also the lay members in giving me some idea of the reactions throughout the country to our suggestions and plans for the improvement of the general health of the people.[62]

Browne was determined rather than stubborn; he believed in keeping the plan free of a means test and saw no logical reason for his party, his government, or the bishops to object. After his resignation, expelled Clann member Peadar Cowan stated

I say deliberately, that Deputy Dr. Browne, if not the most popular Minister, was certainly one of the most popular. The Party to which he belonged, Clann na Poblachta, were claiming credit all over the country for the magnificent work being done by Deputy Dr. Browne in the Department of Health. After the things that have been said about him here this evening, it is only right that I should say that, in my view, Deputy Dr. Noël Browne has built a monument to himself in the health services of this country in a short period of three years and that no other Minister that I know of could have done as much for the people in 20 years as he has done in three...[63]

It is doubtful that Browne would have been so popular if he were so incredibly obstinate. His early accomplishments in eradicating tuberculosis and building and improving hospitals would have been unlikely without some compromise and ability to work constructively with others. Deeny admitted that Browne was 'patently sincere' and possessed 'great energy'.[64] Horgan points out in his biography of Browne that he suffered from partial deafness and though he was comfortable in one-to-one conversations, Browne was withdrawn in meetings because he was not always aware of everything that was being said.[65]

Another interesting aspect of the controversy involves the growing animosity between Browne and MacBride. Both men seemed uncomfortable with those who disagreed with them and personality conflicts would feature heavily in both of their careers. Browne believed that Clann na Poblachta was losing its radicalism and that this development was MacBride's fault. They argued over the Baltinglass scandal, where the Minister for Posts and Telegraphs James Everett appointed a political friend to the postmastership of Baltinglass, County Wicklow over a well-qualified popular local candidate. There was protest throughout the country, and both Browne and Hartnett felt that Clann na Poblachta should fight the government on this issue, but MacBride felt that the scandal was not worth bringing down the government, concluding that 'unsavoury matters are inseparable from politics.'[66] Hartnett resigned from Clann na Poblachta, mainly over MacBride's nonchalance regarding the Baltinglass affair, commenting that he 'had become obsessed with power and had abandoned any political or social philosophy.'[67]

Hartnett and Browne were close; it was Hartnett that brought Browne into the party. After the relationship between Hartnett and MacBride worsened, so did relations between Browne and MacBride. Browne agreed that MacBride 'had fallen in love with the trappings and aura of politics.'[68] The conflict culminated in a dinner at the Russell Hotel in November 1950.[69] According to MacBride, Browne told him that he had failed as a party leader, that the Clann was stagnant, and Browne intended to bring down the government and break the party up. MacBride compiled a memorandum that night to keep the details of the meeting straight. His secretary, Louie O'Brien, confirms this, as she typed the memorandum that night at Iveagh House.[70] Browne remembers the dinner, but does not recall making threats of any kind, merely pointing out that giving in to the bishops may harm the prospects for a united Ireland.[71] In MacBride's letter to Browne asking for his resignation written on 10 April 1951, he wrote that

I should like to assure you that, in reaching the decision that has compelled me to write this letter, I have sincerely sought to eliminate from my mind the other events, not connected with the mother and child services, which have rendered our collaboration increasingly difficult in the course of the last year… In a substantial portion of the time during which we collaborated in the Clann and in the Government, you did valuable work for which you deserve the thanks and gratitude of the Clann and of myself.[72]

Browne's understandably vituperative reply to MacBride declared that the letter was

> in full conformity with the standards of behaviour which I have learned to expect from you... Your letter is a model of the two faced hypocrisy and humbug so characteristic of you... I entered politics because I believed in the high-minded principles which you were expounding on political platforms. I do you no injustice when I state that I have never observed you hearken to any of these principles when practical cases came before us. I have tried to analyse your curious philosophy not very successfully. Expediency is your sole yardstick, and to expediency you are prepared to subordinate all principles sacred and profane...[73]

He resigned from Clann na Poblachta as well, writing, 'I have bidden farewell to your unwholesome brand of politics.'
Browne felt betrayed by his colleagues, stating that

> I as a Catholic accept unequivocally and unreservedly the views of the Hierarchy on this matter, I have not been able to accept the manner in which this matter has been dealt with by my former colleagues in the Government... I trust that the standards manifested in these dealings are not customary in the public life of this or any other democratic nation and I hope that my experience has been exceptional.[74]

Costello informed Browne that 'Whatever about fighting the doctors, I am not going to fight the Bishops and whatever about fighting the Bishops, I am not going to fight the doctors and the Bishops.'[75] As the *Irish Times* points out, 'with a united Cabinet on his side, he might have prevailed against the doctors... but... he was left to fight a single-handed battle once the Church entered the arena.'[76] The scheme was originally welcomed by all parties, yet 'just as soon as the hierarchy intervened, it ceased to be a Fianna Fáil, Fine Gael, Labour Party, or even Clann na Poblachta scheme; it became the Dr. Noël Browne mother and child health scheme.'[77]

What the Outcome Meant

Interpretations vary as much as recollections; several theories exist for why the scheme failed and what that failure meant. The Mother and Child controversy is often cited as an example of the extent of Church control over the State. Coogan sees it as such, believing that 'the Church, and in particular John Charles McQuaid... was the main architect of the Mother and Child Scheme's destruction' and Browne's impertinent independence from the bishops had to be reined in.[78] Coogan also calls attention to the fact that Costello had McQuaid's help in drafting his 15 April Dáil rebuttal of Browne's position. However, the aspect of Church intervention in politics is more complex than it seems. Whyte concludes that on the whole, bishops intervened very rarely and the Irish government does not automatically defer to the hierarchy on any point – there were other factors involved in the Mother and Child controversy; such as Browne's growing unpopularity within the cabinet, the cabinet's dislike of the scheme in general, and the cabinet's willingness to choose their battles.[79] Brian Inglis points out that the hierarchy was asked to comment on the Mother and Child Scheme and 'they had merely been asked for their advice on the Bill, which they had given; politicians, it could be argued, were really to blame for trying to suppress the Bill.'[80]

There may be other reasons why the cabinet did not back Browne besides the distastefulness of tangling with the Church; 'As far as most of his cabinet colleagues are concerned, the hierarchy's decision suited them well. Some of them disliked the mother and child scheme in itself.'[81] Fine Gael Ministers were sympathetic toward IMA arguments; Costello stating several times that 'I would not be a member of a Government or take part in any Government that was in favour of or tried in any way to socialise medicine.'[82] Some had close links with the medical profession; Minister for Defence Dr. Tom O'Higgins was a senior officer of the IMA. At best, Fine Gael was not inclined to fight for the scheme; at worst they encouraged the bishops to intervene because they knew they would find problems with the scheme and anticipated Browne's reaction. According to Cruise O'Brien, Costello, 'in an effort to quash Browne's scheme, called in the help of the Catholic Church,' consulting McQuaid, who called the plan 'contrary to the moral teaching of the Church.' Costello asked Browne to bring the scheme in line, MacBride agreed with Costello and the Clann agreed with MacBride, MacBride demanded and received Browne's resignation.[83] There is no evidence that Costello deliberately planned to sabotage the scheme; this is Cruise O'Brien's reading of the situation, but he is correct in noting that 'issues were aired which were and are, normally discussed behind closed doors. To outsiders, it looked like a case of the Church dictating to the State. It was actually a case of a politician asking for a *public* intervention by the Church, for political reasons, and spectacularly bungling the whole business.'[84] An editorial in the *Irish Times* observed that 'with more tactful treatment, the crisis might have been avoided, and the Government might have been enabled to complete its statutory term of office.'[85] There is no proof that Costello cunningly intended for the Church to do his dirty work, but Cruise O'Brien is correct about perceptions of the controversy; it is still seen as the Church dictating policy to the State and the State unquestioningly obeying.

Another theory posits that not only did the government, especially Fine Gael, dislike the scheme; they may have been trying to encourage Browne to resign. As Seán Lemass later mused, 'I am not so sure that it was not allowed to develop this way because the coalition leaders were anxious to get an excuse to drop Browne who must have been a very difficult colleague in the Government at the time.'[86] Costello, though he had proved his tactical abilities during repeal, was probably not such a schemer and there is no real evidence that it was an attempt to get rid of a fractious colleague. Peadar Cowan posited something very similar, but placed the blame on MacBride:

> Why has Deputy Dr. Browne, from being the Minister that was held up by Clann na Poblachta all over the country as such a wonderful man, been brought to the position that he is described as a scoundrel and a liar, as incompetent, incapable and unfit to be Minister in this or any other Government? What has brought about that change? Is it not clear that what has brought about the change is that Deputy Dr. Browne, because of his great work for the people, was becoming more popular than his Leader? Because he was more popular than his Leader, he must be downed and he must be damned.[87]

Did MacBride set Browne up because he was overtaking him in popularity? It must be kept in mind that Cowan, having been expelled from Clann na Poblachta by MacBride, was probably not the most objective observer. If Cowan's conspiracy theory is correct, it means that MacBride, declining in popularity, was somehow able to encourage Costello, Clann na Poblachta, and the bishops to help get rid of Browne. MacBride should shoulder some of the responsibility - Jackson writes that his 'personal obtuseness as well as uncomplicated religious conviction' turned a problem into a political crisis.[88] Yet his behaviour was that of a shortsighted politician rather than a clever conspirator.

At first glance, MacBride's response to the crisis is surprising for two reasons, the obvious one being that his party took a strong stand on social welfare issues. The other is his close relationship with his strong-willed mother, sometimes regarded as the paragon of an independent woman. This too is more complex than it seems. Maud Gonne MacBride never specifically concerned herself with women's rights; she concentrated more on prisoners' rights and the republican cause. She was a political activist, but never claimed to be a feminist. The only feminist position she publicly took regarded marriage; in an interview during her divorce proceedings, she told the *New York Evening World* that 'I believe any woman with independent instincts with the dream of making her individual personality count for something in the world might just as well shun marriage.'[89] This statement was based more on personal experience and the desire to maintain her own independence rather than any dedication to expanding the rights of single women. She came from a Protestant upper-class background and had never had the experience of an ordinary Irish woman despite her 'lifelong concern for the well-being of children and their mothers.'[90]

Mother and son were not always in agreement politically. In 1917 William Butler Yeats wrote that the 13-year-old MacBride 'is going to be very clever and to my amusement has begun to criticise his mother's politics. He has a confident analytical mind.'[91] He had broken ranks before, joining the IRA at fourteen without his mother's knowledge or permission and opposing the 1921 Treaty while she supported it.[92] Madame MacBride never publicly commented on the Mother and Child scheme, but she was ill at the time. Her biographer Margaret Ward posits that her younger self may have argued with the Church, as she did when they refused to cooperate with her school meals for children campaign.[93] She did contribute to the Clann na Poblacta periodical *Our Nation*, formed to help MacBride in the 1951 general election. When actor Micheál MacLiammóir asked her about her son, she replied, 'Oh, he must go his own way. We all do in the end.'[94] Whatever their political disagreements, she was proud of all he had achieved.

Moreover, MacBride was more traditional than his mother. As a convert to Catholicism, she took what she needed from Catholic dogma and discarded anything else.[95] Yet MacBride, raised a Catholic and educated in French and Irish Catholic schools, took his faith from Rome. MacBride advised Gonne not to include her long-term affair with French politician Lucien Millevoye and the details of her divorce from John MacBride when writing her memoir *A Servant of the Queen*.[96] As a result, her autobiography ends at her marriage to MacBride. She had two illegitimate children with Millevoye, Georges, who died in infancy, and

Iseult, who Gonne refers to in the book as her adopted child or niece. Iseult's true parentage was concealed because the revelation could have damaged Millevoye's political career, Gonne's social and political creditability, and Iseult's social standing. In the conservative Irish atmosphere, MacBride was 'especially anxious that none of the family skeletons should be aired in public.'[97] He did later attempt to ease the stigma of illegitimacy by supporting the introduction of a shortened birth certificate that left out parents' names but would later oppose the 1986 referendum deleting the prohibition of divorce from the Irish Constitution.

Later biographies detail Gonne's arrest and imprisonment in 1918 with a fourteen-year-old MacBride chasing after the van taking his mother to jail. While Gonne was imprisoned, MacBride was at school in Wexford and spent holidays with the Yeats' in Galway. Despite his obvious admiration for his mother and her work, MacBride may have wanted a more traditional upbringing and idealised mothers in this role.

MacBride's wife, Catalina 'Kid' MacBride, never publicly commented on the controversy. An activist before her marriage, she later devoted herself to her husband's causes. Yet, it is likely that they did not have a very close relationship; his work was his first priority and rumours exist as to extramarital dalliances. According to McQuaid biographer John Cooney, 'though he was a married man, [he] was known to be fond of women, especially when in Paris.'[98] Coogan and Jordan also mention this 'fondness' for women.[99] Jordan further comments that their marriage was more of a 'friendly relationship'; when MacBride went to Geneva to head the International Commission of Jurists, he did not ask his wife to go with him.[100] Whether she criticised her husband's behaviour during the Mother and Child controversy behind closed doors remains a mystery.

There is no correspondence at this time between McQuaid and MacBride despite MacBride's offer to be available at any time and McQuaid's reply that 'I shall not fail to take advantage of your generous suggestion that you are at my disposal for any matters in which you could assist.'[101] Now would have been the time to take MacBride up on this offer, but McQuaid chose to communicate through Costello, despite MacBride's position as leader of Browne's party. This may be because McQuaid distrusted MacBride due to his IRA background and his alleged role in the denial of a Red Hat to McQuaid, but there is no extant written evidence to confirm this hypothesis or support any other explanation.[102]

The outcome of the Mother and Child controversy is best seen as another example of the reactive nature of the inter-party government and their willingness to hang together rather than disagree and risk losing power. It became more obvious that there were five political parties with divergent views and the doctors and the bishops exploited these differences.[103] Costello did not dissolve the Dáil after Browne's resignation, the Government managed to continue for a few weeks after expunging Browne and introducing a means test, the element causing most of the controversy. The repeal of the External Relations Act is an earlier example of such reactive behaviour, a hasty compromise in order to keep the government afloat. Repeal worked in the government's and Clann na Poblachta's favour, but now the danger for MacBride was that he would lose the radical element of his party.

Whether or not he was trying to take on the IMA or bring down the government, Browne did succeed in enlarging the area of political discourse in Ireland between Church and State. Two important immediate effects of the fallout were the response of the North and the dissolution of Clann na Poblachta.

The resulting crisis led to accusations in the North of 'Rome Rule' and strengthened the Unionist perception that whenever the Church chooses to interfere, it is able to influence decisions. The 14 April *Irish Times* headline '"We told you so" is Northern View' summed it up well. An editorial in the same newspaper lamented that 'an honest, far-sighted man has been driven out of active politics. The most serious revelation, however is that the Roman Catholic Church would seem to be the effective Government of this country.'[104] That phrase, Horgan affirms, 'has been reprinted thousands of times in the intervening half-century and... helped to define the parameters of analysis for as long.'[105] The Ulster Unionist Council pamphlet proclaimed that 'in any matter where the Roman Catholic Church decides to intervene the Eire Government must accept the Church's policy and decision irrespective of all other considerations.'[106] Harry Midgley, Northern Ireland's Minister of Education, addressed the Unionist Association, 'There is no doubt that the Roman Catholic Hierarchy has entered the political arena and that it is becoming more and more aggressive in extending the pointers of Roman Catholic authority in the fields of medicine and education,' surmising that there would be no spiritual or temporal freedom in a united Ireland.[107] MacBride's assurances that Protestant rights would be protected if partition ended seemed insincere. As Laithwaite observed in his report to the British Government,

The deference paid by the Government to the views of the Hierarchy has gravely disturbed Protestant, and indeed some Catholic, feeling in the Republic, and the Hierarchy's attitude may well supply damaging ammunition to opponents of Catholicism in other countries... Above all, the effect of the incident has been to set back decisively any prospects there might have been... of an understanding between the north and south over Partition.[108]

The dispute also highlighted the difference in availability of social services. The *Belfast Telegraph* wrote that 'this controversy shows how partition is a wise recognition of fundamental differences... a radical difference of outlook between North and South in social reform.'[109] The fact that the skirmishes occurred behind close doors also caused suspicion. Some hard-line publications enjoyed the fracas; the *Unionist* editorial of May 1951 concluded with 'the Dr. Browne affair is the best propaganda Ulster has had for years, let us see that we use it.'[110]

Costello attempted to defend the government's position in the face of such Unionist propaganda:

There will be suggestions made as to the intervention of the Church authorities in State affairs. That, I'm afraid, is now inevitable... I regret that it may be misrepresented in the North but I wanted to make it clear, as the last thing that I say, that there was no intention of the Hierarchy interfering in any way in politics or with the activities of my Government or the activities of the State. They confine themselves strictly to faith and morals.[111]

Yet many felt that the government had chosen between blind obedience to the Church and improving chances of reunification and that 'there should be no more bawling from the anti-partition menagerie.'[112] The *Belfast Telegraph* concluded that 'the division between North and South is wider to-day than it has been for a long time.'[113]

McQuaid felt that the outcome was a triumph for the Catholic Church in Ireland, writing to Papal Nuncio Archbishop Ettore Felici that the defeat of the Mother and Child Scheme was the most important event in Irish history since Daniel O'Connell achieved Catholic Emancipation in 1829.[114] Yet, the 'popular memory remains of McQuaid as a clerical villain and Browne as a medical Robin Hood.'[115] The hierarchy's response to the scheme also demonstrated how out of touch they were with the people they claimed to minister to. As Browne observed after his first meeting with McQuaid:

> Dr McQuaid asked why it was necessary to go to so much trouble and expense simply to provide a free health service for the 10 per cent necessitous poor. This comment was not only wrong, since the percentage involved was 30 not 10, but surely represented a strange attitude from a powerful prelate of a Christian Church towards the life and death of the necessitous poor and their children.[116]

As Laithwaite explained in a letter to London, 'Since the core of the hierarchical objection was the absence of a means test, there are signs... of a degree of underground criticism of the attitude of the bishops among the poorer classes in this country, which is far from usual.'[117] Their response to the plan showed their inability to trust their congregations; their position on the Mother and Child scheme hinted that Catholic women have no judgement on matters of faith and morals and would take the advice of their doctor even if it went against Church teaching. As the *Unionist* put it, 'someday the women of Eire will realize their plight under a religious system which values them only for their prolific family value.'[118] The hierarchy appeared to be 'sheltered from the harsher side of Irish life, fearful of hidden dangers to faith and morals and susceptible to the arguments of the medical profession,' and 'the bishops' objections to the scheme seem wide of the mark.'[119] The controversy also affected the Church in the longer term; the fallout led to 'a reservoir of hostility which is probably only finally overflowing.'[120]

Costello replaced Browne as Minister for Health and attempted to formulate a plan to satisfy both the IMA and the hierarchy. However, weeks after Browne's resignation, rural TDs threatened to withdraw their support unless the government raised milk prices in order to help farm incomes – it was then that Costello decided to hold a general election. The Dáil was officially dissolved on 7 May 1951.

No one was surprised at the dissolution, 'the wonder is that [the inter-party government] has managed to survive for so long.'[121] The government chose to fight the election as a government, rather than individual parties. MacBride delivered speeches on their accomplishments, highlighting lower luxury taxes, increased pensions, lower unemployment, the absence of military courts or political prisoners, and the declaration of the Republic; 'From being a part of the British Empire this State was now an independent sovereign Republic recognised as such by the nations of the world.'[122] Other than this reference, the election was silent on partition and international affairs.

De Valera and Fianna Fáil fought the election on the premise that a coalition was an unstable form of government and one party would provide a greater degree of stability. MacBride countered by stating that 'our first inter-party government would indicate that it is more stable than those which were provided by the Fianna Fáil party.'[123] Fianna Fáil candidate Gerald Boland accused both Fine Gael and Clann na Poblachta of letting down their supporters while in power; Fine Gael by leaving the Commonwealth, the Clann by abandoning Browne.[124] Browne,

an Independent and was crowds at his speeches. speeches, but did write to ny reckless and malicious grity, honesty of purpose only intended to confuse

addressed in the election a clear picture of what it hman's Diary' in the *Irish* a duller election... there sh elections; but this time y.'[127] The *Irish Independent* Both the *Irish Times* and pointing out that there was nent and an inter-party had refused to enter a

voted than in the last 89,558 in 1948.[130] The ned to the Dáil as an 1951 election, the Clann Peadar Cowan and Jack

chta saw the decline of the uise O'Brien was correct of Noël Browne was Patrick Smith called him

'Pontius Pilate' in the Dáil[132] and the image of him washing his hands is very evocative. Both the government and MacBride wanted to avoid controversy and he showed little of the radicalism of Clann na Poblachta in founding days. It made sense for Fine Gael (who gained from participation in the inter-party government) to bow to vested interests, but it did not for Clann na Poblachta. What might have happened if MacBride brought the government down? He would have been justified in doing so; the no-means test principle was agreed-upon Clann policy. In a letter to the *Irish Times*, Michael ffrench-O'Carroll, who would later run for a Dáil seat in 1951 as an Independent in MacBride's Dublin constituency, wrote 'It must come as a great surprise to members of Clann na Poblachta that Mr. Seán MacBride and the National Executive of the party are not supporting Dr. Browne in his refusal to introduce a means test' as it had been declared party policy at the last ard-fhies.[133]   Bringing down the government probably would have been the wisest course of action for the longevity of his party, as Coogan colourfully declares, 'MacBride would have been better advised to support his stormy petrel minister and lead the Clann out of government in defiance of the brandished crosiers.'[134] The coalition had lasted longer than anyone thought possible in 1948 and withdrawing support would have satisfied the social welfare element in the party; as the republicans had already been placated somewhat by the declaration of the Republic and leaving may have soothed the hurt feelings of those who had questioned the wisdom of coalescing with Fine Gael. Browne's resignation was a pyrrhic victory for both the government and MacBride.

Why then did he choose to stay in government? His reasoning is unclear. Perhaps he remembered his godfather John O'Leary's advice to William Butler Yeats that in Ireland a man must have the Catholic Church or the Fenians on his side. He had lost much of the Fenian backing with Clann's decision to join the inter-party government. The republicans in Clann na Poblachta felt betrayed when Clann went into government and the radical section dissipated because of the official Clann response to the Mother and Child scheme. Supporters looking toward the party for radical change revolted against his alleged yielding to the Church; old IRA and republican supporters were unhappy with the Fine Gael alliance.

Of the ten Clann TDs in 1948, three became Independents and one joined the Labour Party. The party had only two seats after 1951, including MacBride's, whose vote fell substantially. Fine Gael were the winners, getting nine extra seats and it looked like another inter-party government would convene. Both the *Irish Times* and the *Irish Independent* pointed out that people had preferred an inter-party government to a single-party one.[135] Fianna Fáil got only one extra seat, but was able to form a government with Independent support. MacBride made a mistake in jettisoning the radical Clann vote and chose to split the party's support base rather than the government.[136] MacBride had sacrificed long-term gain for short-term reward. He was re-elected as TD in 1951 and 1954, but was never again to hold a position of political importance in the Republic. Browne remained in Irish politics in the Dáil and Seanad until 1982, though a *Manchester Guardian* editorial predicted in 1951 that 'he can command much sympathy in the country, but no politician of ordinary prudence after reading his reply to MacBride will ever be willing to have him for a colleague.'[137] The prediction was somewhat accurate in that Browne had very few long-term colleagues. Browne joined Fianna Fáil in 1954, then formed his own party, the National Progressive Democrats in 1958, finally joining the Labour Party in 1969. However, he would end his political career as an Independent.

Cruise O'Brien offered a remarkable, if cruel, appraisal of MacBride's time in office. 'Shortly after MacBride's fall, I wrote a comment on his career which appeared anonymously in a local periodical *The Leader*' where he compared MacBride to both Charlie Chaplin and Don Quixote, inspired by lofty and chivalrous but false or unrealisable ideals:

There are those who say... that he is in fact constantly acting a part... This gibe, although it often merely voices the envy of the inarticulate and drab, is not altogether unjust. The professions of law, politics and diplomacy are not conducive to unconditional sincerity... Certainly the new, purged, party follows its leader with uncritical devotion, unsupported by either talent or numbers. [138]

He did credit MacBride with building up his Department:

He managed, with the aid of General Marshall, to induce these gentlemen to put their fingers into the pies of various other Departments... and he got Mr. Blowick to plant a great deal of Sithca Spruce. He also – and it was not an inconsiderable achievement – got the money for Dr. Browne to build his hospitals... In the sphere of justice... his interventions were aimed at saving men from the gallows... The gaunt knight, wistful yet severe, in the dilapidated La Mancha of Roebuck, has been reading tales of chivalry, from Standish O'Grady to Patrick Pearse. He will rescue the fair lady Cathleen Ni

Houlihan from the castle Discrimination, where the British giant Gerrymandering, holds her thrall. The ogre Sterling bars the way with his famous Link, which will have snapped. The good fairies from America will help to accomplish this. (They have all been expelled from the State Department, but Quixote does not know this.) He saddles his spavined mare, Poblaclante, and gallops down the drive. But something is missing. He calls aloud for Sancho Panza. But Sancho will never come again. Sancho has locked himself into the lodge.

Years afterward, Cruise O'Brien felt a bit ashamed of the piece. Seeing himself as the Sancho Panza character, 'hoping that in serving his master in his wild career, he might attain the governorship of an island. But unlike Sancho Panza I not merely obtained from my master the civil service equivalent of the governorship of an island, but retained that prize after my master's fall.'[139]

MacBride campaigned during the general election of 1954 on familiar themes such as emigration, partition, protecting natural resources, and allowing representatives from the North to join the Dáil and Seanad. Clann na Poblachta still advocated making partition an international issue. Though MacBride received enthusiastic receptions wherever he spoke, he did not attract the crowds that de Valera or Costello did and the *Irish Times* called 1954 'the dullest election campaign in recent years.'[140] That newspaper half-heartedly endorsed de Valera and Fianna Fáil, admitting that it was a 'less of two evils' vote, as the alternative was an inter-party government with vague policies and principles.[141]

Despite the apparent lack of enthusiasm, the usual polling level of 70 percent was exceeded in many places.[142] Fine Gael increased its representation. MacBride also saw an increase of support and the Clann gained one seat from 1951. After the results were in, MacBride urged all parties to form a National Government similar to Switzerland's, with the main planks of encouraging reunification and full employment, increasing productivity, reducing emigration, and preserving the Gaeltacht. He conceded that 'by reason of the small representation of my party in the Dáil, I would not seek or expect representation in such a National Government.'[143] The *Irish Independent* liked the idea, writing that 'one-party rule has not solved the nation's problems; it has kept alive old feuds and old personal spleens.'[144]

Instead, a second inter-party government took power with a cabinet consisting of Fine Gael, Labour, and Clann na Talmhan, a party formed in

1938 to represent the interests of small farmers. Clann na Poblachta lent 'external support' to the government, but did not join it. In the spring of 1957, Clann na Poblachta decided to withdraw support from the government due to the poor economic situation and the government's offensive against the IRA. MacBride opposed the decision, but was outvoted. A general election resulted. By then the Clann had lost much of its freshness and innovation. Only eleven Clann candidates stood. MacBride was not re-elected; his defeat and the subsequent failure to get re-elected in a by-election in 1959 and a general election in 1961 meant the end for the party.

Talks of a Labour-Clann merger came to nothing, as they could not agree on the focus of a merged party; republican or Labour, the composition of the alliance, and the inclusion of Sinn Féin or Noël Browne's newly formed National Progressive Democrats. John Tully continued as the only Clann TD in the Dáil until 1965. An ard-fhies of 10 July 1965 officially dissolved Clann na Poblachta, but by then MacBride had other concerns.

7

A Statesman of International Status: Seán MacBride's Later Career

'Sometimes people carry to such perfection the mask they have assumed that in due course they actually become the person they seem.'[1]

W. Somerset Maugham

After the fall of the inter-party government in 1951 and the collapse of Clann na Poblachta in 1965, it seemed that Seán MacBride's career in Irish politics was over. However, his legal skills, his diplomatic experience, and his fluency in French made it possible for him to take up a new international role as a spokesman for human rights issues. MacBride developed into a respected diplomat and became the first Irishman to receive the Nobel Peace Prize in 1974. Despite gaining fame outside Ireland, he continued to impact the country, indirectly through his prominence and directly by returning to the Irish bar in the 1980s, participating in the New Ireland Forum in 1983, and sponsoring the MacBride Principles to encourage American investors to employ fair hiring practices in Northern Ireland.

MacBride's later career reinforces the idea of transition; the shift from concentrating on Ireland to involvement in more universal concerns is similar to his earlier transformation from insurgent to constitutional politician. Conor Cruise O'Brien posits that MacBride needed a niche once his political career was at a standstill. Was his later vocation motivated by altruism or was it a calculated way of ensuring that his fame would continue? This, like many other aspects of MacBride's career, is subject to debate. Some, like MacBride's biographer Anthony Jordan thought the conversion was genuine while others like former colleague Noël Browne believed that it was mere opportunism; use of MacBride's skill as a 'versatile performer'.[2] Regardless of the motivation, it is undeniable that he accomplished a substantial amount not only within international politics, but he continued to impact Irish foreign policy as well.

Writings on MacBride's later life are few and scattered. MacBride himself wrote several prefaces and introductions to Amnesty International pamphlets and other non-fiction material. His later life is covered reverently, if briefly, by Jordan in his *Seán MacBride: A Biography*. MacBride's colleagues and acquaintances also provide portrayals in their various memoirs, some flattering, some certainly not.[3] The Seán MacBride Collection at Iona College in New York, consisting of books, pamphlets, and journals, was presented to the American Fund Raising Institute by MacBride's family after his death and provides some clue as to what his concerns were.[4] Most of the material he collected and saved concerns disarmament, poverty, and discrimination, showing the range of his later interests, from copies of the Commission of Enquiry into the Irish Penal System to reports on renewable energy resources in developing countries. Recent books on Amnesty International, the organisation MacBride helped to establish, are sparse and focus more on the group's achievements rather than its founding and history.[5]

Assessments of MacBride's life emphasise his international role, which is not surprising as that is where he made his most public and long-lasting contributions. As yet, there is no real examination of MacBride's impact on Ireland at this time, which seems incomplete because, even though his most notable achievements occurred outside the island, it can be argued that he influenced events within the country as well.

MacBride's Role as an International Advocate

After his defeat in 1957, MacBride became disillusioned with Irish politics and began to broaden his perspective. His

> failure in home politics to build up a stable political base or to maintain for himself for long a significant role in Irish parliamentary affairs, left him free to pursue with a success denied to him at home a new and impressive career on an international level, where his considerable diplomatic and legal skills could be used in the cause of a better world order.[6]

MacBride's interest in human rights, the treatment of prisoners (no doubt influenced by his and his mother's experiences in prison), and work towards European integration led him to return to the legal profession. He began to practice in Irish and European courts as an advocate. One of his most celebrated cases took place in 1958 when the Greek government asked him to challenge the deportation of Archbishop Makarios, the Cypriot nationalist leader whom the British government claimed was actively supporting terrorism. The case came before the European Court where MacBride was able to prove that conditions in Cyprus, then a British crown colony, did not justify Makarios' deportation. In 1959, Makarios became the President of an independent Cyprus.

The achievement MacBride is most recognised for is his co-founding and help with the development of Amnesty International (AI). English lawyer Peter Benenson's concern for political prisoners provided the impetus for the formation of the organisation, a worldwide movement campaigning for internationally recognised human rights. Benenson was concerned with law reform and cases of injustice; in the 1950s he worked at helping those persecuted for political and religious beliefs in various countries, acting as an observer and defence counsel and writing and broadcasting about abuses of autocratic governments. In 1959 he founded Justice, an all-party organisation of British lawyers to campaign for the maintenance of the rule of law and observation of the United Nations Universal Declaration of Human Rights. While travelling to work one morning on the London Underground, Benenson read an article about two Portuguese students arrested for raising their glasses in a toast to freedom.[7] He recalled that

> it was on the 19th November 1960 as I was reading [the *Daily Telegraph*] in the Tube... that I came on a short paragraph that related how two Portuguese students had been sentenced to terms of imprisonment for no other offence than having drunk a toast to liberty in a Lisbon restaurant. Perhaps because I am particularly attached to liberty, perhaps because I am fond of wine, this news-item produced a righteous indignation in me that transcended normal bounds.[8]

Benenson was not only profoundly shocked, he decided that he would try to help the two young men who had been the victims of this violation of justice. His initial idea involved a one-year campaign to draw public attention to the plight of political and religious prisoners. Benenson's London office would collect and publish information on 'prisoners of conscience' in a year-long 'Appeal for Amnesty.'

He decided to begin by publicising the appeal through a newspaper article published in *The Observer* of 28 May 1961. Entitled 'The Forgotten

Prisoners,' it began, 'Open your newspaper any day of the week and you will find a report from somewhere in the world of someone being imprisoned, tortured or executed because his opinions are unacceptable to his government.' He maintained that common action was necessary; a world campaign to mobilise public opinion quickly with a 'broadly based, international, non-sectarian and all-party' movement that would not publicise any political views, instead they would focus on humanitarian concerns. The aims of the 'Appeal for Amnesty 1961' were to work impartially for the release of those imprisoned for their opinions, to seek for them a fair and public trial, to enlarge the Right of Asylum and help political refugees find work, and to urge effective international machinery to guarantee freedom of opinion. Success 'depends... upon the campaign being all-embracing in its composition, international in character and politically impartial in direction.'[9] A simultaneous article was published in France's *Le Monde*.

The articles generated an unexpected number of letters, donations, information on other prisoners, and editorial support. *The New York Times, Irish Independent, The Times, New York Tribune*, West Germany's *Die Welt*, Switzerland's *Journal de Genève*, and Sweden's *Politiken* commented favourably and appealed to their readers for help. The *Irish Times* editorial stated that 'no reasonable and humane person could quarrel with these objectives'[10] and *The Guardian* editorial pointed out that 'there are few countries today which can proudly boast that they have no prisoners of conscience in their gaols, and the fact demonstrates eloquently a deep malaise in our world.'[11] The first international meeting was in Luxembourg in July 1961, where it was decided to turn the appeal into a permanent international movement, named Amnesty International the following year.

MacBride and Benenson had much in common. Both were lawyers with an interest in human rights issues and both were Catholic, Benenson having converted in 1958. MacBride helped plan the first Amnesty 'Missions', formulating what tactics to use to aid individual prisoners.[12] His high profile helped both in publicising the movement and gaining access to world leaders, especially in Amnesty's early years.

The idea was to collect information on prisoners incarcerated for political views and bombard the offending governments with letters, postcards, and telegrams calling for the prisoner's release.[13] Amnesty's regional offices never adopted prisoners in their own countries or accepted the cases of those who had advocated the use of violence. Amnesty did not widely publicise its victories for fear of government reprisals on remaining prisoners or unwillingness to respond to later pressure. Yet, the movement was going well and Amnesty soon established itself as the leading organisation protecting the rights of political refugees and dissidents and opposing arbitrary imprisonment and torture. MacBride said in 1964, 'Although it cannot be said that the release of two or three thousand people was the actual work of Amnesty International, its influence is obvious.'[14]

Though the organisation was meeting with some success, problems developed. In 1966 Benenson began to suspect that British Intelligence was infiltrating Amnesty and he accused the British Government of tapping Amnesty's phone lines the following year.[15] He expressed a desire to move the organisation to a neutral country, but he was unable to convince anyone else.[16] He then decided to resign, not just because of Amnesty International remaining based in London, but also because of a rift with MacBride and his desire to retire. Benenson reconsidered soon after and decided to stay. He later learned that CIA money had helped fund the International Commission of Jurists (ICJ), where MacBride was Secretary. He grew paranoid about MacBride being linked to the CIA, despite the fact that when MacBride found out about the ICJ's links to the CIA, he protested and resigned.[17] However, Benenson himself was not without fault; it was later discovered that he had accepted money from the British government to help British subjects in Rhodesia and Nigeria. This situation was notable, as the idea of Amnesty was to be independently funded and apolitical. MacBride acknowledged that Benenson was responsible for 'a number of erratic actions.' Benenson refused to attend Amnesty International's March 1967 meeting, resigning instead. His relationship with the organisation was eventually restored, but he continued to believe that Amnesty should be headquartered in a neutral country.

MacBride chaired Amnesty International for 13 years, resigning in November 1974, one month before he received the Nobel Peace Prize. Jonathan Power calls MacBride 'critically important' to the movement by keeping it going, managing to straddle the Cold War East-West ideological divide better than most, and helping establish high-level contacts as well as undertaking regular missions to explore human rights abuses.[18] The founding and development of Amnesty International is credited among the great successes of MacBride's career.

Ironically, Amnesty could not alter the problem that so concerned MacBride while in government. Remarking on their work in Northern Ireland, Power believes that Amnesty has not profoundly altered or slowed the conflict.[19] He points out the irony in this situation as Amnesty, based in Britain, has had 'more success in foreign parts than it did in its own backyard.'[20] Additionally Amnesty has not been very effective in improving the treatment of prisoners in Northern Ireland. A *Sunday Times* article in 1971 revealed that torture was taking place in prisons in Northern Ireland. After establishing a Committee of Enquiry chaired by Sir Edmund Compton, which found that 'a large number of specific complaints of ill-treatment were justified,'[21] Edward Heath's government banned the practices of hooding, the use of high-pitched noises, standing for long periods against a wall, and the deprivation of food and sleep. Amnesty's own report revealed that the British government provided very limited access and cooperation.[22] While British activity does not reach the same level as the treatment of prisoners in Chile or Guatemala, 'in the course of the effort to stop the fighting much of Britain's proud heritage of fair play and the rule of law was trampled on.'[23] As AI is partly dependent on mobilising public opinion, Power has argued that the British public's indifference is partially culpable for the situation; Northern Ireland was viewed as a world apart, 'a colonial conflict in a faraway place, about which most of the British knew little and cared less.'[24]

MacBride also served as Secretary General for the previously mentioned International Commission of Jurists, a non-governmental organisation devoted to promoting throughout the world the understanding and observance of the Rule of Law and legal protection of human rights, from 1963 to 1970. Though not allied to any government, the Commission was seen as pro-Western, concerned more with the abuses of human rights in Eastern Europe. Yet MacBride would later take stands on issues that were decidedly anti-American. For example, he denounced the United States bombing of Vietnam. In 1969 he traveled to North Vietnam and was appalled by the use of civilian targets and anti-personnel weapons.[25] He also met with the Shah of Iran, whose Prime Minister informed him that the regime used torture, but only employed the most modern scientific techniques under the guidance of their American and British advisors.[26] Later, MacBride did not approve of the Ayatollah Khomeini's repressive regime, but he viewed it as a result of the Shah's rule, supported for so many years by the West.

He became United Nations Commissioner for Namibia (South West Africa) from 1973 to 1976, gaining the title of Assistant Secretary General of the UN. Namibia was a German colony until the 1919 Treaty of Versailles. The League of Nations placed it under the protection of South Africa. In 1966, the United Nations declared that South Africa's mandate to administer Namibia had expired. South Africa refused to adhere to the

UN request to vacate the territory and the UN set up a Council for Namibia to implement its policy. As MacBride maintained later, 'South Africa has been systematically flouting the international law and the decisions of the International Court of Justice and the United Nations.'[27]

The appointment of MacBride is not as surprising as it first appears. The International Commission of Jurists had taken cases relating to Namibia so he was familiar with the situation. MacBride had visited South Africa in 1958 and condemned their policy of apartheid. He was a good publicist, proven by his work with Amnesty International, and the United Nations wanted MacBride to organise international opinion against South African rule. In addition, there was the instinctive sympathy he felt for an illegally occupied nation.

He concluded that the foreign policy followed by NATO countries was partly responsible for the situation and the procrastination of Western nations allowed South Africa to hold out against the UN's request.[28] His public relations work on Namibia allowed him to express a larger opinion that 'be it in Afghanistan, Angola, El Salvador or Cambodia – no superpower has the right to intervene by direct or covert actions. These are matters which should be referred to and dealt with by the United Nations.'[29] Free elections should be organised under UN control to let the people decide the government they desired. He distinguished himself in the post and Namibia gained independence in 1990.

He was also the Chairman of the International Peace Bureau, the parent body for pacifist organisations worldwide dedicated to resolving international conflicts in a non-violent way, from 1968 to 1974 and its President from 1974 to 1985. In the late 1970s he chaired the UNESCO International Commission for the Study of Communication Problems culminating in its report 'Many Voices - One World' in 1980. The report criticised the imbalances in world information flows and attacked Western news agencies' reporting of Third World issues, which led to criticism from the American government, as did his protest of the bombing campaign in Vietnam. Not all of his endeavours met with success; despite his skills as a negotiator, he was unable to break the deadlock between the United States and Iran over the holding of American hostages at the American Embassy in Teheran.

The role of international diplomat suited MacBride well. Cruise O'Brien makes the point that in his previous career in Irish parliamentary politics, he had been striving to please 'ghosts', his mother's reputation and his father's martyrdom rather than a sincere desire to be a politician.

When MacBride was Secretary-General of the ICJ, they had dinner together;

> Looking back on it now, I can see that MacBride, as Minister in Dublin, had been doomed to appease ghosts... at a high cost to himself as a person. But by driving him from office into exile, the Irish people had set MacBride free for a time at least from the ghost-appeasing business. He was now free to be his natural, humorous and pleasant self.[30]

Nobel Peace Prize

MacBride shared the 1974 Nobel Peace Prize with Eisaku Sato of Japan. The prize was awarded in December in Oslo, Norway. The Nobel Committee commended him for his 'many years of efforts to build up and protect human rights all over the world.'[31] The honour was well received in Ireland; no Irish political figure had achieved such international recognition since Éamon de Valera's tenure as president of the League of Nations Assembly in the 1930s.[32] The *Irish Independent* reported that 'most people here see Mr. MacBride as a very deserving Prize winner.'[33] An *Irish Times* editorial praised the achievement:

> Ireland can take a proper pride in Mr. Seán MacBride's latest distinction... With his legal talents, he could have easily made a fortune at the Bar and relapsed into selfish, moneyed complacency... Instead he looked outward at the tormented world, and immersed himself in it. He will not feel proud himself, so Ireland has the right to feel proud on his behalf.[34]

In the Dáil, Fianna Fáil TD and future Minister of Foreign Affairs Michael O'Kennedy congratulated MacBride:

> Finally, it is noteworthy that a former Minister for External Affairs in this House has been nominated for the Nobel Peace Prize. This is a great honour for our country, and on behalf of the Fianna Fáil Party I would like to convey to him publicly our appreciation of what he has done and our best wishes for future achievements by him.[35]

MacBride was surprised at the honour, 'It came as a bombshell and I did not even know that I was being considered.'[36] He hoped that the Prize would give him greater prestige in putting forward proposals for

Namibia's future. He donated his share of the £45,000 Prize to Amnesty International and other various humanitarian organisations.

The presentation speech was given by Aase Lionæs, Chairman of the Norwegian Nobel Committee, who noted that MacBride was a 'citizen of a country that for many years had been the scene of bitter, grievous conflict.' Strangely, for a 'sore thumb' strategy advocate who once believed in publicising partition at every opportunity, MacBride did not mention partition or the Troubles in the North in his acceptance speech, despite the fact that the conflict was intensifying. Perhaps this is because he was not receiving the Prize for work done in Ireland and he had been unable to alter that situation in his previous interventions; 'MacBride came to Oslo very much as the president of the International Peace Bureau and as the United Nations Commissioner for Namibia.'[37] His acceptance speech, entitled 'The Imperatives of Survival' and delivered on 12 December 1974, reported knowledgably and at length about disarmament and ways to improve world problems:

> The tremendous scientific and material developments that have taken place in this period have altered radically the whole structure of human society - and even threatened the survival of the human race. This stupendous scientific and material revolution has brought basic changes into every aspect of our lives and of the ecology in which we live. These scientific developments were accompanied by equally radical changes in our social and political structures.[38]

Not surprisingly, MacBride mentioned the treatment of prisoners and the resulting cycle of violence,

> Force, or threat of force, are constantly used to dominate other countries... Prisoners are not only ill-treated but are tortured systematically in a worse manner than at any barbaric period of history. In many cases this is done with the direct or tacit approval of governments that claim to be civilized or even Christian... If those vested with authority and power practice injustice, resort to torture and killing, is it not inevitable that those who are the victims will react with similar methods?[39]

He emphasised some immediate steps that could be taken and some of the problems with present endeavours:

I have drawn attention to these philosophical and ethical issues to underline the responsibility that rests on the religious leaders of the world in this situation. The breakdown in public and private morality is in no small measure due to their failure to adjust to the tremendous scientific revolution through which we are passing... Often they have remained silent when they should have led the demand for justice; often they have resisted reform when they should have been leading the demand for it. It is the duty of the religious to give an unequivocal lead in the struggle for justice and peace.[40]

He also made statements that would later be perceived as anti-Western:

The socialist countries do not have a profit-motivated industrial-military complex. They can therefore adjust more readily to disarmament. The military industrial complex is state owned and controlled. To them disarmament means an automatic switch from increased arms production to increase in production for industrial development and for the consumer and export markets. They cannot lose by disarmament, they can only gain... This, no doubt, accounts for the much more sincere and far-reaching approach of the Soviet Union to General and Complete Disarmament than that of the Western powers.[41]

These views represented a vast change from his anti-communist stance while in government. Why had his view altered so completely? Much of MacBride's anti-communist posturing may have been done to please the electorate. Perhaps his new research on disarmament and the knowledge about the dangers of building and storing weapons of mass destruction influenced his opinion. However it is more likely that MacBride's ability to compartmentalise allowed him to comfortably hold this viewpoint. He had demonstrated this ability on previous occasions; while in government, he disliked the British stance on partition, but was on friendly terms with Clement Attlee and Ernest Bevin and partnered with Britain in the Council of Europe and the OEEC, he founded a political party based on social welfare reform, but did not support Noël Browne during the Mother and Child controversy. Similarly, he disliked the atheistic and repressive parts of communist philosophy, but recognised the benefits of their approach to disarmament.

MacBride also addressed familiar themes from his own work:

Structures which deprive persons of their human rights and dignity prevent justice from being realized; and systems which condemn people to starvation or to substandard conditions are a denial both of human rights and human dignity.

The Universal Declaration of 1948 is both universal and comprehensive... It provides a basis for the relationship between human beings and states inter se. The political and religious leaders of the world should utilize it as part of an effort to rebuild standards of morality that have crumbled in the decadence of this age.[42]

He praised non-governmental organizations both for their achievements and their lack of political bias and suggested what could be done to make the United Nations more effective:

In recent years the non-governmental organizations have been playing an increasingly important role. They are virtually the only independent voices that are heard and that can alert public opinion through the press and the media. The International Commission of Jurists and the International Association of Democratic Lawyers have rendered valuable services in the process of integrating human rights into the practical application of the Rule of Law. Amnesty International has succeeded in focusing attention very successfully on the torture of prisoners. These three organizations have also rendered invaluable humanitarian service by sending missions to areas where human rights were being violated and by sending observers to trials... In my view the role of voluntary organizations is becoming more and more essential. They are the only bodies that will have the necessary independence and initiative to restore some faith and idealism in our world. They deserve a great deal more support and encouragement.[43]

MacBride's speech demonstrates just how universal and comprehensive his later concerns became. Perhaps his time away from the country educated him and made him aware of problems greater than partition. The lecture was well received at home, the *Irish Times* calling it 'a wide-ranging and profound survey of present discontents and life enhancing expectations... rich in humane passion and reasoned argument.'[44]

Three years after MacBride's award, Amnesty International won the
Nobel Peace Prize in 1977. The presentation speech was again given by
Lionæs, who commented that Amnesty deserved the prize because the
organisation had 'sprung spontaneously from the individual's deep and
firmly rooted conviction that the ordinary man and woman is capable of
making a meaningful contribution to peace.'[45] The Nobel Lecture was
delivered on 11 December by Mümtaz Soysal, a Turkish politician and law
professor who was Chairman of Amnesty International from 1974 to
1978.

MacBride also won the 1977 Lenin Peace Prize, which had been
established in 1928 as a socialist rival to the Nobel Peace Prize. He was
chosen for his 'outstanding merits in the struggle for maintaining and
strengthening peace.'[46] He responded that the honour was 'an indication
of the interest which the Soviet Union has in putting an end to the arms
race and in pursuing the goal of general and complete disarmament.'[47] The
award was presented to MacBride in Dublin by Nicolai Blokhain,
Chairman of the International Lenin Committee for his work in Namibia
and his policy on disarmament. He is among a few Westerners to be given
the award from a Soviet government-approved committee and the first to
win both prizes. Though there were no Irish newspaper editorials praising
the achievement, there was also no protest at MacBride's acceptance of
the award. MacBride was popular with the Soviet government due to his
denouncement of the Western military-industrial complex, but he
protested just as strongly the Soviet occupation of Afghanistan and martial
law in Poland. MacBride was also the first non-American to win the
American Medal for Justice in 1978.

MacBride in Ireland

Brian Inglis remarks in his memoir *Downstart* that 'I thought it safe to label
MacBride as the Grey Subsidence of Irish politics – as politically he was,
and remained, though he was to bounce back into international eminence
in his old age.'[48] Such labelling was only partially accurate because, despite
its international scope, his later career also had an immense impact on
Ireland. MacBride's participation in non-governmental and peace-keeping
bodies and his role in founding and developing Amnesty International
served as a counterpoint to growing tensions in the North, and his Nobel
Peace Prize improved Ireland's image; the *Irish Times* commented that 'it is
no bad time for the world to be reminded that there are Irishmen
dedicated to peace and order.'[49] The *Irish Independent* observed that 'in a
way too Ireland is being honoured through Mr. MacBride.'[50] The Prize

gave credit to the nation as well as MacBride. In addition to the reflected glory of MacBride's international achievements, he also had more direct involvement in events happening within the country.

In 1957, the Fianna Fáil government reintroduced internment. MacBride took the case of internee Gerard Lawless to the European Commission on Human Rights. It was the first case to be heard by the European Court in 1959. MacBride lost, but the proceedings established the principle that the Court could investigate whether a state of emergency exists in a country that is sufficient to allow the use of internment or other measures.

During the Irish Presidential election of 1966, Tom O'Higgins proposed MacBride as a potential candidate that Opposition parties could support against incumbent Éamon de Valera. Liam Cosgrave's response to the suggestion was, 'Are you mad?'[51] Whoever ran against de Valera would most likely lose and there was talk of allowing him to run unopposed, 'but the party [Fine Gael] would never consent to giving Dev a free run.'[52] Eventually O'Higgins was chosen as the Fine Gael candidate and came within 10,000 votes of de Valera.

MacBride strongly opposed the renewed IRA campaign in Northern Ireland in the 1970s, stating that 'I think violence is justified only in certain circumstances. I do not think it is justified in Northern Ireland.'[53] In 1976, he and Northern QC Desmond Boal acted on behalf of the IRA and Ulster Loyalist Central Coordinating Committee in an attempt to find a peaceful solution to the conflict, a negotiated settlement not involving politicians or third parties.[54] Secret talks continued for several months but the initiative was ultimately unsuccessful. In the early 1980s, he resumed practice at the Irish Bar, defending political prisoners in Irish law courts, just as he had at the beginning of his career. Consistently, he supported Ireland's entry into the European Community, but did not want Ireland to participate in any common European defence or security policy.[55] MacBride no longer spoke publicly regarding Irish affairs when he was out of the country, but in later life proved willing to share his opinions with the media.

He did not publicly involve himself in one of the most controversial events in Northern Ireland in the 1980s, the H-Block hunger strikes, where IRA prisoners in Long Kesh prison, demanding the right to recently denied 'special category' status as political prisoners, protested by fasting.[56] MacBride stated that 'I do not agree with violence. Throughout the hunger strikes, I did not participate in any of the H Block Committee activities lest this might be construed as an approval of violence... I did make my views known to the British authorities in no uncertain terms but did not do so publicly.'[57]

MacBride did contribute to the introduction to *Bobby Sands: Writings From Prison* published in 1988 and reiterated his position on partition. He wrote that the British public is 'oblivious to the fact that the partition of Ireland has been created, imposed and fostered by the British establishment.'[58] MacBride's position on partition remained firm; he never changed his mind about the issue, both about the necessity of its immediate end and who was to blame. C.S. Andrews remarked that, 'on the question of separation, MacBride never lost his Fenian faith.'[59] He still applied the concept of 'self-determination' to the entire island. He had been away form political office for quite a few years; he no longer needed to 'bang the anti-partition drum' for the electorate – either he had made anti-partition statements so often that they became second nature or he sincerely believed in his position.

In 1983, Irish political parties Fianna Fáil, Fine Gael, Labour, and the SDLP met to review their position on the national question. They were seeking a peaceful solution to renewed IRA violence and were also looking for a way to curb growing support for Sinn Féin as a result of the hunger strikes. The New Ireland Forum was 'established for consultations on the manner in which lasting peace and stability could be achieved in a new Ireland through the democratic process and to report on possible new structures and processes through which this objective might be achieved.'[60] These new structures did not necessarily mean the end of partition. As Taoiseach Garret FitzGerald explained, the goal was to 'seek in discussion with all in Northern Ireland who may see merit in reducing tension within our island their help in identifying those aspects of the Constitution, laws and social arrangements of our state which pose obstacles to understanding amongst the people of this island.'[61] Participation was open to all democratic parties that rejected violence; the four parties together represented over 90 percent of the nationalist population in the North and almost three-quarters of the entire population of Ireland.[62]

The Forum brought together for the first time elected nationalist representatives from the North and the Republic to deliberate on the form of a new Ireland. The first session took place at Dublin Castle on 30 May 1983. The convenors visited the North on 26-27 September 1983, then from 23-24 January 1984 travelled to London for discussions with groups from Conservative, Labour, Liberal, and Social Democratic Parties.

MacBride was invited to attend the New Ireland Forum Public Session on 4 October 1983 to communicate his views on the partition issue and the continuing violence in the North. He suggested a Swiss cantonal model for the government of a united Ireland, with a strong emphasis on decentralisation and each county having more autonomy.[63] He also advocated more cooperation between the Republic and the North in areas like afforestation, environmental protection, and the arts. His position on partition remained; he asked the Forum to reiterate 'Ireland's claim to national unity and independence' and still believed the responsibility for ending partition rested with the British.[64] The *Irish Independent* did not take to MacBride's cantonal suggestion, pointing out that 'the Swiss have arrived at their present system through a process of trial and error over a couple of centuries' and such a structure could not be instantly imposed on Ireland, but the *Irish Times* praised the Forum as a whole for its 'impressive variety of ideas' which would help 'stimulate debate and fresh thinking.'[65]

The Forum concluded by suggesting new structures accommodating two sets of legitimate rights, 'the rights of nationalists to effective political, symbolic and administrative expression of their identity' and 'the right of unionists to effective political, symbolic and administrative expression of their ethos and way of life.'[66] Despite all the effort put into the Forum, after the second meeting with FitzGerald, British Prime Minister Margaret Thatcher's summary dismissal of the proposals, 'the unified Ireland was one solution - that is out. A second solution was a confederation of the two States - that is out. A third solution was joint authority - that is out,' made it appear that it was wasted time.[67]

Yet, despite Thatcher's seeming unwillingness to include the Republic in the governance of the North, 'it was precisely after the second meeting between Thatcher and FitzGerald that work began in earnest toward the establishment of a treaty of co-operation between Great Britain and the Republic of Ireland regarding the political and security problems afflicting both countries and Northern Ireland,' the 1985 Anglo-Irish Agreement.[68] The Agreement was a precedent-setting document due to Britain's recognition that the Republic of Ireland did have some say in the affairs of Northern Ireland and Irish acknowledgement of the Unionist position. Structures proposed by the Forum can be found in the current power-sharing government instituted by the Good Friday Agreement.[69]

MacBride also became an active supporter of the Irish National Caucus, an American lobby formed to fight discrimination against Catholics in the North. He lent his name to a series of conditions for

American companies operating in Northern Ireland to follow in order to prevent discrimination. These became known as the MacBride Principles because 'his nationalist and human rights credentials gave him unrivalled credibility among the constituency which the leaders of the campaign sought to mobilize – Irish-American groups and US human rights groups.'[70]

The MacBride Principles are American in origin, consisting of fair employment measures, affirmative action principles, a corporate code of conduct for American companies doing business in Northern Ireland; a direct, meaningful and non-violent means of addressing injustice and discrimination. The idea began with New York City Comptroller Harrison Goldin in 1983, and was embraced by the Irish National Caucus, headed by Fr. Sean MacManus. They were modelled on the Sullivan Principles for American companies with subsidiaries in South Africa.

The Principles included increasing the representation of individuals from underrepresented religious groups (namely Catholics) in the work force, adequate security for the protection of minority employees both at the work place and while travelling to and from work, the banning of provocative religious or political emblems from the work place, and layoff, recall and termination procedures should not in practice favour a particular religion, abolition of job reservations, apprenticeship restrictions and differential employment criteria which discriminate on the basis of religion.

Most groups responded favourably to the idea. The European Parliament issued a report in March 1994 endorsing the campaign's moral principles, stating that American pressure was 'responsible for reopening the question of discrimination in Northern Ireland... Northern Ireland Catholics see the worldwide "MacBride Principles" campaign as a great source of support in overcoming their problems.' They have been passed in sixteen states, passed and endorsed in forty cities, and are pending in more. They have been adopted by state legislatures, city, councils, church groups, including the Archdiocese of New York, the American Baptist Convention, the Episcopal Church in America, the Society of Jesus, and American companies such as AT&T, Federal Express, Ford, General Motors, IBM, McDonalds, Philip Morris, P&G, Texaco, and Xerox among others.

The Irish government supported the aims of the Principles, but worried that they could discourage investment in Northern Ireland. Foreign Minister Peter Barry commented in the Dáil, 'we believe that, while the philosophy underlying the MacBride Principles presents no difficulties for us, any action which, in the serious economic situation of Northern Ireland, might lead to disinvestment and to the discouragement of US firms investing in Northern Ireland should be avoided.'[71] However, a change of government in Dublin and America's favourable response to the Principles led to a new attitude; Brian Lenihan remarked in the Dáil three years later that 'the Government's view is that there is nothing objectionable in the MacBride principles. We fully understand and share the anxieties of Irish Americans about discrimination in employment in Northern Ireland.'[72]

However, the MacBride Principles were not wholly welcomed in Northern Ireland or Britain. The use of MacBride's name was controversial due to his previous IRA connections and he was still perceived as a symbol of some of the worst aspects of Irish Catholic social conservatism.[73] The Principles themselves appeared too vague about how to achieve a fair proportion of Catholics and Protestants employed and it was feared that they may discourage new investment or cause already established companies to pull out. They were opposed by Irish Protestant Churches as well as the SDLP, as John Hume felt that depriving Protestants of jobs would not alleviate the plight of jobless Catholics.[74] Not surprisingly, Sinn Féin endorsed the Principles. The Catholic bishops took no formal position. The MacBride Principles were successful at putting pressure on the British as new anti-discrimination legislations was introduced and the Principles remain a force for change in Northern Ireland should the British government's own efforts falter in the future.[75]

In late 1983, MacBride volunteered to stand for the presidency of Ireland, an offer that was not accepted by the parties. This snub was probably due more to the popularity of the outgoing President Dr. Patrick Hillery than to any problem with MacBride's candidacy. In fact, the leaders of the major Irish parties, Fine Gael's FitzGerald, Fianna Fáil's Charles Haughey, and Labour's Dick Spring, persuaded Hillery to stand for a second term.[76] Though he made it known in the *Sunday Press* newspaper that he wanted to contest the office, only Hillery was nominated and was declared re-elected for a second seven-year term of office without the need for a popular vote.

Conclusion

The 'Petition to the United Nations 1998 by 32 County Sovereignty Movement' demonstrates just how influential MacBride remained within Irish politics. The movement, founded in December 1997, was formed by Sinn Féin members who felt that the Northern Ireland Peace Process did not allow for full Irish sovereignty and would ensure that the six counties would be forever marginalised. As their manifesto explains,

> Simply put we are a group of individuals who recognise that the root cause of the conflict in Ireland is Britain's refusal to respect the Sovereignty of all-Ireland. We believe that the only way in which Britain can show respect for Irish Sovereignty is to declare publicly its intention to withdraw from Ireland permanently.[77]

The 32 County Sovereignty Movement's petition to the United Nations included MacBride's introduction to the Bobby Sands book, posthumously appropriating him as an example of a non-violent Irishman.

The petition neglects to mention that the passage was taken from the Bobby Sands book and not written by MacBride specifically for their organisation. This omission makes it seem that MacBride was in-line with their cause, which he could not have been, as he had died ten year earlier. Moreover, the 32 County Movement supported the re-formation of the IRA, which MacBride would not have done. Finally, the authors misspelled 'McBride' and mentioned that he was 'an international jurist; a former U.N. High Commissioner and winner of both the Nobel and the Lenin Peace Prizes.'

MacBride is chiefly remembered for his international work, as shown by his obituaries.[78] Yet he still left an important legacy within Ireland which was contentious. As Charles Lysaght said, 'I wrote his obit in the London *Times* but I found it difficult to reach a firm view about him. Different people assessed him so differently.'[79]

Most agree that he was controversial. Most also agree that he was charming, but differ on whether his charm was sincere. Noël Browne wrote of him:

> Though a forbidding-looking figure he was a man of much personal charm, and impeccable drawing-room manners, reserved for whomever he wished to impress. As I came to know him better, he seemed to me to be an insecure person, a product, no doubt, of his disturbed and turbulent upbringing.[80]

Browne's wife Phyllis recalled meeting him for the first time; 'he wore an air of seriousness, as though he was carrying the troubles of the world on his shoulders. I could see no sense of humour in his face, but he did display a little charm, at times – which I felt was false.'[81] Former government colleague Tom O'Higgins reflected that, 'when he was with you he was forceful and charming, but when the sun went in he was a different man.'[82]

Some contemporaries have questioned the sincerity of his later career as a humanitarian. Phyllis Browne wondered, 'How MacBride was given the Lenin Peace Prize and the Nobel Peace Prize also, is a mystery to me, and many others.'[83] Brian Inglis, who worked with MacBride at the Irish News Agency, wrote of his 'slippery political manoeuvrings – which survived all his climb to international fame and to a Nobel Prize.'[84] As mentioned above, many feel that he lived his life to please ghosts as well as his formidable mother. As Browne, who was interested in psychology, wrote in his memoirs,

> His later campaign for peace following [his mother's] death, is hard to reconcile with his former violent lifestyle... To what extent was the powerful and dominating personality of this notorious rebel mother responsible for his earlier career of violence?.. Was it that, subsequently deprived of all political power – he had lost his Cabinet post, his Dáil seat and his party – he was left with no choice but to play peacemaker?[85]

Cruise O'Brien, who called a chapter in his *Ancestral Voices* 'Son of Maud Gonne' wrote that MacBride was under the spell of 'the power of the ghosts of a nation... Seán MacBride was brought up under that power...You could sense the presence of ghosts all right; his face, when in repose, had a perpetually haunted expression.'[86] Gonne once showed Phyllis Browne a photo of MacBride at about age 10 with 'Seán, Man of Destiny' written across it, leading her to comment, 'I wonder did he live up to her expectations?'[87] As his contemporary C.S. Andrews noted, 'whatever one may think of MacBride's role in Irish politics, Nobel and Lenin Prizes are not conferred on people of no merit.'[88] It is doubtful that he was insincere in his beliefs; he devoted so much time and energy to human rights causes. Whether or not MacBride was motivated by the desire for distinction, it cannot be questioned that he and the organisations he was involved with accomplished a great deal and his interventions benefited a great many people.

Conclusion

'Yesterday's terrorist is today's statesman.'[1]

Neil Jordan

After Seán MacBride's death on 15 January 1988, a remarkable number of tributes were paid to him from around the world, reflecting the strength of his commitment to a variety of causes. United Nations Secretary General Javier Pérez de Cuéllar declared that 'Sean MacBride was widely recognised in the international community as a champion of peace, justice and the universal respect for human rights. Indeed, these concerns of his, and the non-violent settlement of disputes, lie at the very heart of the United Nation's Charter of which he was a most eloquent partisan.'[2] The President of the African National Congress, Oliver Tambo saluted 'the contribution of Sean MacBride to the cause of freedom and human emancipation throughout the world. He was a great beacon, guiding and assisting oppressed people to the path of national liberation and self-determination.'[3] Sergei Losev, director-general of the Soviet News Agency Tass said that MacBride was widely known in the Soviet Union and Soviet journalists wholeheartedly respected him.[4] The Green Alliance praised his support of ecological causes 'long before it was fashionable to do so.'[5] Massachusetts Congressman Joseph Kennedy declared that 'he was a man who dedicated his life to the pursuit of peace and justice... his voice and compassion will be missed' and Congressman Hamilton Fish Junior of New York said that MacBride 'rightly understood that ability and religion should be the basis for employment opportunity in Ireland.'[6]

Most obituaries focused on his career as an international statesman. Yet some did mention his IRA past and the idea of transition in his career. The *Irish Times* wrote that the young gunman came to be the most fervent convert to peace. His commitment to the rule of law and to the protection of human rights was absolute... His conversion from unconstitutional to constitutional methods in his vision of Ireland's future was matched by a recognition that the evolution of all civilised society had to be similarly grounded.[7]

The *Irish Independent* 'Weekender' section contained articles about MacBride and assessments of his career, including an article by Ronan Fanning entitled 'A man for his times,' which maintained that 'he reflected the dreams of a young nation' and 'the long life of Sean MacBride is best seen as a personification of the history of the 20th century Irish Republicanism.' He described MacBride's role in the IRA during the Civil War and stated that his 'finest hour as Minister for External Affairs was when the Republic of Ireland Act of 1948 severed Ireland's last link with the Commonwealth.' MacBride's 'international acclaim which he enjoyed in later life as an elder statesman was closely linked with his reputation as one of Ireland's most famous radical republicans.'

John A. Murphy, a Professor at University College Dublin commented in the 'Tributes' box that MacBride was one of the outstanding Irish men of the twentieth century, but 'really a Chief of Staff of the IRA at heart, it seems to me, in his attitude toward the National question.' This statement is true in the sense that he always held the British responsible for partition, but incomplete, as it ignores his rejection of violence later in life.

MacBride was also mentioned in newspapers abroad, yet those tributes hardly mentioned his political career in Ireland. A 16 January *Times'* article mentions that he was a former IRA chief of staff as well as being the 'Irish Republic's most celebrated constitutional and criminal lawyer... he was also a principal architect of the European Convention on Human Rights.'[8]

Another *Times* article, entitled 'Irreconcilable Irish Republican' mentions his prominence as an 'international advocate of human rights and disarmament,' then details his career in the Irish Republican movement, as a 'suave and sophisticated' foreign Minister and a 'shrewd tactician and a tireless worker,' but 'neither an outstanding advocate nor a specially acute lawyer' who 'indulged in the luxury of advocating ideal solutions without having to accept responsibility for the tasks involved in dismantling Western defences.'[9] The article concluded that 'he seemed oblivious to positions other than his own, and in argument he showed little understanding of opposing viewpoints' but 'never hesitated to commit his own money to causes which he supported.'

The *Times* editorial of 18 January 1988, entitled, 'His Infamous Career' was even less flattering. The 'interpretations of the career of Mr. Sean MacBride... have tended to suggest that his life was synonymous with the short history of his own Republic of Ireland... His biographical trajectory, which took him from IRA chief of staff to recipient of both the Nobel and Lenin peace prizes, has been seen as mirroring the transformation of a state born in violence to fully fledged democracy.' However, the editorial went on to claim that MacBride's international reputation 'was not put to the service of reconciling the state he had helped to found, nor to the service of its future' and his absence will help put away Ireland's violent past and the romantic appeal of violence. [10] This assessment seems unfair, as MacBride had altered his position on violence as an effective means of change.

There were responses to the editorial. On 23 January 1988, Reverend Dr. Vincent Twomey of St. Patrick's College, Maynooth wrote that MacBride had a beneficial influence on Ireland's development; 'the violent revolution which eventually brought the Irish State into being has been transformed over the past five decades into authentic democratic republicanism of the classical and Christian traditions which can only be a source of pride to any self-respecting Irish man or woman... His championship of human rights throughout the world was his most significant contribution to that development since rights are the basis of democracy.' Another response, from former Secretary-General of Amnesty International Martin Ennals, maintained that the editorial was 'too dismissive of his international role, particularly in the field of human rights,' as MacBride had worked 'tirelessly' for Amnesty, the Council of Europe, and the United Nations. [11]

Both the *New York Times* and the *Boston Globe* published MacBride's obituary, both emphasising his later life; the *Globe* obituary contained nothing at all about his political career in Ireland.

Like his contemporaries, his obituaries would assess him differently, but most would agree that "In all that he touched, MacBride showed extraordinary dedication and tenacity,' and 'He worked tirelessly without thought for any tangible reward and never hesitated to commit his own money to causes which he supported. Of him it can truly be said that he was faithful to the tradition of passionate political commitment in which he had been nurtured.' [12]

The Irish papers provided extensive coverage of his funeral; 'the variety of accents and indeed languages to be heard at the graveside bore ample testimony to the unrivalled international esteem in which Sean

MacBride was held.'[13] Cardinal Tomás Ó Fiach declared in his sermon in Glasnevin Cemetery, 'He would be equally at home among the patriots, the jurists, the politicians, the international statesmen, the defenders of human rights, the protagonists of peace and spokesmen of minorities'

The editorial in 19 January's *Irish Times* reported the 'huge crowds' at MacBride's 'scarcely standing room' funeral with its long, varied list of attendees; 'no one's funeral could have drawn together so many people so far from each other in mind.' Presidents, Taoisigh, other dignitaries, even Noël Browne attended. If further proof was needed, his significance as a humanitarian can be seen by U2's Bono attending the funeral.

Praise also came in from Irish politicians. Fianna Fáil Taoiseach Charles Haughey led the tributes, stating that MacBride was 'a statesman of international status and was listened to with respect around the world.'[14] President Patrick Hillery praised his 'exemplary commitment and generosity' and Tánaiste Brian Lenihan mused that if he was a controversial figure,

> it may have been because his thinking was too challenging, his perspective too broad for conventional wisdom. He was often ahead of his time in his awareness of the position in international affairs of the newly independent nations, in his determination to bridge the divide between East and West, and in his belief in the force of justice in international relations.[15]

Tributes were heard in the Seanad and the Dáil. Senator Mick Lanigan called MacBride 'a statesman of international standard. His work for the underprivileged, not alone here but abroad, has been acknowledged through the world.'[16] Senator Maurice Manning admitted that 'Perhaps by conventional Irish standards his political career was not a great success... The party he founded did not make a lasting impact.' However, 'at almost every stage when he entered Irish politics he made a lasting mark; in his work in the courts in the thirties and in his work in the first inter-Party Government. Most of all he will be remembered for his work in the international forum, his work for humanitarian, libertarian causes right around the world.'[17] He relayed a story about MacBride merely glancing at his Nobel Peace Prize cheque, signing his name on the back, and sending the prize money to Amnesty International. Professor John A. Murphy, though praising MacBride's achievements, disliked 'the absurd attempts at instant canonisation over the weekend,' calling it hypocritical because 'In Seán MacBride's cause it has to be recorded, regrettably, that his contribution to the cause of peace at home, to the national debate on the North, was in inverse proportion to his service to peace worldwide. It is a pity that his thinking in the area of this tragic problem remained dangerously simplistic to the end.'[18]

In the Dáil, Haughey summarised his international human rights achievements while also recognising his contributions during the inter-party government;

> He did much to foster economic and social progress in this country at an important stage in its development, and his contributions to international economic co-operation were numerous and distinguished... He was an important influence in the creation of the Council of Europe and also served as Vice-President of the Organisation for European Economic Co-Operation. He helped to draft the European Convention on Human Rights.[19]

Fine Gael leader Alan Dukes also paid tribute,

> There are very few of us who can look back over a lifetime that contained three separate identifiable careers. I think that it is mostly for his career as a former Member of this House and Minister and for his later career as an international jurist of wide repute that we would remember Seán MacBride. ... He was a man who was involved in many controversies during his lifetime. On many issues there are many of us who are here today who disagreed very strongly with him but all of us would recognise that, in our personal dealings with him, we always found him — whether he agreed with us or not — to be a man of very considerable personal charm and warmth.[20]

Tomás MacGiolla of the Workers Party said that 'few Irish people have made a greater contribution to world affairs than Seán MacBride. It is for that that he will be remembered most.'[21]

Yet it was Labour leader Dick Spring who gave the most precise assessment:

> Seán MacBride was a man of many parts. At one time he appeared to be on the verge of engineering a fundamental change in the development of the Irish political system but ultimately it was on the world stage that he made his greatest contribution... Throughout his

career he was a man in search of change for the better, as he saw it. In his later years I, together with many others in the House, found myself on the opposite side to Seán MacBride on a number of important social issues. I did not agree with the position he adopted and he was not always an easy man to disagree with but I respect the sincerity with which he held and maintained his views. It is difficult to sum up a career as varied as his in the few moments available to us. Perhaps, in the fullness of time he will be remembered at home for things that are not so obvious now. He may be remembered, for instance, for his commitment to the development of our natural resources or he may be remembered as one who believed passionately that there was room on this island for every one of its young people and that we had an economy that could provide for all.[22]

MacBride's obituaries and testimonials focused on his international reputation and his contributions to world peace and human rights. Few emphasised his career in Irish politics. Perhaps Spring was correct; his political accomplishments in Ireland were not so obvious. MacBride's legacy in Irish politics was mixed. Both J.J. Lee and Dermot Keogh point out that MacBride entered the cabinet in 1948 with an enormous reputation, Keogh even calling him a 'rival Taoiseach.'[23] Why did his influence diminish?

Personality conflicts, which seemed a common feature of his political career, were a key factor. During his career in government, MacBride had fallen out with Clann members Peadar Cowan, Noel Hartnett, and Noël Browne as well the Secretary of his Department Frederick Boland. Hence MacBride lacked an effective team around him both in his party and in government. Perhaps MacBride was not enough of a politician; he did not seem able to compromise and tended to take disagreement personally.

Part of the problem was the reactive nature of the inter-party government, which is especially seen in the management of the repeal of the External Relations Act and the declaration of the Irish Republic and the handling of the Mother and Child controversy. Such reactivity is not difficult to understand; an inter-party government was a new phenomenon and its loose structure allowed MacBride leeway in establishing his authority and show interest in topics outside his portfolio, such as finance, environment, and social welfare. However, as the government settled, it was inevitable that Costello would assert his authority as Taoiseach and 'MacBride's wings would be clipped as other departments tried to assert their command in their traditional areas.'[24]

The government as a whole made mistakes. They did not respond skilfully to the invitation to join NATO, overestimating the American willingness to become involved in solving the partition issue. The increase of anti-partition rhetoric did not solve the problem and it can be argued that their policy further entrenched the border. Instead of taking advantage of opportunities for rapprochement with the North, the government misjudged the strength of Northern Unionism and fell prey to bellowing louder instead of slow but constructive solutions. The 'sore thumb' policy was counterproductive; it alienated other countries and made Ireland appear insular. It also affected the relationship with Belfast, where the real decision-making power to end partition lay. The government's reliance on rhetoric instead of attempting cross-border cooperation demonstrates a conservatism echoed in their behaviour during the Mother and Child controversy. They were not willing to risk offending the Church, the Irish medical lobby, or their constituents.

The repeal of the External Relations Act, though considered one of the government's major achievements, should be viewed as a mixed blessing. The Irish were fortunate that other Commonwealth countries were willing to lend support and an otherwise preoccupied Britain decided to be generous. While declaring Ireland a Republic was an important psychological step, it was not ideal for ending partition and the manner in which it was handled caused confusion, which still remains.

However, the inter-party government did more than give Fianna Fáil a short holiday and, because of one spectacular failure, has not been recognised for smaller successes. The inter-party government showed that coalition government was a workable option and they managed to make it last longer than most contemporary observers thought possible. The government ended sixteen years of Fianna Fáil domination and restored true parliamentary democracy to Ireland, providing hope for a genuine party system. The emergence of Clann na Poblachta began a decline of civil war-influenced politics. The coalition achieved success in revitalising land policy, developing agriculture, and introducing the Industrial Development Authority and Córas Trachtála, established to promote Irish exports. MacBride helped bring about an increased awareness of economic planning and cooperation, energised his department, and his later awards and accomplishments reflected well upon the Irish nation. He also helped bring Ireland into Europe and European Union funding would help the Irish economy at later stage. Many of these activities would bear fruit later; particularly Seán Lemass' enthusiasm for European integration and T.K. Whitaker's venture at economic planning.

My motivation for beginning this volume was to discover what, if any, influence Seàn MacBride had over the development of Irish foreign policy. I hope I have demonstrated that he had an unequivocal impact for which he has not been fully credited. Although his most enduring legacy will be his international reputation; the Irish Amnesty International section is now located in Seán MacBride House in Dublin and an annual peace prize is awarded in his name by the International Peace Bureau, a lasting influence in Irish politics can be seen in the continued enthusiasm for European integration and the willingness of the Irish people to accept a substantial commitment to the United Nations, though, as Kevin Nowlan points out, it was not just MacBride who inspired this development.[25] Perhaps this was not the legacy his mother envisioned when she emblazoned his childhood photo with the words 'Man of Destiny', yet it is an impressive and substantial one.

Notes

Introduction
1. Dáil Éireann Debates, vol. 5, col. 1944, 14 December 1923.
2. C.S. Andrews, *Man of No Property: An Autobiography (Vol. Two)* (Dublin, 1982), p. 35.
3. See Tom Garvin, *1922: The Birth of Irish Democracy* (Dublin, 1996) and *The Nationalist Revolution in Ireland* (Oxford, 1997) for an analysis of the Irish nationalist tradition and how it resulted in the establishment of a stable, well-structured democracy.
4. This is also a term Noël Browne uses to describe MacBride, though in a much less flattering way!
5. See Seán Cronin, *Washington's Irish Policy 1916-1986* (Dublin, 1987), Troy D. Davis, *Dublin's American Policy: Irish-American Diplomatic Relations 1945-1952* (Washington D.C., 1998), Ian McCabe, *A Diplomatic History of Ireland 1948-1949: The Republic, the Commonwealth and NATO* (Dublin, 1991), Bernadette Whelan, *Ireland and the Marshall Plan 1974-57* (Dublin, 2000), and Michael Kennedy and Joseph Morrison Skelly (eds.), *Irish Foreign Policy 1919-1969: From Independence to Internationalism* (Dublin, 2000).
6. Lee, *Ireland 1912-1985: Politics and Society* (Cambridge, 1989), p. 318.
7. Noël Browne, *Against the Tide* (Dublin, 1986), p. 96.
8. Browne, *Against the Tide*, p. 96.
9. Maud Gonne to William Butler Yeats, 11 May 1916. Anna MacBride White and A. Norman Jeffares (eds.), *Always Your Friend: The Gonne-Yeats Letters 1893-1938* (London, 1992), p. 375.
10. Cruise O'Brien, *Memoir: My Life and Themes* (Dublin, 1998), p. 143.
11. Cruise O'Brien, *Memoir*, p. 168.
12. The collection consists of a group of books, magazines, and pamphlets he owned in the early 1980s. Petronio Room, Iona College Libraries, New Rochelle, New York.
13. Kevin Rafter, *The Clann: The Story of Clann na Poblachta* (Cork, 1996), p. 134 and Eithne MacDermott, *Clann na Poblachta* (Cork, 1998), p. 135.

Chapter One
1. RTÉ Documentary, 'A History of Clann na Poblachta,' 5 November 1976.
2. Reported in *Irish Times*, 18 March 1943.
3. Noël Browne, *Against the Tide* (Dublin, 1986), p. 97.

4. F.S.L. Lyons, *Ireland Since the Famine* (London, 1985), p. 558.
5. *The Times*, 17 July 1948.
6. John A. Murphy, *Ireland in the Twentieth Century* (Dublin, 1975), p. 107.
7. *The Times*, 2 February 1948.
8. Dermot Keogh, *Twentieth-Century Ireland* (Dublin, 1994), p. 173. Seán MacBride and Noel Hartnett served as counsel during McCaughey's inquest.
9. Conor Cruise O'Brien, *Memoir: My Life and Themes* (Dublin, 1998), p. 168.
10. Brian Inglis, *West Briton* (London, 1962), p. 100.
11. Ian McCabe, *A Diplomatic History of Ireland 1948-1949: The Republic, the Commonwealth and NATO* (Dublin, 1991), p. 25. It can be argued that Fine Gael, as the dominant party in the inter-party government, would later benefit.
12. *Irish Times*, 8 July 1946.
13. Cruise O'Brien, *Memoir*, p. 134. Cruise O'Brien was Head of Information in the External Affairs Department during MacBride's ministry.
14. Inglis, *West Briton*, p. 105.
15. Eithne MacDermott, *Clann na Poblachta* (Cork, 1998), p. 40.
16. All major political parties in the Irish Free State chose Irish names, with the exception of the Irish Labour Party, perhaps because their party ethos was more international, though Labour in Ireland never wanted to appear too far to the left. Lyons points out that the Irish political community was deeply opposed to communism (*Ireland Since the Famine*, p. 591) and John Coakley and Michael Gallagher remark on the 'absence of a significant classical revolutionary left' in Ireland [*Politics in the Republic of Ireland*, 2nd edition (Limerick, 1996), p. 18]. As Seán Lemass once commented, Labour in Ireland was always 'a harmless shade of pink.'
17. MacDermott, *Clann na Poblachta*, p. 14.
18. Alvin Jackson, *Ireland 1798-1998* (Oxford, 1998), p. 305.
19. Kees van Kersbergen, 'The Distinctiveness of Christian Democracy' in David Hanley (ed.), *Christian Democracy in Europe: A Comparative Perspective* (London, 1994), p. 35. For other treatments of the phenomenon and influence of Christian Democracy in Europe, see R.E.M. Irving, *Christian Democracy in France* (London, 1973), R.A. Webster, *Christian Democracy in Italy 1860-1960* (London, 1961), Emiel Lamberts, *Christian Democracy in the European Union 1945-1995: Proceedings of the Leuven Colloquium* (Leuven, 1997), M.P. Fogarty, *Christian Democracy in Western Europe 1820-1953* (London, 1957), and Geoffrey Pridham, *Christian Democracy in Western Germany: The CDU/CSU in Government and Opposition 1945-1976* (London, 1977).
20. See Dermot Keogh, 'Ireland, the Vatican and the Cold War: The Case of Italy 1948,' *Irish Studies in International Affairs* 3 (1991).
21. Quoted in Keogh, 'Ireland, the Vatican, and the Cold War,' pp. 77-78.
22. Keogh, 'Ireland, the Vatican, and the Cold War,' p. 110.
23. Desmond Dinan, 'After the Emergency: Ireland in the Post-War World, 1945-1950,' *Éire-Ireland*, vol. 24 (Fall 1989), p. 88.
24. J.H. Whyte, *Church and State in Modern Ireland 1923-1979*, 2nd ed. (Dublin, 1980), p. 158.

25. 29 February 1948, Copy found in John A. Costello Papers, University College, Dublin, P190/357 (29).
26. MacBride to McQuaid, 30 October 1947, Seán MacBride file, John Charles McQuaid Papers, Dublin Diocesan Archives.
27. McQuaid to MacBride, 1 November 1947, Dublin Diocesan Archives.
28. MacBride to McQuaid, 7 February 1948, Dublin Diocesan Archives.
29. *Irish Times*, 13 November 1999.
30. Caitriona Lawlor, MacBride's personal assistant, responded with an article of her own, writing that Bowman's comments were 'unfair', that MacBride 'deliberately avoided getting too closely involved with the hierarchy concerning matters regarding political developments,' and that Bowman had taken MacBride's letters out of context of the period (*Irish Times*, 20 November 1999). Bowman replied that Lawlor merely summarised MacBride's own self-assessment of his career so 'that he emerges from this scrutiny without blemish is hardly surprising.' (*Irish Times*, 29 November 1999).
31. *Irish Independent*, 24 November 1947.
32. Whyte, *Church and State*, p. 159.
33. Whyte, *Church and State*, p. 160.
34. *Irish Times*, 8 July 1946.
35. Newspaper clipping, undated, found in Seán MacEntee Papers, University College, Dublin, P67/542 (28).
36. Newspaper clipping, undated, found in Seán MacEntee Papers, P67/542 (29).
37. See the *Irish Independent*, 18 January 1932, 22 January 1932, and the *Irish Times*, 18 January 1932, 25 January 1932, and 30 January 1932.
38. Quoted in Ronan Fanning, *Independent Ireland* (Dublin, 1983), p. 105.
39. *Irish Times*, 16 January 1932.
40. T. Desmond Williams, Conclusion, in Francis MacManus, (ed.), *Years of the Great Test 1926-1939* (Cork, 1962), p. 173.
41. *Irish Times*, 10 May 1947, 6 February 1947.
42. *Irish Times*, 6 April 1968.
43. Phyllis Browne, *Thanks for the Tea, Mrs. Browne: My Life with Noël* (Dublin, 1998), p. 103.
44. See Coakley and Gallagher, *Politics in the Republic of Ireland*, Basil Chubb, *The Government and Politics of Ireland* 3rd ed. (Stanford, 1992), J. Lee, *The Modernisation of Irish Society*, (Dublin 1973), pp. 74-79, and Tom Garvin, 'Continuity and Change in Irish Electoral Politics 1923-1969,' in *Economic and Social Review* vol. III, (March 1972) for studies of the importance of constituency politics.
45. *Irish Independent*, 27 October 1947. MacBride's comment on the family unit was an odd statement to make, considering that MacBride and his half-sister were raised by a single parent. As he lived in France until his father's death, perhaps he did not consider France as 'Christian' a state as Ireland.
46. MacBride to McQuaid, 1 November 1948, Dublin Diocesan Archives. McQuaid referred the matter to the Youth Unemployment Council, but did not offer any advice directly to MacBride.
47. *Irish Independent*, 25 November 1947.

210   AN IRISH STATESMAN AND REVOLUTIONARY

48. In 1944, this amount stood at £130.9 million. Kevin Rafter, *The Clann: The Story of Clann na Poblachta* (Cork, 1996), pp. 33-34.
49. *Irish Independent*, 13 December 1947.
50. Browne, *Against the Tide*, p. 97.
51. Lee, *Ireland 1912-1985*, p. 241.
52. *Irish Independent*, 5 January 1948.
53. *Irish Independent*, 2 January 1948.
54. *The Economist*, 8 November 1947.
55. 29 December 1980, quoted in MacDermott, *Clann na Poblacta*, p. 63.
56. F.S.L. Lyons, 'The Years of Readjustment 1945-51' in K.B. Nowlan and T.D. Williams (eds.), *Ireland in the War Years and After 1939-1951* (Dublin, 1969), p. 69.
57. See J. Bowyer Bell, *The Secret Army: The IRA* (Dublin, 1998) and Tim Pat Coogan, *The IRA* (London, 2000).
58. MacDermott, *Clann na Poblachta*, p. 23.
59. Cruise O'Brien, *Memoir*, p. 138.
60. Lee, *Ireland 1912-1985*, p. 318.
61. *Irish Times*, 27 January 1948.
62. *Irish Independent*, 9 October 1947.
63. *Irish Independent*, 25 October 1947.
64. Interview with Eithne MacDermott in *Clann na Poblachta*, p. 79.
65. *Irish Times*, 27 October 1947.
66. *Irish Times* 8 November 1947.
67. From mid-January until polling day on 4 February, the *Irish Press* gave 94 column inches to Fianna Fáil and 22 to Clann na Poblachta while the *Irish Independent* gave 41 inches to Fianna Fáil and 9 to Clann na Poblachta.
68. MacDermott, *Clann na Poblachta*, p. 39.
69. Moynihan to MacBride, 15 January 1948, Department of the Taoiseach, S14204, National Archives, Dublin.
70. *Irish Times*, 16 October 1947.
71. *Irish Times*, 18 October 1947. At various times, MacEntee labelled MacBride a communist, fascist, socialist, and Nazi sympathiser, which makes for an interesting political philosophy!
72. *Irish Times*, 29 October 1947.
73. *Irish Independent*, 29 October 1947.
74. *Irish Independent*, 29 October 1947.
75. *Irish Independent*, 1 November 1947.
76. *Irish Times*, 1 November 1947.
77. *Irish Times*, 31 October 1947.
78. *Irish Independent*, 1 November 1947.
79. Dáil Éireann Debates, vol. 108, col. 1379, 5 November 1947.
80. Dáil Éireann Debates, vol.108, cols. 1443-1444, 5 November 1947.
81. Ran in the *Irish Independent*, 30 January 1948.
82. Quoted in David McCullagh, *A Makeshift Majority: The First Interparty Government 1948-1951* (Dublin, 1999), p. 20.
83. MacDermott, *Clann na Poblachta*, p. 57.
84. Browne, *Against the Tide*, p. 99.

85. Inglis, *West Briton*, p. 114.
86. Editorial, *Irish Times* 17 January 1948.
87. Colm and Liam Ó Laoghaire in conversation with MacDermott, in *Clann na Poblachta*, p. 62.
88. *Irish Times*, 4 February 1948.
89. *Irish Independent*, 13 December 1947.
90. Browne, *Against the Tide*, p. 103.
91. Rafter, *The Clann*, p. 35.
92. *Irish Independent*, 6 January 1948.
93. Lord Rugby to the Commonwealth Relations Office, 1 November 1947, Dominions Office, 35.3955, p.3, National Archives, Kew.
94. *The Observer*, 18 January 1948.
95. Inglis, *West Briton*, p. 114.
96. *Limerick Leader*, 31 January 1948.
97. Ballina was close to Westport, Co. Mayo, the birthplace of John MacBride.
98. *Irish Independent*, 4 February 1948.
99. *Irish Independent*, 29 January 1948.
100. John A. Murphy, 'The Irish Party System' in Nowlan and Williams (eds.), *Ireland in the War Years*, pp. 158-159.
101. Ronan Fanning, *Independent Ireland*, p. 165. Italics his.
102. *Irish Independent*, 25 November 1947.
103. Murphy, *Ireland in the Twentieth Century*, p. 119.
104. *Irish Times*, 1 January 1979.
105. Fanning, *Independent Ireland*, p. 165.
106. Ernest Blythe to John Costello, 19 February 1948, John A. Costello Papers, P190/363 (23).
107. Keogh, 'Ireland, the Vatican, and the Cold War,' p. 68.
108. Voice recording of speech, February 1948, John A. Costello Papers, P190/428 (4).

Chapter Two

1. Quoted in *Jawaharal Nehru's Speeches, vol. 1 September 1946-May 1949* (New Dehli, 1949), p. 241.
2. Repeal receives substantial analysis in J.J. Lee's *Ireland 1912-1985: Politics and Society* (Cambridge, 1989), Tim Pat Coogan, *Ireland in the Twentieth Century* (London, 2003), F.S.L. Lyons' *Ireland Since the Famine* (London, 1985), less so in Alvin Jackson's *Ireland 1798-1998* (Oxford, 1998) and R.F. Foster's *Modern Ireland 1600-1972* (London, 1988) because those surveys examine a wider time period.
3. Notably Patrick Keatinge's *The Formulation of Irish Foreign Policy* (Dublin, 1973), Ronan Fanning's *Independent Ireland* (Dublin, 1983) and *The Irish Department of Finance 1922-58* (Dublin, 1978), a thorough examination of an administrative system that wields much influence on foreign policy, Dermot Keogh's *Twentieth Century Ireland* (Dublin, 1994) and *Europe, 1919-1989: A Diplomatic and Political History* (Cork, 1990), which places foreign policy outside the scope of Anglo-Irish relations, Nicholas Mansergh's *Nationalism and Independence* (Cork, 1997) and *The Unresolved Question: the Anglo-Irish Settlement and its Undoing*

(New Haven, CT, 1991), and Bernadette Whelan's *Ireland and the Marshall Plan* (Dublin, 2001). Mansergh's focus is on Commonwealth relations whereas Whelan emphasises Ireland's dealings with the United States with regard to the European Recovery Programme. Both Fanning and Keogh have authored journal articles on specific issues in Irish foreign policy; Keogh's 'Ireland, the Vatican, and the Cold War' in *Irish Studies in International Affairs* 3 (1991) and Fanning's 'The Response of the London and Belfast Governments to the Declaration of the Republic of Ireland 1948-1949,' *International Affairs* 58 (Winter 1981-1982) provide insight into the inter-party government's well-meaning yet short-sighted diplomatic efforts.

4.   Anthony Jordan, *Seán MacBride: A Biography* (Dublin, 1993), p. 105.

5.   H. Duncan Hall, *A History of the British Commonwealth of Nations* (London, 1971), p. 811.

6.   Donal Lowry, 'New Ireland, Old Empire and the Outside World, 1922-49: The Strange Evolution of a "Dictionary Republic,"' in Mike Cronin and John M. Regan (eds.), *Ireland: the Politics of Independence, 1922-49* (London, 2000), p. 168.

7.   Jackson, *Ireland 1798-1998*, p. 309.

8.   Dáil Éireann Debates, vol. 97, col. 2570, 17 July 1945.

9.   *Irish Times*, 27 January 1948.

10. Dáil Éireann Debates, vol. 113, col. 25, 18 February 1948.

11. *Irish Times*, 19 February 1948.

12. Dáil Éireann Debates, vol. 112, col. 910, 20 July 1948.

13. Copy found in Frank Aiken Papers, University College, Dublin, P104/4442 (2).

14. Dáil Éireann Debates, vol. 110, cols. 27-28, 18 February 1948.

15. Nicholas Mansergh, *Nationalism and Independence*, pp. 188-189.

16. Lyons, *Famine*, p. 564.

17. Dáil Debates, vol. 112, col. 992, 21 July 1948.

18. Dáil Debates, vol. 112, col. 2441, 06 August 1948.

19. Cabinet Minutes, 10 August 1948, CAB 2/10, pp. 99-102, National Archives, Dublin.

20. Michael McInerney profile of John Costello, *Irish Times*, 4 September 1967. Copy of Costello's initial answers to McInerney's questions found in Patrick McGilligan Papers, University College, Dublin, P35c/205 (3).

21. Eithne MacDermott, *Clann na Poblachta* (Cork, 1998), pp. 115-116.

22. *Ireland in International Affairs*, text found in John A. Costello Papers, University College, Dublin, P190/532.

23. Costello to F.S.L. Lyons, 6 January 1967, in Lyons, *Famine*, p. 565.

24. 'Dinner on 4 September, Diary of Taoiseach's visit to the USA and Canada,' John A. Costello Papers, P190/526 (3).

25. Patrick Lynch, 'Pages from a Memoir' in P. Lynch and J. Meenan (eds.), *Essays in Honour of Alexis Fitzgerald* (Dublin, 1987), pp. 50-52.

26. 'Memorandum for the Secretary of State for External Affairs,' 28 February 1949, Department of External Affairs, File 50021-40 (Record Group 25, vols. 4480-4481), National Archives of Canada, Ottawa.

27. Lynch, 'Pages', pp. 52-53.

28. Memorandum, 15 June 1972, written by Costello, John A. Costello Papers, P190/546 (14). In an *Irish Times* interview on 25 March 1961 the Governor-General denied ever intending an 'insult to this country.' Costello later acknowledged the statement and accepted the apology.

29. Memorandum, 15 June 1972, by Costello, John Costello Papers, P190/546 (14).

30. John J. Hearne to Costello, 23 January 1949, John A. Costello Papers, P190/414 (11).

31. Noël Browne, *Against the Tide* (Dublin, 1986), pp. 130-132 and Mansergh, 'Conversation with Frederick Boland – 1952,' *Nationalism and Independence*, pp. 188-189.

32. Mansergh, *The Unresolved Question*, p. 331.

33. Attlee, *As It Happened*, p. 190.

34. Lyons, *Famine*, p. 562.

35. Editorial, *Ottawa Journal*, 23 February 1948, copy in John A. Costello Papers, P190/355 (12).

36. 29 July 1948, quoted in Ian McCabe, *A Diplomatic History of Ireland 1948-9: The Republic, the Commonwealth and NATO* (Dublin, 1991), p. 36.

37. 'Memorandum for file,' 28 February 1949, Department of External Affairs, File 50021-40 (Record Group 25, vols. 4480-4481), National Archives of Canada, Ottawa.

38. Jordan, *Seán MacBride*, pp. 106-107.

39. Mansergh, *Nationalism and Independence*, p. 187.

40. Responding to allegations that MacBride had secretly leaked the story, Legge wrote to the *Irish Times* that 'MacBride knew me well enough to talk to me direct. Backdoor methods would not have been necessary.' *Irish Times*, 11 January 1992.

41. Maffey report to the Commonwealth Relations Office, 12 June 1948, CAB 134/118. National Archives, Kew.

42. Patrick Lynch to Sean MacBride, 12 March 1981, courtesy of Caitriona Lawlor.

43. Second draft of memo, July 1972, John A. Costello Papers, P190/546 (16).

44. *Irish Times*, 8 September 1948.

45. *Irish Times*, 5 April 1999.

46. Memorandum, 15 June 1972, by Costello, John A. Costello Papers, P190/546 (14).

47. John Murphy, *Ireland in the Twentieth Century* (Dublin, 1975), p. 126.

48. Lyons, *Famine*, p. 567.

49. *Irish Times*, 4 July 1962.

50. *Irish Times*, 19 January 1979.

51. *Irish Times*, 10 July 1962.

52. Noël Browne, *Against the Tide*, p. 131.

53. *Sunday Independent* 1 February 1984.

54. Patrick Lynch to Sean MacBride, 17 January 1984, courtesy of Caitriona Lawlor.

55. MacDermott, *Clann na Poblachta*, p. 130.

56. Lynch, 'Pages', p. 39.

57. Brian Farrell, *Chairman or Chief: The Role of the Taoiseach in Irish Government* (Dublin, 1971), p. 46-47.
58. Coogan, *Ireland*, p. 349.
59. Cabinet Minutes, 11 October 1948, CAB 2/10, pp. 159-160, National Archives, Dublin.
60. Attlee, *As It Happened*, p. 190.
61. Coogan, *Ireland*, p. 349.
62. Garret FitzGerald, *All In A Life: An Autobiography* (Dublin, 1991), p. 45.
63. Seanad Éireann Debates, vol. 36 col. 84, 9 December 1948.
64. *Irish Times*, 1 January 1979.
65. *Irish Times*, 25 November 1948.
66. Nicholas Mansergh 'The Implications of Eire's Relationship with the British Commonwealth of Nations' *International Affairs* January 1948, p. 4.
67. Nicholas Mansergh, *The Unresolved Question*, p. 328.
68. Quoted in the *Irish Times*, 27 October 1948.
69. Fitzgerald to Costello, Wednesday, October 1949, John A. Costello Papers, P190/390.
70. Michael Gallagher, *Political Parties in the Republic of Ireland* (Manchester, 1985), p. 49.
71. MacDermott, *Clann na Poblachta*, p. 96.
72. Conor Cruise O'Brien, *Memoir: My Life and Themes* (Dublin, 1998), pp. 141-142. It is questionable as to whether MacBride still had any direct or indirect connections with the IRA while in the Dáil. MacEntee claims MacBride was in close association with the IRA as late as 1944. [Seán MacEntee Papers, University College, Dublin, P67/539 (2)].
73. Quoted in Fanning, *Independent Ireland*, pp. 168-169.
74. *Irish People*, 14 February 1948.
75. Report to the Department of External Affairs by John Dulanty, 7 October 1948. Frank Aiken Papers, P104/4449 (2).
76. *The Citizen*, May 1967.
77. Copy found in Sighle Humphreys Papers, University College, Dublin, P106/2148 (1).
78. De Valera's occupancy of both roles can be interpreted two ways – the ministry was so important that the Taoiseach himself had to manage it (Patrick Keatinge, *Formulation of Irish Foreign Policy*, pp. 71-72) or the position was relatively unimportant so it could be controlled by someone as busy as the Taoiseach (Brian Farrell, *Chairman or Chief*, p. 11).
79. Patrick Keatinge, *Formulation of Irish Foreign Policy*, pp. 80-81.
80. Cruise O'Brien, *Memoir*, p.159.
81. *Irish Times*, 26 October 1948.
82. Keatinge, *Formulation of Irish Foreign Policy*, p. 63.
83. MacDermott, *Clann na Poblachta*, p. 131.
84. Alexis Fitzgerald to Costello, Wednesday, October 1949, John A. Costello Papers, P190/390. Underline his.
85. Browne, *Against the Tide*, p. 133.
86. Dáil Éireann Debates, vol.113, col. 347, 24 November 1948.
87. *Irish Times*, 22 December 1948.

88. The conference took place from 2 April to 3 May. Easter Monday fell on 18 April in 1949.
89. McCabe, *Diplomatic History*, p. 92.
90. MacBride had a close relationship with his mother – they lived together in Roebuck House until her death in 1953 and though they did not always agree on political matters, she was very proud of his accomplishments. See Nancy Cardozo, *Lucky Eyes and a High Heart: The Life of Maud Gonne* (New York, 1978), pp. 401-404 and Anthony Jordan, *Seán MacBride*, p. 143, where he states that Gonne 'supported her son in all his political ventures.' Also Samuel Levenson, *Maud Gonne* (London, 1976), p. 405. Levenson mentions a photo in *Life* magazine detailing the Easter Monday celebrations: 'important figures leaving the Pro-Cathedral after Mass on that day; among them was Maud Gonne MacBride, leaning on the arm of her son.' This was most likely Seán's son Tiernan MacBride. (*Life*, 2 May 1949)
91. *Life*, 2 May 1949.
92. The *Times*, 19 April 1949.
93. *Irish Times*, 19 April 1949.
94. Records of the Cabinet Office, 129/29 CP(48) 205, National Archives, Kew.
95. Browne, *Against the Tide*, p. 134.
96. Report by High Commissioner for Ireland John J. Hearne to External Affairs, 5 October 1949. Department of Foreign Affairs 313/3A, National Archives, Dublin.
97. Maffey to Sir Eric Machtig, 27 January 1948, CAB 134/118/annex 11, National Archives, Kew.
98. Fanning, 'The Response of the London and Belfast Governments,' p. 113.
99. Clement Attlee, *As It Happened* (London, 1954), p. 190-191. Attlee's memoirs in general are not very detailed.
100. Stephen Howe, *Anticolonialism in British Politics* (London, 1993), pp. 147-148.
101. Kenneth O. Morgan, *Labour in Power 1945-1951* (London, 1985), p. 188.
102. Morgan, *Labour in Power*, p, 226.
103. Copy found in Frank Aiken Papers, P104/4442 (2).
104. 'Notes of a conversation between the Prime Minister of Canada and the Prime Minister of Ireland,' 9 September 1948, Department of External Affairs, File 50021-40 (Record Group 25, vols. 4480-4481), National Archives of Canada, Ottawa.
105. Copy found in Frank Aiken Papers, P104/4443 (1).
106. Quoted in Mansergh, *Nationalism and Independence*, p. 208.
107. Frank Moraes, *Jawaharal Nehru: A Biography* (New York, 1956), p. 42.
108. Report to External Affairs by Dulanty, 27 October 1948. Frank Aiken Papers, P104/4458 (1).
109. Report to External Affairs by Dulanty, 23 September 1948. Frank Aiken Papers, P104/4447 (3), Report to External Affairs by Dulanty, 22 November 1948. Frank Aiken Papers, P104/4464 (1).
110. Report to External Affairs by Dulanty, 20 October 1948. Frank Aiken Papers, P104/4451 (2).
111. Report to External Affairs by Dulanty, 8 November 1948. Frank Aiken Papers, P104/4463 (1).

112. House of Commons Debates, 15 December 1948, vol. CLIX, col. 1090.
113. CAB 128/13/143-4, National Archives, Kew.
114. The *Times*, 18 October 1948, *Irish Times*, 18 October 1948.
115. Ronan Fanning, 'Anglo-Irish Relations – Partition and the British Dimension in Historical Perspective,' *Irish Studies in International Affairs* vol. 2 no, 1 1985, p. 15.
116. Dáil Éireann Debates, vol. 113, col. 715, 26 November 1948.
117. *The Times*, 26 November 1948.
118. Dominions Office 35.3976, National Archives, Kew.
119. Clement Attlee Papers, Bodleian Library, Oxford, MS Attlee, dep. 82, 172.
120. D.G. Boyce, *The Irish Question and British Politics 1868-1996*, 2nd ed., (London, 1996), pp. 97-98.
121. Report to External Affairs by Dulanty, 10 May 1949. Department of Foreign Affairs 305/14/36, National Archives, Dublin.
122. Northern Ireland House of Commons Debates, vol. XXXII, col. 3665-6, 30 November 1948.
123. Records of the Prime Minister's Office, 8/1464, National Archives, Kew.
124. Attlee Papers, MS Attlee, dep. 82, 177.
125. Attlee Papers, MS Attlee, dep. 74, 42.
126. Attlee Papers, MS Attlee dep. 74, 44.
127. Attlee, *As It Happened*, p. 190.
128. *Irish Times*, 27 January 1948.
129. Lyons, *Famine*, p. 567.
130. Dáil Éireann Debates, vol. 113, col. 385, 24 November 1948.
131. Mansergh, *Unresolved Question*, p. 341.
132. Telegram from Noel-Baker to Maffey, 9 May 1949, CAB, 21/184, National Archives, Kew.
133. MacBride to Dulanty, 15 May 1949, Department of Foreign Affairs 305/14/36, National Archives, Dublin.
134. Reply to the British Lord Chancellor, 23 May 1949, Patrick McGilligan Papers, P35b/146 (1).
135. Report to External Affairs by Dulanty, 10 May 1949. Department of Foreign Affairs 305/14/36, National Archives, Dublin.
136. R.F. Foster, *Modern Ireland 1600-1972*, p. 567.
137. House of Commons Debates, vol. 464, col. 1858, 11 May 1949. Fanning arrives at a similar conclusion, 'Response of London and Belfast Governments,' p. 114.
138. *Irish Times*, 4 May 1949.
139. 'Notes in Relation to the Ireland Bill,' copy in Patrick McGilligan Papers, P35b/146 (3).
140. Dáil Éireann Debates, vol. 115, cols. 785-786, 10 May 1949.
141. *Irish Times*, 8 September 1967.
142. David Harkness, *Ireland in the Twentieth Century: Divided Island* (London, 1966), p. 80.
143. Attlee, *As It Happened*, p. 190.
144. Attlee Papers, MS Attlee, dep 83, 15.
145. Copy found in Patrick McGilligan Papers, P35b/148.

146. Attlee, *As It Happened*, pp. 186-187.
147. Nicholas Mansergh, *The Commonwealth Experience, Vol.2. 2nd ed.*, (London, 1982), p. 144.
148. Mansergh, 'Ireland: the Republic Outside the Commonwealth,' in *Nationalism and Independence*, p. 176.
149. Lee, *Ireland 1912-1985*, p. 300.
150. *Kilkenny People* 30 April 1949, copy found in Seán MacEoin Papers P151/613 (10). Italics mine.
151. Browne, *Against the Tide*, p. 149.
152. Lee, *Ireland 1912-1985*, p. 301.
153. Copy found in Patrick McGilligan Papers, P35b/148.
154. Lyons, *Famine*, p. 570.
155. *Irish Times*, 7 Sept. 1967.
156. 14 April 1949 radio interview reprinted in 16 April *Irish Times*. Seán MacEoin Papers, P151/619 (1).
157. Lee, *Ireland 1912-1985*, p. 301.
158. Foster, *Modern Ireland 1600-1972*, p. 567.
159. Coogan, *Ireland*, p. 350.
160. McCabe, *Diplomatic History*, p. 149.
161. MacDermott, *Clann na Poblachta*, p. 113.
162. *Irish Times*, 20 November 1999.
163. *Irish Times*, 19 April 1949.
164. Speech in Mulligar, Westmeath, undated, Seán MacEoin Papers, P151/615 (2).
165. *Manchester Guardian* 21 September 1948.
166. *Irish Times*, 2 October 1948.
167. Cruise O'Brien, *Memoir*, p. 141.
168. *Irish Times*, 6 May 1949.
169. Attlee, *As It Happened*, p.190.
170. Fanning, *Independent Ireland*, p. 180.
171. Seán MacEoin Papers, P151/618.

Chapter Three

1. Most notably David Harkness' *Ireland in the Twentieth Century: Divided Island* (London, 1966), David Fitzpatrick's *The Two Irelands 1912-1939* (Oxford, 1998), Clare O'Halloran's *Partition and the Limits of Irish Nationalism* (Dublin, 1987), and Nicholas Mansergh's *The Unresolved Question: The Anglo-Irish Settlement and Its Undoing 1912-72* (New Haven, CT, 1991). Partition is also explored in survey histories such as Lee's *Ireland 1912-1985* (Cambridge, 1989), Foster's *Modern Ireland 1600-1972* (London, 1988), Lyons' *Ireland Since the Famine* (London, 1985), and Jackson's *Ireland 1798-1998* (Oxford, 1998).
2. Eithne MacDermott, *Clann na Poblachta* (Cork, 1998), p. 135.
3. MacDermott, *Clann na Poblachta*, p. 135.
4. Ian McCabe, *A Diplomatic History of Ireland 1948-49: The Republic, the Commonwealth and NATO* (Dublin, 1991), pp. 150-151.
5. Recent writings on this subject include Bernadette Whelan's *Ireland and the Marshall Plan* (Dublin, 2000), Seán Cronin's *Washington's Irish Policy* (Dublin,

1987), and Troy D. Davis' *Dublin's American Policy: Irish-American Diplomatic Relations 1945-1952* (Washington D.C., 1998).

6. Davis, *Dublin's American Policy*, p. 218.

7. Anthony Jordan, *Seán MacBride: A Biography* (Dublin, 1993), p. 122. The memoirs of Conor Cruise O'Brien and Brian Inglis provide valuable firsthand insight into MacBride's Irish News Agency and the development of government policy regarding partition as well as opinions of the personality and motivation of MacBride himself. See Conor Cruise O'Brien, *Ancestral Voices: Religion and Nationalism in Ireland* (Dublin, 1994), *Memoir: My Life and Themes* (Dublin, 1998), Brian Inglis, *West Briton* (London, 1962), and *Downstart: The Autobiography of Brian Inglis* (London, 1990).

8. Nicholas Mansergh, *Nationalism and Independence* (Cork, 1997), p. 174, David McCullagh, *A Makeshift Majority: The First Interparty Government 1948-51* (Dublin, 1999), p. 128.

9. See especially Fitzpatrick, *The Two Irelands 1912-1939*, Harkness, *Ireland in the Twentieth Century: Divided Island*, and Mansergh, *The Unresolved Question*.

10. Quoted in Fitzpatrick, *The Two Irelands 1912-1939*, p. 32.

11. Foster, *Modern Ireland*, p. 503.

12. Lyons, *Ireland Since the Famine*, p. 445.

13. Lecture to Royal Institute of International Affairs, Chatham House 24 February 1949 – given by MacBride (Patrick McGilligan Papers, University College Dublin, P35b/148).

14. Pamphlet, 'Ulster is British: A Re-affirmation of Ulster's political outlook,' February 1949. Frank Aiken Papers, University College Dublin, P1/4623 (1).

15. O'Halloran, *Partition*, p. xv.

16. Dáil Éireann Debates, 13 July 1949, vol. 117, col. 853.

17. Hugh Seton-Watson, *Nations and States: An Enquiry into the Origins of Nations and the Politics of Nationalism* (London, 1977), p. 1. Seton-Watson's approach is more relevant in this context, but see also Benedict Anderson, *Imagined Communities: Reflections on the Origin and Spread of Nationalism* (London, 1983), which concentrates on emerging nationalisms in Southeast Asia and provides an analysis of popular theories on the concept of nationalism, Anthony D. Smith, *Nationalism and Modernism: A Critical Survey of Recent Theories of Nations and Nationalism* (London, 1998), and E.J. Hobsbawm, *Nations and Nationalism since 1780: Programme, Myth, Reality* (Cambridge, 1990).

18. Seton-Watson, *Nations and States*, p. 4.

19. Seton-Watson, *Nations and States*, pp. 41-42.

20. Tom Nairn, *The Break-up of Britain: Crisis and Neo-Nationalism*, 2nd edition, (London, 1981), pp. 237-238.

21. Timothy J. White, 'Nationalism vs. Liberalism in the Irish Context: From a Postcolonial Past to a Postmodern Future,' *Eire-Ireland* vol. XXXVII (Fall/Winter 2002), p. 26.

22. O'Halloran, *Partition*, p. 26.

23. Donald Akenson, *Conor: A Biography of Conor Cruise O'Brien* (London, 1994), p. 129.

24. H. Duncan Hall, *A History of the British Commonwealth of Nations* (London, 1971), p. 778.

25. Cruise O'Brien, *Memoir*, p. 145.
26. John Bowman, *De Valera and the Ulster Question 1917-1973* (Oxford, 1982), p. 128.
27. *Freeman's Journal*, 19 June 1916.
28. Dáil Éireann Debates, vol. 112, col. 95, 20 July 1948.
29. O'Halloran, *Partition*, p. 7.
30. 24 February 1949, Copy found in Patrick McGilligan Papers, University College Dublin, P35b/148.
31. McGilligan Papers, P35b/148.
32. Dáil Éireann Debates, vol. 113, col. 397, 24 November 1948.
33. *Irish Press*, 6 May 1949.
34. Hall, *History of the British Commonwealth*, p. 819, fn.
35. Copy found in Sighle Humphreys Papers, University College, Dublin, P106/2148.
36. Speech delivered on 7 October 1951. Copy found in Richard Mulcahy Papers, University College Dublin, P7/c/123.
37. *Irish Times*, 29 October 1948.
38. *Irish Times*, 19 March 1947.
39. J.H. Whyte, *Church and State in Modern Ireland 1923-1979*, 2nd edition (Dublin, 1980), p. 48.
40. O'Halloran, *Partition*, p. 175.
41. Dáil Éireann Debates, vol. 67, col. 1890, 4 June 1937.
42. Dáil Éireann Debates, vol. 67, col. 1890, 4 June 1937.
43. Joseph Lee, 'The Irish Constitution of 1937,' Seán Hutton and Paul Stewart (eds.), *Ireland's Histories: Aspects of State, Society and Ideology* (London, 1991), p. 83.
44. Lee, 'Irish Constitution,', p. 83.
45. It was suggested in an *Irish Times* editorial that Unionists would 'nourish a deep dislike' of these Articles, (4 June 1937) and would 'postpone the day of [unification]… by slights which cannot fail to be resented across the border.' (3 May 1937).
46. *Irish Independent*, 10 June 1937.
47. *Irish Times*, 5 June 1937.
48. O'Halloran, *Partition*, p. 176.
49. Whyte, *Church and State*, p. 57.
50. Lee, 'Irish Constitution,' p. 82.
51. Dáil Éireann Debates vol. 111, col. 2447, 8 July 1948.
52. The special position of the Catholic Church was removed in 1972. Articles 2 and 3 were amended in 1998 as part of the Good Friday Agreement. A referendum to lift a ban on divorce was approved by a slim margin in November 1995. After a contentious court battle contesting the referendum, legalized divorce was finally enacted on 27 February 1997. Ireland's divorce referendum is a very conservative piece of legislation, one of the most conservative in any Western country, requiring at least four years separation and the courts must be satisfied that there is no prospect of reconciliation.
53. British note to Eire Government, 26 June 1940, Records of the Prime Minister's Office 3/131/2, Public Record Office.

54. British note to Eire Government, 26 June 1940, PREM 3/131/2, National Archives, Kew.
55. British note to Eire Government, 26 June 1940, PREM 3/131/2, National Archives, Kew.
56. Robert Fisk, *In Time of War* (London, 1985), p. 201.
57. Ronan Fanning, 'Irish Neutrality: An Historical Perspective,' in *Irish Studies in International Affairs* vol. 1 no. 3 (1982), p. 31.
58. Chamberlain memorandum, 25 June 1940, Records of the Cabinet Office, 66/9, National Archives, Kew.
59. Fisk, *In Time of War*, p. 202.
60. Fisk, *In Time of War*, p. 202.
61. Cabinet Meeting, 27 June 1940, CAB 2/3, pp. 159-160, National Archives, Dublin.
62. De Valera to Chamberlain, 4 July 1940, PREM 3/131/2, National Archives, Kew.
63. Fisk, *In Time of War*, pp. 207-208.
64. Craigavon telegram to Chamberlain, 27 June 1940, PREM 3/131/2, National Archives, Kew.
65. Clement Attlee, *As It Happened* (London, 1954), p. 190.
66. Attlee wrote in his memoirs that 'I am sure that the spirit of the people was with the Allies.' *As It Happened*, p. 190.
67. Fanning, 'Irish Neutrality: An Historical Perspective,' p. 37.
68. In 1945, the War Office estimated that 42,665 Irish soldiers served in the British Armed Forces during the war, quite high for a neutral country. See Fisk, *In Time of War*, pp. 523-524.
69. There was secret military cooperation between the British and Irish Armies to repel a German invasion of Ireland, known as the 'W' Plan. The operational papers for the plan were destroyed in the Luftwaffe bombing of Belfast in 1941. See Fisk, *In Time of War*, pp. 233-244.
70. As of September 1939, the Department of Defence, Dublin estimated the Irish Army to number 19,783 – 7494 Regulars, 5066 A and B Reservists, and 7223 Volunteers with 21 armoured vehicles, two tanks, a tiny air force, and no navy.
71. Lee, *Ireland: 1912-1985*, p. 270.
72. Nicholas Mansergh, *Survey of British Commonwealth Affairs: Problems of War-time Cooperation and Postwar Change, 1939-1952* (Oxford, 1958), p 75.
73. *The Economist*, editorial, 27 November 1948.
74. John Hickerson to George Garrett, 24 May 1948, State Department Decimal File, 841D 00/3.2448, National Archives, Washington DC.
75. In a celebrated exchange between Churchill and de Valera, Churchill took credit for British 'restraint and poise' in not invading Ireland during the war, blaming de Valera for not allowing the British to use Irish ports and airfields (13 May 1945). De Valera replied three days later, declaring that 'Mr. Churchill makes it clear that, in certain circumstances, he would have violated our neutrality... All credit to him that he successfully resisted the temptation... instead of adding another horrid chapter to the already bloodstained record of the relations between England and this country.' De

Valera praised Britain's resolve during the early years of the war and added, 'Could he [Churchill] not find in his heart the generosity to acknowledge that there is a small nation that stood alone, not for one year or two, but for several hundred years against aggression; that endured spoliations, famine, massacres in endless succession; that was clubbed many times into insensibility, but that each time... took up the fight anew; a small nation that could never be got to accept defeat and has never surrendered her soul?' Maurice Moynihan, ed., *Speeches and Statements by Eamon de Valera 1917-73* (Dublin, 1980), pp. 470-476.

76. *Irish Times*, 19 March 1947.
77. Troy Davis, 'Anti-partitionism, Irish America and Anglo-Irish Relations, 1945-51' in *Irish Foreign Policy: From Independence to Internationalism* (Dublin, 2000), p. 195. Brian Inglis, *West Briton*, pp. 135-136.
78. Quoted in Cronin, *Washington's Irish Policy*, p. 183.
79. Letter to Minister of External Affairs from E. McAteer, 5 March 1949. Copy found in McGilligan Papers, P35b/146 (4).
80. Dáil Éireann Debates, vol. 117, col. 2, 5 July 1949.
81. Memorandum from Taoiseach to Government, 12 March 1949, McGilligan Papers, P35/146 (5).
82. Copy found in Mulcahy Papers, P7c/122.
83. Quoted in Cronin, *Washington's Irish Policy*, p. 201.
84. John Dulanty to External Affairs – 8 November 1948 (Aiken Papers, P104/4463).
85. McCabe, *Diplomatic History*, p. 36.
86. Memoranda of conversations, 11 April 1949, Dean Acheson Papers, Box 73, Harry S. Truman Library.
87. Lord Rugby report of General Election in Eire, Report from Lord Rugby to Commonwealth Relations Office, 1 November 1947, Foreign Office 371.707175, National Archives, Kew.
88. Bowman, *De Valera*, pp. 274-275.
89. Westmeath Examiner, 21 August 1948.
90. Attlee, *As It Happened*, pp. 190-191, the *Times*, 26 November 1948.
91. Mansergh, *The Unresolved Question*, p. 335.
92. Attlee report to Cabinet, 7 December 1948, CAB 129/31/124, National Archives, Kew.
93. Cabinet meeting, 25 November 1948, CAB 4/769/11, Public Record Office Northern Ireland.
94. Cabinet minutes, 6 January 1949, CAB 130/44/262, National Archives, Kew.
95. Mansergh, *The Unresolved Question*, p. 341.
96. Tim Pat Coogan, *Ireland in the Twentieth Century* (London, 2003), p. 350.
97. Dáil Éireann Debates, vol. 115, col. 786, 10 May 1949.
98. Lyons, *Famine*, p. 563.
99. Dáil Éireann Debates, vol. 113, col. 385, 24 November 1948.
100. NSC Report, 17 October 1950, NSC 83/1 PSF Box 209, Truman Papers, HSTL. Italics mine.
101. *Irish Independent*, 4 May 1948.
102. *Manchester Guardian*, 15 October 1947.

103. Lee, *Ireland: 1912-1985*, p. 304.
104. Garrett to Acheson, 21 January 1949, State Department Decimal File, 840.20/1-2149, A-19, National Archives, DC.
105. *Ireland's Position in Relation to the North Atlantic Treaty* (Dublin, 1950), p. 5.
106. Referenda only take place in matters of Constitutional alteration.
107. Fanning, 'Irish Neutrality: An Historical Perspective,' p. 34.
108. Quoted in Ronan Fanning, 'The United States and Irish Participation in NATO: The Debate of 1950,' *Irish Studies in International Affairs* 1 (1979), p. 39.
109. Reprinted in *Irish Echo*, 27 March 1948.
110. Dáil Éireann Debates, vol. 112, col. 903, 20 July 1948.
111. Memorandum of conversation, 23 March 1951, Dean Acheson Papers, Box 66, HSTL.
112. Oral History, Theodore Achilles, 13 November 1972, Box, OH-170, p. 62, HSTL.
113. Lyons, *Famine*, pp. 557-558.
114. NSC note, *Irish Times* 5 November 1980.
115. NSC Report, 17 October 1950, NSC 83/1 PSF Box 209, Truman Papers, HSTL. See Fanning, 'The United States and Irish Participation in NATO: The Debate of 1950.'
116. Quoted in Davis, *Dublin's American Policy*, p. 151.
117. Conor Cruise O'Brien, 'Ireland in International Affairs' in Owen Dudley Edwards, ed., *Conor Cruise O'Brien Introduces Ireland* (New York, 1969), pp. 124-125.
118. Quoted in Cronin, *Washington's Irish Policy*, p. 254.
119. Department of Foreign Affairs, 305/72/5 Part 1, National Archives, Dublin.
120. Davis, *Dublin's American Policy*, p. 171.
121. Voice recording of speech, February 1948, John A. Costello Papers, University College, Dublin, P190/428 (4).
122. Copy found in Mulcahy Papers, P7/c/123.
123. Dáil Éireann Debates, vol. 113, col. 392, 24 November 1948.
124. Bowman, *De Valera*, pp. 258-260.
125. Cronin, *Washington's Irish Policy*, p. 194.
126. Inadequate representation was not entirely the fault of the Stormont Government. Most Nationalist parties followed an absentionist policy until 1925, which allowed the Government to tighten control.
127. *Irish Independent*, 28 January 1949.
128. *Irish Press*, 28 January 1949.
129. *Irish Times*, 3 February 1949.
130. *Irish Independent*, editorial, 26 January 1949.
131. *Irish Times*, editorial, 28 January 1949.
132. CAB, 9F/123/11, PRONI.
133. Franks to Ernest Bevin, 2 June 1950, FO 371/81648, National Archives, Kew.
134. Dáil Éireann Debates, vol. 117, col. 757, 13 July 1949.
135. Dáil Éireann Debates, vol. 117, col. 761, 13 July 1949.
136. Inglis, *West Briton*, p. 138.

137. Cruise O'Brien, *Memoir*, p. 145.
138. Hartnett was Clann na Poblachta's Campaign Director and deserved much of the credit for Clann's early success. After losing the Dáil seat he was vying for in the 1948 election, he hoped to receive one of the two Clann-nominated Seanad seats. MacBride did not choose him and he was hurt by the slight. Cruise O'Brien described Hartnett as 'able but angry and bitter' and believed that their falling out culminated in Hartnett being abruptly relieved of his speechwriting duties on MacBride's American tour. Cruise O'Brien, *Memoir*, pp. 144-148, Noël Browne, *Against the Tide*, (Dublin, 1986), pp. 106-107, 137-138.
139. As Cruise O'Brien explains in his memoirs, 'to have been favoured by MacBride and then be dropped by him was not a promising career option.' Cruise O'Brien, *Memoir*, p. 147.
140. Cruise O'Brien, *Memoir*, p. 148.
141. Akenson, *Conor*, p. 137.
142. Akenson, *Conor*, p. 137.
143. Inglis, *West Briton*, p. 142.
144. Inglis, *Downstart*, p. 175.
145. Inglis, *West Briton*, p. 142.
146. Cruise O'Brien, *Memoir*, p. 150.
147. Cruise O'Brien, *Memoir*, pp. 152-155.
148. Inglis, *West Briton*, p. 187.
149. Miriam Hederman, *The Road to Europe: Irish Attitudes 1948-61* (Dublin, 1983), p. 78.
150. Douglas Gageby, 'The Media 1945-70' in J.J. Lee, ed. *Ireland 1945-70* (Dublin, 1979), p. 130.
151. *Irish Times*, 8 March 1948.
152. Dáil Éireann Debates, vol. 112, col. 2113, 5 August 1948.
153. David Mitrany, *Functional Theory of Politics* (London, 1975), p. 356.
154. Mitrany, *Functional Theory*, p. 358.
155. Dáil Éireann Debates, vol. 112, col. 2113, 5 August 1948.
156. CAB 9F/140/28, PRONI.
157. McWilliam to Brooke, 23 August 1950, CAB 9F/140/28, PRONI.
158. Cabinet meeting, 8 March 1951, CAB 9F/140/29, PRONI.
159. *Irish Independent*, 9 May 1950.
160. *Irish Times*, 10 May 1950.
161. Curran to Lavery, 4 April 1949, Department of the Taoiseach, S 14414 A, National Archives, Dublin.
162. Quoted in McCabe, *Diplomatic History*, p. 129.
163. Unfortunately, Cosgrave goes on to say that 'These three instances demonstrate the absurdity of Partition and the necessity for ending it as quickly as possible.' Dáil Éireann Debates, vol. 126, col. 2227, 19 July 1951.
164. McCullagh, *A Makeshift Majority*, p. 128.
165. John Whyte, 'Dynamics of Social and Political Change in Northern Ireland,' in Dermot Keogh and Michael H. Haltzel (eds.), *Northern Ireland and the Politics of Reconciliation* (Cambridge, 1993), p. 116.
166. *Irish Times*, 8 May 1950.

167. Basil Chubb, *The Politics of the Irish Constitution* (Dublin, 1991), p. 81.
168. *Irish Independent*, 8 May 1950.
169. Copy found in Mulcahy Papers, P7/c/123, 7 October 1951.
170. McCabe, *Diplomatic History*, p. 150.

Chapter Four

1. Tip O'Neill and William Novak, *Man of the House: The Life and Political Memoirs of Speaker Tip O'Neill* (London, 1987), p. 26.
2. P.J. Drudy's *The Irish in America: Emigration, Assimilation, Impact* (Cambridge, 1985) contains a varied and interesting collection of articles on the Irish-American relationship. See also Donald Harmon Akenson, *The United States and Ireland* (Cambridge, MA., 1973), Owen Dudley Edwards and David N. Doyle (eds.), *America and Ireland 1776-1976* (Westport, CT., 1980), Kevin Kenny, *The American Irish: A History* (Harlow, 2000), and Seán Cronin, *Washington's Irish Policy 1916-1986* (Dublin, 1987).
3. See especially Cronin, *Washington's Irish Policy*, Robert Fisk, *In Time of War* (London, 1985), Trevor Salmon, 'Neutrality and the Irish Republic: Myth or Reality?' in *Round Table* 290 (1984), and *Unneutral Ireland: An Ambivalent and Unique Security Policy* (Oxford, 1989), Troy D. Davis, *Dublin's American Policy: Irish-American Diplomatic Relations 1945-1952* (Washington D.C., 1998), John Bowman, *De Valera and the Ulster Question 1917-1973* (Oxford, 1982), T. Ryle Dwyer, *Strained Relations: Ireland at Peace and the USA at War, 1941-45* (Dublin, 1988), Ronan Fanning, 'Irish Neutrality: An Historical Perspective,' in *Irish Studies in International Affairs* vol. 1 no. 3 (1982), Joseph Carroll 'US-Irish Relations 1939-45,' in *Irish Sword* 19 (1993-94), and Carrolle J. Carter, 'Ireland: America's Neutral Ally,' in *Éire-Ireland* XII (1977).
4. See Cronin, Bernadette Whelan, *Ireland and the Marshall Plan* (Dublin, 2000), Davis, *Dublin's American Policy*, Till Geiger and Michael Kennedy (eds.), *Ireland, Europe and the Marshall Plan* (Dublin, 2004), and Ian McCabe, *A Diplomatic History of Ireland 1948-1949: The Republic, the Commonwealth and NATO* (Dublin, 1991).
5. Donal Lowry, 'New Ireland, Old Empire and the Outside World 1922-49: The Strange Evolution of a "Dictionary Republic"' in Mike Cronin and John M. Regan (eds.), *Ireland: The Politics of Independence, 1922-49* (London, 2000), p. 195.
6. Quoted in Dermot Keogh, 'Ireland' in Zara Steiner's *Times Survey of Foreign Ministries of the World* (London, 1982), p. 279.
7. Dáil Éireann Debates, vol. 4, col. 11, 18 August 1921.
8. Akenson, *United States and Ireland*, p. 34.
9. Akenson, *United States and Ireland*, p. 37.
10. Davis, *Dublin's American Policy*, p. 92.
11. T.N. Brown, *Irish-American Nationalism 1870-1890* (New York, 1966), pp. 63-64.
12. Patrick J. Blessing, 'Irish Emigration to the United States, 1800-1920: An overview' in Drudy, *The Irish in America*, p. 31.
13. Akenson, *United States and Ireland*, p. 44.

14. Though no reliable published work on the Irish ancestry of American Presidents exists, nineteen American Presidents have claimed Irish ancestry. However, their backgrounds were 'Scotch-Irish' and only one American President was an Irish-American Catholic.
15. Daniel Patrick Moynihan, 'The Irish' in Daniel Patrick Moynihan and Nathan Glazer (eds.), *Beyond the Melting Pot: The Negros, Puerto Ricans, Jews, Italians, and Irish of New York City*, (Cambridge, MA, 1963), p. 241.
16. Thomas N. Brown, 'Social Discrimination Against the Irish in the United States,' quoted in Moynihan, p. 241.
17. Lawrence J. McCaffrey, 'Irish-American Politics: Power with or without Purpose?' in Drudy, *The Irish in America*, p. 169.
18. Moynihan, 'The Irish,' p. 229.
19. Lowry, 'New Ireland,' p. 195.
20. Lowry, 'New Ireland,' p. 164.
21. Memorandum from Matthew Connelly to Secretary of State George Marshall, 18 June 1947, Harry S. Truman Papers (HSTP), White House Central Files, Official File 218, Box 823, Harry S. Truman Library (HSTL), Independence, Missouri.
22. Hickerson to Gray, 1 January 1945, Record Group 59, Box 20, File UK D-5 (B), National Archives and Records Administration, Washington DC.
23. British Embassy to Foreign Office, 10 March 1949, Foreign Office (FO) 371 1967, 74190, National Archives, Kew.
24. Dwyer, *Strained Relations*, p. 172, Davis, *Dublin's American Policy*, pp. 29-57.
25. Davis, Dublin's American Policy, pp. 58-59.
26. Oral History, Nathan M. Becker, State Department, 19 January 1973, Box 27, OH-159, p. 7a, HSTL.
27. Hickerson to Garrett, 4 May 1948.
28. Memorandum for the President, 11 April 1949, Myron C. Taylor File, HSTP, White House Confidential Files, Box 47, HSTL.
29. Memorandum on the state of Ireland, 10 October 1942, President Secretary's Files, Vatican Diplomatic Files, Box 51, Franklin Delano Roosevelt Library, Hyde Park, New York.
30. Raymond J. Raymond, 'The Marshall Plan and Ireland 1947-1952,' in Drudy, The Irish in America, p. 297.
31. Moynihan, 'The Irish,' p. 244.
32. *New York Times*, 1 May 1945.
33. Memorandum, 21 May 1945, Dominions Office (DO) 130/56, National Archives, Kew.
34. Dáil Éireann Debates, vol. 96, col. 2037, 13 April 1945.
35. Dwyer, *Strained Relations*, p. 161.
36. Quoted in Earl of Longford and Thomas P. O'Neill, *Eamon de Valera* (London, 1970), p. 411.
37. Lewis W. Douglas to Ernest Bevin, April 6, 1948 BEVN II 6/5, Misc. Correspondence, 1948 Foreign Office #7, Ernest Bevin Papers, Churchill College, Cambridge.
38. Ronan Fanning, *Independent Ireland* (Dublin, 1983), p. 177.

39. Memorandum for the President, Subject Policy Manual, p. 46, 16 April 1945, HSTP, President Secretary Files, Subject File Cabinet, Box 138, HSTL.
40. MacBride to Nunan, 26 October 1948, Department of Foreign Affairs 305/74, National Archives, Dublin.
41. Cronin, *Washington's Irish Policy*, p. 191.
42. Quoted in Cronin, *Washington's Irish Policy*, p. 248.
43. *Congressional Record* – House of Representatives, vol. 96, 81st Congress, 2nd session, March 29, 1950, p. 4344.
44. The Amendment was passed by a teller vote. According to Congressional Quarterly's *American Congressional Dictionary*, this procedure required Members to pass through the centre aisle to be counted, but not recorded by name. The teller vote is no longer practiced in the House of Representatives.
45. Truman cleverly ran his 1948 Presidential campaign not against Republican opponent Thomas E. Dewey, but against a 'do-nothing' Republican Congress. See David McCullough, *Truman* (New York, 1993).
46. *New York Times*, 30 March 1950.
47. *Washington Post*, 30 March 1950.
48. *Irish Times*, 30 March 1950.
49. *Irish Times*, 31 March 1950.
50. See Department of Foreign Affairs, File D24, National Archives, Dublin.
51. *New York Times*, 2 April 1950.
52. *New York Times*, 31 March 1950.
53. *Washington Post*, 30 March 1950.
54. *Irish Times*, 31 March 1950.
55. See *Congressional Record* – House of Representatives, vol. 96, 81st Congress, 2nd session, March 31, 1950, p. 4552.
56. Jack K. McFall, Assistant Secretary of State, to Tom Connally, 13 April 1951, United States State Department Decimal File, 740A.00, National Archives, Washington DC.
57. Michael Farrell, 'The Extraordinary Life and Times of Sean MacBride, Part 2' *Magill* (January, 1983), p. 31.
58. American League to Marshall, 12 May 1948, HSTP, HSTL.
59. HSTP, White House Central Files, Official File 218, Box 823, HSTL.
60. 'Ireland' written by Colonel HD Kehm, Dublin Army Attaché to Psychological Strategy Board, dated 20 September 1951, HSTP, Psychological Strategy Board Files, Box 7, 091.
61. J.J. Lee, *Ireland 1912-1985: Politics and Society* (Cambridge, 1989), p. 301.
62. CIA Situation Report Ireland April 1949, p. 15, HSTP, PSF, Intelligence File 1946-1953, Box 219.
63. Rugby to Sir Eric Machtig, Under-Secretary of State at Dominions Office, 30 March 1948, DO 35/3928, National Archives, Kew.
64. Troy Davis, 'Anti-partitionism, Irish America and Anglo-Irish Relations, 1945-51' in Michael Kennedy and Joseph Morrison Skelly (eds.), *Irish Foreign Policy 1919-1969: From Independence to Internationalism* (Dublin, 2000), p. 193.
65. Memorandum for Truman, dated 22 March 1951, re: MacBride appointment for meeting of 23 March Signed by Dean Acheson. HSTP, President Secretary's File, Subject File, Foreign Affairs 1945-1953 'Ireland' Box 157.

66. HSTP, White House Confidential Files, State Department Correspondence, Box 42, HSTL.
67. Truman to Sir Basil Brooke, 23 September 1949, HSTP, White House Central Files, Official File 218, Box 823, HSTL.
68. HSTP, White House Central Files, Official File 218, Box 823, HSTL.
69. Cronin, *Washington's Irish Policy*, p. 220.
70. Davis, *Dublin's American Policy*, p. 134.
71. Conor Cruise O'Brien 'Ireland in International Affairs,' in Owen Dudley Edwards, ed., *Conor Cruise O'Brien Introduces Ireland* (New York, 1969), p. 127.
72. Dáil Éireann Debates, vol. 126, col. 2024, 19 July 1951.
73. 'Against hunger, poverty, desperation and chaos,' George C. Marshall's speech at the Harvard University Commencement, 5 June 1947, reprinted in *Foreign Affairs*, May-June 1997, vol.76, p.160.
74. Bernadette Whelan, 'Integration or Isolation? Ireland and the Invitation to Join the Marshall Plan' in *Irish Foreign Policy*, p. 204.
75. Marshall never explicitly stated this in his speech; aid was not directed 'against any country or doctrine.' However, Sallie Pisani convincingly argued that the Marshall Plan was 'coordinated intervention' used to combat communism. Sallie Pisani, *The CIA and the Marshall Plan* (Lawrence, Kansas, 1991).
76. Geiger and Kennedy, *Marshall Plan*, p. 29.
77. Whelan, 'Integration' in *Irish Foreign Policy*, p. 221 and *Ireland and the Marshall Plan*, p. 17.
78. HSTP, President's Secretary File, Box 256, SR 48, CIA Ireland, 1 April 1949, HSTL.
79. Raymond, 'Marshall Plan,' pp. 299-300.
80. This was possibly because Spain, as a fascist dictatorship under Franco, was not invited to participate in the OEEC and by association, the Marshall Plan.
81. HSTP, PSF: Intelligence File 1946-1953, Box 219, CIA: Situation Report, Ireland April 1949, p. 13, HSTL.
82. Dáil Éireann Debates, vol. 114, col. 324, 23 February 1949.
83. Whelan, 'Integration,' p. 213.
84. 4 July 1947, Department of External Affairs to the Government, Department of the Taoiseach, S 14106/A, National Archives, Dublin.
85. *Irish Independent*, 17 April 1948.
86. MacBride's role in the OEEC is more fully explored in chapter five.
87. Memorandum, Hickerson to Marshall, 18 May 1948, State Department Decimal Files 841D.021, National Archives, Washington DC.
88. Oral History, W. John Kenney, Chief of Mission, ECA 1949-1950, OH 322, Box 56, 29 November 1971, HSTL.
89. Raymond, 'Marshall Plan,' p. 306.
90. MacBride – submitted to ECA, May 1948, p. 1, HSTP, White House Central Files, Official File 218, Box 823, HSTL.
91. MacBride – submitted to ECA, May 1948, p. 3, HSTP, White House Central Files, Official File 218, Box 823, HSTL.
92. Northern Ireland was receiving three-fourths of its aid in grant form in 1949-1950.

93. Memorandum, Department of Finance to Government, 18 April 1952, Taoiseach S 141061, National Archives, Dublin.
94. Lee, *Ireland 1912-1985*, p. 304.
95. Alan S. Milward, *The Reconstruction of Western Europe*, 1945-51 (London, 1987), p. 83.
96. Memorandum for Government from Finance, 8 June 1948, Department of Finance, 121/21/48 F Series, National Archives, Dublin.
97. Hickerson, Memorandum of Conversation, 20 May 1948, quoted in Cronin, *Washington's Irish Policy*, pp. 196-197.
98. Geiger and Kennedy, *Marshall Plan*, p. 21.
99. Daniel Davies, "'It is More Important to us that Eire Should Receive Adequate Aid than it is for Eire Herself:" Britain, Ireland and the Marshall Plan,' in Geiger and Kennedy, *Marshall Plan*, p. 69.
100. HSTP, PSF: Intelligence File 1946-1953, Box 219, CIA: Situation Report, Ireland April 1949, p. 38, HSTL.
101. HSTP, PSF: Intelligence File 1946-1953, Box 219, CIA: Situation Report, Ireland April 1949, p. 11, HSTL.
102. Memoranda of conversations, 13 February 1951, with John J. Hearne, Dean Acheson Papers, Box 77, HSTL.
103. Quoted in Ronan Fanning, *The Irish Department of Finance 1922-58* (Dublin, 1978), p. 411.
104. Quoted in Fanning, *Finance*, p. 406.
105. 3 February 1948, Department of Finance 121/10/48, National Archives, Dublin.
106. Fanning, *Finance*, pp. 434-442.
107. Lee, *Ireland 1912-1985*, p. 305, Copy of *Long-Term Recovery Programme* found in John A. Costello Papers, University College, Dublin, P190/414 (8).
108. Quoted in Fanning, *Finance*, p. 405.
109. Text found in HSTP, Foreign Affairs File, Ireland – General News Clippings, Box 151.
110. Raymond, 'Marshall Plan,' p. 321.
111. Fanning, *Finance*, p. 406.
112. Michael Kennedy, 'The Challenge of Multilateralism: The Marshall Plan and the Expansion of the Irish Diplomatic Service,' in Geiger and Kennedy, *Marshall Plan*, p. 103.
113. HSTP, President's Secretary's File, Intelligence File, Box 219, CIA Situation Report, Ireland, April 1949, p. 1, HSTL.
114. 8 February 1949, Department of Foreign Affairs 305/74, National Archives, Dublin.
115. Dáil Éireann Debates, vol. 114, col. 324, 23 February 1949.
116. Quoted in Cronin, *Washington's Irish Policy*, p. 225.
117. Hickerson to Nunan, 31 March 1949, Department of Foreign Affairs 305/72/5 part 1, National Archives, Dublin.
118. McCabe, *Diplomatic History*, p. 97.
119. HSTP, PSF: Intelligence File 1946-1953, Box 219, CIA: Situation Report, Ireland April 1949, p. 38, HSTL.

120. Noël Browne, *Against the Tide* (Dublin, 1986), p. 134. Browne was unhappy about MacBride overlooking 'the hardworking and experienced' Noel Hartnett for a Seanad nomination. He goes so far as to suggest that Denis Ireland may have been 'a secret member of British Intelligence whose job it was to bring the Republic into NATO.' (p. 135)

121. Garrett to Truman, 10 July 1950, HSTP, White House Central Files, Official File 218, Box 823, HSTL.

122. Cronin interview with MacBride, 12 February 1986 in *Washington's Irish Policy*, p. 248.

123. Memoranda of conversations, 11 April 1949, Dean Acheson Papers, Box 73, HSTL.

124. Department of Foreign Affairs, 305/74, National Archives, Dublin.

125. HSTP, PSF, Subject File, NSC Meetings, 2 November 1950, NSC Staff Study, Box 181, HSTL.

126. HSTP, PSF, Subject File, NSC Meetings, 2 November 1950, NSC Staff Study, Box 181, HSTL.

127. NSC note, reported in *Irish Times* 5 November 1980.

128. HSTP, PSF, Subject File, NSC Meetings, 2 November 1950, NSC Staff Study, Box 181, HSTL.

129. Cronin, *Washington's Irish Policy*, p. 233.

130. Report 'Eire and the Paris Conference' 12 March 1948, FO, 371.70175, National Archives, Kew.

131. Dáil Éireann Debates, vol. 106, col. 2333, 20 June 1947.

132. Francis H. Heller and John R. Gillingham (eds.), *NATO: The Founding of the Atlantic Alliance and the Integration of Europe* (New York, 1992), p. 2.

133. 14 March 1951, Text can be found in HSTP, Foreign Affairs File, Ireland – General News Clippings, Box 151, HSTL.

134. Quoted in McCabe, *Diplomatic History*, p. 108.

135. Cronin interview with MacBride, 12 February 1986, *Washington's Irish Policy*, pp. 247-248.

136. *Irish Times*, 29 January 1949.

137. *Irish Times*, 19 March 1949

138. 28 January 1949, 'outline of conversation between MacBride and Garrett,' FO 371.79224, National Archives, Kew.

139. Garrett to Truman, 10 July 1950, HSTP, White House Central Files, Official File 218, Box 823, HSTL.

140. HSTP, PSF, Subject File, NSC Meetings, 2 November 1950, NSC Staff Study, Box 181, HSTL.

141. Memoranda of conversations, 13 March 1951, Dean Acheson Papers, Box 77, HSTL.

142. This was approved by Truman on 3 November 1950. HSTP, PSF, Subject File, NSC Meetings, 2 November 1950, Box 181, HSTL.

143. Cronin, *Washington's Irish Policy*, pp. 248-249.

144. Boland to Walsh, 9 February 1949, Department of Foreign Affairs, 305/72/5, part 1, National Archives, Dublin. Canadian intervention also proved elusive; the Canadian High Commissioner in London told MacBride that repeal of the External Relations Act coupled with the refusal to join

NATO meant that 'not only are the United Kingdom and Northern Ireland less disposed to discuss partition, but other North Atlantic countries, including Canada, have, for the first time, a strategic interest in maintaining partition.' (Quoted in McCabe, *Diplomatic History*, p. 112)

145. Cronin, *Washington's Irish Policy*, p. 249.
146. Dwyer, *Strained Relations*, p. 1.
147. Dermot Keogh, *Twentieth Century Ireland* (Dublin, 1994), p. 194.
148. Desmond Dinan, 'After the Emergency: Ireland in the Post-War World, 1945-50,' *Éire-Ireland*, vol. 24 (Fall 1989), p. 98.
149. 'Eire and the Paris Conference' 12 March 1948, FO, 371.70175, National Archives, Kew.
150. McCabe, *Diplomatic History*, p. 107.
151. Quoted in Cronin, *Washington's Irish Policy*, p. 254.
152. *Irish Times*, 19 March 1949.
153. Conor Cruise O'Brien, 'Ireland in International Affairs' in Owen Dudley Edwards, ed., *Conor Cruise O'Brien Introduces Ireland*, pp. 124-125.
154. Memorandum to Department of External Affairs from John Dulanty, 10 May 1949, Department of Foreign Affairs 305/14/36, National Archives, Dublin.
155. Cronin, *Washington's Irish Policy*, p. 239.
156. *Irish Times*, 19 June 1951.
157. Farrell, 'Life and Times,' p. 33.
158. Richard Bourke, *Peace in Ireland: The War of Ideas* (London, 2003), p. 17. See also George Mitchell, *Making Peace* (London, 1999).
159. Record Group 84 File (2) 1948, Box 703. National Archives, Washington DC.
160. Keogh, 'Ireland' in *Foreign Ministries*, p. 279.

Chapter Five

1. Dáil Éireann Debates, vol. 11, col. 1415, 13 May 1925.
2. Michael Kennedy and Joseph Morrison Skelly (eds.), *Irish Foreign Policy 1919-1966: From Independence to Internationalism* (Dublin, 2000), p. 23.
3. As J.J. Lee wrote in 1989, Ireland 'has chosen to ignore the study of international relations, including the study of neutrality, to an extent unparalleled in any other small Western European neutral.' J.J. Lee, *Ireland 1912-1985: Politics and Society* (Cambridge, 1989), p. 605.
4. See especially Miriam Hederman, *The Road to Europe: Irish Attitudes 1948-1961* (Dublin, 1983), Michael Kennedy and Eunan O'Halpin, *Ireland and the Council of Europe: From Isolation Towards Integration* (Strasbourg, 2000), Till Geiger and Michael Kennedy (eds.), *Ireland, Europe and the Marshall Plan* (Dublin, 2004), Dermot Keogh, *Ireland and Europe, 1919-1989: A Diplomatic and Political History* (Cork, 1990), Michael Kennedy and Joseph Morrison Skelly (eds.), *Irish Foreign Policy* and Bernadette Whelan, *Ireland and the Marshall Plan* (Dublin, 2000).
5. See Dermot Keogh, *Ireland and Europe 1919-1989*, R. F. Foster, *The Irish Story: Telling Tales and Making It Up In Ireland* (London, 2001), and the journal *Irish Studies in International Affairs* published by the Royal Irish Academy.

6. Kennedy and Skelly, *Irish Foreign Policy*, p. 17.

7. Eithne MacDermott, *Clann na Poblachta* (Cork, 1998), p. 135, Kevin Rafter, *The Clann: The Story of Clann na Poblachta* (Cork, 1996), p. 134.

8. David McCullagh, *A Makeshift Majority: The First Interparty Government 1948-1951* (Dublin, 2000), p. 139.

9. Alvin Jackson, *Ireland 1798-1998* (Oxford, 1998), p. 309.

10. D.J. Maher, *The Tortuous Path: The Course of Ireland's Entry into the EEC 1948-73* (Dublin, 1986), p. xiii.

11. R.F. Foster, *Modern Ireland 1600-1972* (London, 1988), p. 567.

12. F.S.L. Lyons, *Ireland Since the Famine* (London, 1985), p. 563.

13. Daniel Davies, "'It is More Important to us that Eire Should Receive Adequate Aid than it is for Eire Herself:" Britain, Ireland and the Marshall Plan,' in Geiger and Kennedy, *Marshall Plan*, p. 72.

14. Patrick Keatinge, *The Formulation of Irish Foreign Policy* (Dublin, 1973), p. 81.

15. Basil Chubb, *The Government and Politics of Ireland* (Oxford, 1974), p. 46. Trevor Salmon and Patrick Keatinge also make this point. Salmon, *Unneutral Ireland: An Ambivalent and Unique Security Policy* (Oxford, 1989), p. 1.

16. Kennedy and O'Halpin, *Council of Europe*, p. 12.

17. Michael Kennedy, *Ireland and the League of Nations 1919-1946: International Relations, Diplomacy, and Politics* (Dublin 1996), p. 27.

18. Norman MacQueen, 'Ireland's Entry to the United Nations' in Tom Gallagher and James O'Connell, eds., *Contemporary Irish Studies* (Manchester, 1983), p. 77. See also Robert Fisk, *In Time of War* (London, 1985), Ronan Fanning, 'Irish Neutrality: An Historical Perspective,' in *Irish Studies in International Affairs* vol. 1 no. 3 (1982), Trevor Salmon, *Unneutral Ireland*, and Dennis Driscoll, 'Is Ireland Really Neutral?' in *Irish Studies in International Affairs*, vol. 1 no. 3 1982.

19. Desmond Dinan, 'After the Emergency': Ireland in the Post-War World, 1945-50,' *Éire-Ireland*, vol. 24 (Fall 1989), p. 85.

20. Interview with United Press, 12 February 1949, Department of the Taoiseach, S 14291 A/1, National Archives Dublin.

21. Dáil Éireann Debates, vol. 102, col. 1374, 24 July 1946.

22. Irish aide-mémoire, 25 May 1949 in *Texts Concerning Ireland's Position in Relation to the North Atlantic Treaty*, (Dublin, 1950). Italics mine.

23. Dáil Éireann Debates, vol. 112, col. 903, 20 July 1948.

24. See Dermot Keogh, 'Ireland, the Vatican and the Cold War: The Case of Italy 1948,' *Irish Studies in International Affairs* 3 (1991), pp. 931-952.

25. Conor Cruise O'Brien, 'Ireland in International Affairs' in Owen Dudley Edwards, ed., *Conor Cruise O'Brien Introduces Ireland* (London, 1969), p. 124.

26. Miriam Hederman, 'The Beginning of the Discussion on European Union in Ireland,' Walter Lipgens and Wilfred Loth, (eds.), *Documents on the History of European Integration, Vol.3, The Struggle for European Union by Political Parties and Pressure Groups in Western European Countries, 1945-1950* (Berlin, 1988), p. 766.

27. The Labour Party is an exception, though Irish Labour had little in common with other European Labour movements. Clann na Poblachta's connection with European Christian Democrats is another exception.

28. Hederman, *Road*, pp. 22-23.

29. Basil Chubb, *A Source Book of Irish Government* (Dublin, 1983), pp. 157-8.
30. Keatinge, *Formulation*, p. 224.
31. Dermot Keogh, *Ireland and Europe 1919-1989*, p. 219.
32. MacBride speech in Sligo, 17 November 1950, Department of Foreign Affairs, GIS/1/255, National Archives Dublin.
33. Keogh, *Ireland 1919-1989*, p. 218.
34. Seanad Éireann Debates, vol. 35, col. 748, 5 August 1948.
35. Hederman, *Road*, p. 16.
36. In conversation with Mansergh in 1952, *Nationalism and Independence* (Cork, 1997), p. 189.
37. John Bowman, *De Valera and the Ulster Question 1917-1973* (Oxford, 1982), p. 273.
38. Mansergh, *Nationalism and Independence*, p. 209.
39. Mansergh, *Nationalism and Independence*, p. 209.
40. Though Spain and Portugal were currently under authoritarian regimes, both Franco and Salazar allied themselves with Catholicism and Fascist Catholic countries appeared to be lesser evils than Communist Russia. Ireland had diplomatic relations with both Spain and Portugal during MacBride's tenure and worked with both in the OEEC.
41. 29 December 1948, Department of Foreign Affairs 305/62/1, National Archives Dublin.
42. Joseph Walshe to Secretary of the Department of External Affairs, 20 January 1949, Department of Foreign Affairs, 305/62/1, National Archives Dublin.
43. Dermot Keogh, *Ireland and Europe 1919-48*, p. 212.
44. Mansergh, *Nationalism and Independence*, p. 184.
45. MacBride speech in Sligo, 17 November 1950. Department of Foreign Affairs, GIS/1/255, National Archives Dublin.
46. MacBride speech in Sligo, 17 November 1950. Department of Foreign Affairs, GIS/1/255, National Archives Dublin.
47. Dáil Éireann Debates, vol. 117, col. 850, 13 July 1949.
48. See Hederman, *Road*, pp. 21-23.
49. As Bevin stated on 25 January 1949 at a speech to the Foreign Press Association, London, 'It had always been my obsession – a United States of Europe. If Europe is to be saved it has to be in the end one entity: it must be together' (text found in Department of Foreign Affairs, 14/72, National Archives Dublin). However, Bevin later rejected the Schuman Plan because he believed it undermined British power and maintained that the European Movement's vision of Britain's role was for her to 'sponsor foreign rapprochement rather than became part of a United States of Europe.' (Richard Weight, *Patriots: National Identity in Britain 1940-2000* (London, 2002), pp. 176-177).
50. Paul-Henri Spaak, 'Strasbourg: The Second Year,' Stevenson Memorial Lecture, delivered 30 October 1950, Chatham House (Oxford, 1952), p. 13.
51. Attlee to Churchill, 4 February 1948, Winston Churchill Collection, Churchill College, Cambridge, CHUR 2/21.

52. Memorandum from External Affairs, 13 June 1950, Department of Foreign Affairs, 4/17, National Archives Dublin.
53. European Parliamentary Union Memorandum on the Structure of Europe, 16 December 1949, Department of Foreign Affairs, 417/24 Part I, National Archives Dublin.
54. *Irish Independent*, 8 May 1948.
55. *Irish Times*, 15 May 1948.
56. Seanad Éireann Debates, vol. 35, col. 815, 5 August 1948. See also Kennedy and O'Halpin, *Council of Europe*, p. 26.
57. Kennedy and O'Halpin, *Council of Europe*, p. 23.
58. Dáil Éireann Debates, vol. 112, col. 903, 20 July 1948.
59. 16 June 1949, Department of Foreign Affairs, 417/39, National Archives Dublin.
60. Whelan, *Marshall Plan*, p. 172.
61. Seanad Éireann Debates, vol. 35, col. 805, 5 August 1948.
62. Frederick Boland to John Costello, 11 August 1948, Department of Foreign Affairs, 417/24 Part I, National Archives Dublin.
63. Hederman, *Road*, p. 29.
64. Dáil Éireann Debates, vol. 112, col. 2435, 6 August 1948.
65. Dáil Éireann Debates, vol. 112, col. 903, 20 July 1948.
66. Seanad Éireann Debates, vol. 35, col. 813, 5 August 1948.
67. Dáil Éireann Debates, vol. 117, cols. 696-706, 12 July 1949.
68. *Irish Times*, editorial, 14 July 1949.
69. *Irish Times*, editorial, 16 July 1949.
70. Dáil Éireann Debates, vol. 122, col. 1601, 12 July 1950.
71. *Irish Times*, 16 February 1949.
72. Conor Cruise O'Brien, *To Katanga and Back: A UN Case History* (London, 1962), p. 14.
73. Cruise O'Brien, 'Ireland in International Affairs,' p. 126.
74. Lyons, *Famine*, p. 591.
75. *Official Reports of Council of Europe Consultative Assembly*, 10 August – 8 September 1949, p. 238.
76. *Irish Independent*, 12 August 1950.
77. Quoted in Hederman, *Road*, p. 31.
78. *The Leader*, editorial, 27 August 1949.
79. *Irish Times*, editorial, 13 August 1949.
80. *Irish Times*, 10 May 1948.
81. Dáil Éireann Debates, vol. 122 col. 1592, 12 July 1950.
82. Dáil Éireann Debates, vol. 122 col. 1592, 12 July 1950.
83. Kennedy and O'Halpin, *Council of Europe*, p. 80.
84. *Irish Independent*, 10 September 1949.
85. *Summary of the Debates in the Consultative Assembly of the Council of Europe*, August 1950, Winston Churchill Collection, Churchill College, Cambridge, CHUR 2/76.
86. *Irish Times*, 3 August 1949.
87. James P. O'Donnell, 'Ireland's New Man of Destiny,' *Saturday Evening Post*, 23 April 1949.

88. 'With Churchill and Spaak, whose popularity is enormous, it is Sean MacBride, the brilliant Foreign Minister of Ireland, who has the most success.' (vol. 34, 20 August 1949)
89. Kennedy and O'Halpin, *Council of Europe*, p. 59.
90. Bevin to MacBride, 30 October 1950, Department of Foreign Affairs, 417/39/64, National Archives Dublin.
91. Anthony Jordan, *Seán MacBride: A Biography* (Dublin, 1993), p. 120.
92. *Irish Independent*, 8 November 1950.
93. Dáil Éireann Debates, vol. 117, col. 746, 13 July 1949.
94. Quoted in Eire/Ireland, Bulletin of Department of External Affairs, No. 136, 19 May 1952.
95. Quoted in Hederman, *Road*, p. 33.
96. Hederman, *Road*, p. 147.
97. 'Against Hunger, Poverty, Desperation and Chaos,' George C. Marshall speech at Harvard University Commencement, June 5, 1947, reprinted in *Foreign Affairs*, May-June 1997, vol.76, n.3, p.160.
98. CIA - Ireland, 1 April 1949, Harry S. Truman Papers, President's Secretary File, Box 256, SR 48, Harry S. Truman Library, Independence, Missouri.
99. Bernadette Whelan, 'Integration or Isolation? Ireland and the Invitation to Join the Marshall Plan' in *Irish Foreign Policy*, p. 213.
100. External Affairs to the Government, 4 July 1947, Department of the Taoiseach, S 14106/A, National Archives Dublin.
101. External Affairs to the Government, June 1947, Department of the Taoiseach, S 14106/A, National Archives Dublin.
102. *Irish Independent*, 17 April 1948.
103. MacBride's role in the Marshall Plan is more fully explored above, pp.140-148.
104. Report of final session of the Conference on European Economic Cooperation, reported in the *Irish Independent*, 17 March 1948.
105. Address to Institute of International Affairs, 24 February 1949, Department of the Taoiseach S 14406, National Archives Dublin.
106. MacBride to Spaak, 6 September 1948, Department of the Taoiseach, S 14106, National Archives Dublin.
107. MacBride to Spaak, 6 September 1948, Department of the Taoiseach, S 14106, National Archives Dublin.
108. Keogh, *Ireland and Europe 1919-1989*, p. 222.
109. Department of External Affairs Report, 28 February 1949, Department of Foreign Affairs, 305/57/140, National Archives Dublin.
110. Quoted in Cronin, *Washington's Irish Policy*, p. 241.
111. Dáil Éireann Debates, vol. 110, cols. 331-335, 10 March 1948.
112. Speech before the OEEC Council on 25 July 1948, File: OEEC 1010;106, C(48)106, European University Institute Archives, Florence.
113. Dermot Keogh, *Twentieth Century Ireland* (Dublin, 1994), p. 196.
114. *Irish Times*, editorial, 22 February 1950.
115. Department of External Affairs Report, 31 March 1951, Department of the Taoiseach S 15067B, National Archives Dublin.
116. Dáil Éireann Debates, vol, 117, cols. 857-858, 13 July 1949.

117. Dáil Éireann Debates, vol. 117, cols. 850-851, 13 July 1949.
118. Dáil Éireann Debates, vol. 117, cols. 850-851, 13 July 1949.
119. Dáil Éireann Debates, vol. 117, col. 857, 13 July 1949.
120. Keatinge, *Formulation*, pp. 80-82.
121. *Irish Times*, 25 July 1946.
122. Dáil Éireann Debates, vol. 102, col. 1312, 24 July 1946.
123. *Irish Independent*, 25 July 1946.
124. *Irish Times*, 25 July 1946.
125. MacQueen, 'Ireland's Entry,' p. 69.
126. Article 4 of the Charter states, 'Membership in the United Nations is open to all other peace-loving states which accept the obligations contained in the present Charter and, in the judgment of the Organization, are able and willing to carry out these obligations.'
127. Dáil Éireann Debates, vol. 110, col. 622, 14 April 1948.
128. 'Record of a conversation between the Secretary of State and Sean MacBride,' 16 June 1948, DO 35/3958, National Archives, Kew.
129. Dáil Éireann Debates, vol, 110, col. 623, 14 April 1948.
130. Dáil Éireann Debates, vol. 112, cols. 903-904, 20 July 1948.
131. Department of Foreign Affairs 417/33/Part 3, National Archives Dublin.
132. *The Leader*, editorial, 13 March 1948.
133. Dáil Éireann Debates, vol. 112, col. 904, 20 July 1948.
134. Dáil Éireann Debates, vol.116, cols. 865-866, 21 June 1949.
135. Dáil Éireann Debates, vol 117, col. 999, 14 July 1949.
136. Dáil Éireann Debates, vol. 117, col. 851,13 July 1949.
137. Joseph Morrison Skelly, 'National Interests and International Mediation: Ireland's South Tyrol Initiative at the United Nations 1960-1' in *Irish Foreign Policy*, p. 288.
138. Joseph Morrison Skelly, *Irish Diplomacy at the United Nations 1945-65* (Dublin, 1997), p. 15.
139. In several cases, for example Cyprus, Korea, Vietnam, Germany, West New Guinea, and Algeria, Irish delegates 'in a mature diplomatic fashion' argued against partition as a way of resolving political conflicts. See Skelly, 'National Interests and International Mediation' in *Irish Foreign Policy*.
140. Conor Cruise O'Brien, *Memoir: My Life and Themes* (Dublin, 1998), pp. 156-160, quotes from his anonymous piece in *The Leader*, also in Jordan, pp. 138-139.
141. Cruise O'Brien, 'Ireland in International Affairs', p. 134.
142. Michael Gallagher, *Political Parties in the Republic of Ireland* (Manchester, 1985), p. 49.
143. Lee, *Ireland: 1912-1985*, p. 308.
144. Robinson is perhaps dating Irish independence from the 1937 Constitution rather than the official declaration on Easter Monday 1949.
145. Quoted in Rosemary Mahoney, *Whoredom in Kimmage: Irish Women Coming of Age* (New York, 1993), p. 290.
146. *Irish Independent*, 17 April 1948.

Chapter Six

1. Quoted in Grattan Freyer (ed.), *A Prose and Verse Anthology of Modern Irish Writing* (Dublin, 1979), p. xi.

2. See Noël Browne, Against the Tide (Dublin, 1986), Phyllis Browne, *Thanks for the Tea, Mrs. Browne: My Life with Noël* (Dublin, 1998), Brian Inglis, *West Briton* (London, 1962), James Deeny, *To Cure and to Care: Memoirs of a Chief Medical Officer* (Dublin, 1989), Conor Cruise O'Brien, *Ancestral Voices: Religion and Nationalism in Ireland* (Dublin, 1994) and *Memoir: My Life and Themes* (Dublin, 1998).

3. J.H. Whyte's *Church and State in Modern Ireland 1923-1979*, 2nd edition (Dublin, 1980) provides excellent insight into Irish Catholicism and the Church's role in the mother and child controversy as well as intriguing theories about Noël Browne and the inter-party government's motivations, which may not be obvious at first glance. Ruth Barrington's *Health, Medicine and Politics in Ireland 1900-1970* (Dublin, 1987) focuses on the scheme itself and Browne's problems with the Irish Medical Association. John Horgan's *Noël Browne: Passionate Outsider* (Dublin, 2000) is a useful counterpoint to Browne's memoirs.

4. See especially the controversial *Irish Times* editorial of 12 April 1951 entitled 'Contra Mundum.'

5. Anthony Jordan, *Seán MacBride: A Biography* (Dublin, 1993), p. 139.

6. Eithne MacDermott, *Clann na Poblachta* (Cork, 1998), p. 133.

7. Browne, *Against the Tide*, p. 128.

8. MacDermott, *Clann na Poblachta*, p. 133.

9. Sir Gilbert Laithwaite, 8 March 1950, cited in *Irish Press*, 1 and 2 January 1981.

10. C.S. Andrews, *Man of No Property: An Autobiography (Vol. Two)* (Dublin, 1982), p. 192.

11. In the Dáil, Costello stated 'that I have seldom listened to a statement in which there were so many – let me say it as charitably as possible – inaccuracies, misstatements and misrepresentation.' (Dáil Éireann Debates, vol. 125, col. 675, 12 April 1951) He was referring to Browne's resignation speech, but his statement could also be applied to the controversy in general. Whyte tries to sort out who knew what when and to clarify the misunderstandings between Costello, MacBride, Browne and the hierarchy, Whyte, *Church and State*, p. 214-231. See also MacDermott, *Clann na Poblachta*, pp. 149-161, Browne, *Against the Tide*, pp. 141-188, Jordan, *Seán MacBride*, pp. 125-139, Horgan, *Noël Browne*, pp. 92-158, and Barrington, *Health, Medicine and Politics*, pp. 201-219.

12. See John Cooney, *John Charles McQuaid: Ruler of Catholic Ireland* (Dublin, 2003), pp. 258-260, and Browne, *Against the Tide*, pp. 143-147 for vastly differing recollections of the 11 October 1950 meeting between Browne and Archbishop McQuaid.

13. Tim Pat Coogan, *Ireland in the Twentieth Century* (London, 2003), p. 365.

14. Statement of the Hierarchy on the Health Act 1947, 13 October 1947, Éamon de Valera Papers, P150/2904(2), University College Dublin.

15. Coogan, *Ireland*, p. 366.

NOTES 237

16. Reply to Dr. Staunton, 16 February 1948, Éamon de Valera Papers, P150/2904(2).
17. Dáil Éireann Debates, vol. 111, col. 2264, 6 July 1948.
18. Dáil Éireann Debates, vol. 111, cols. 2400-2401, 7 July 1948.
19. Dáil Éireann Debates, vol. 111, cols. 2540-2541, 8 July 1948.
20. Dáil Éireann Debates, vol. 117, col. 91, 5 July 1949.
21. Cabinet Minutes, 25 June 1948, CAB 2/10, National Archives Dublin.
22. Browne, *Against the Tide*, p. 124.
23. *Irish Times*, 11 April 1951.
24. *Irish Times*, 9 April 1951.
25. Eamonn McKee, 'Church-state relations and the development of Irish health policy: the mother-and-child scheme, 1944-53,' *Irish Historical Studies*, vol. 25 (November 1986), p. 194.
26. Whyte, *Church and State*, p. 230.
27. Whyte, *Church and State*, p. 207.
28. Barrington, *Health, Medicine and Politics*, p. 205.
29. Dáil Éireann Debates, vol. 125, col. 789, 12 April 1951.
30. Barrington, *Health, Medicine and Politics*, p. 220.
31. Deeny, *To Cure*, p. 175.
32. Browne, *Against the Tide*, p. 143.
33. Letter from Dr. James Staunton, Bishop of Ferns to Taoiseach, 10 October 1950, Éamon de Valera Papers P150/2904 (2), Appendix E.
34. Barrington, *Health, Medicine and Politics*, p. 191.
35. McKee, 'Church-state relations,' p. 177. Cabinet ministers Richard Mulcahy, Seán MacEoin, William Norton, and Joseph Blowick were also members.
36. Cooney, *John Charles McQuaid*, p. 252.
37. Letter from Dr. James Staunton, Bishop of Ferns to Taoiseach, 10 October 1950, Éamon de Valera Papers P150/2904 (2), Appendix E.
38. Browne, *Against the Tide*, p. 167.
39. F.S.L. Lyons, *Ireland Since the Famine* (London, 1985), p. 577.
40. J.J. Lee, *Ireland 1912-1985: Politics and Society* (Cambridge, 1989), p. 316.
41. Browne, *Against the Tide*, p. 153.
42. Correspondence, Department of Health 1948-70, Government Box 4. AB 8/B, Dublin Diocesan Archives.
43. Whyte, *Church and State*, p. 150.
44. Browne, *Against the Tide*, pp. 163-164.
45. Horgan, *Noël Browne*, p. 142.
46. At the time Costello declared in the Dáil, 'I want to say here that if Deputy MacBride had not taken that course, I myself would, under the Constitution, have requested Deputy Dr. Browne to give me his resignation. It is only right and it is only just to my loyal colleagues that I should make that quite clear.' (Dáil Éireann Debates, vol. 125, col. 777, 12 April 1951) Yet, years later, his take on the situation was very different. In a 1974 interview with the *Irish Times*, he said, 'And don't forget it wasn't me that sacked Noël Browne, it was his own party and Mr. Sean MacBride.' (*Irish Times*, 2 November 1974)
47. Dáil Éireann Debates, col. 739, vol. 125, 12 April 1951.
48. Letter to the *Irish Times*, 14 April 1951, signed 'A Catholic.'

49. Cruise O'Brien, *Ancestral Voices*, p. 140.
50. Whyte, *Church and State*, pp. 197-198.
51. Quoted in MacDermott, *Clann na Poblachta*, p. 146.
52. Dáil Éireann Debates, vol. 125, col. 910, 17 April 1951.
53. Deeny, *To Cure*, p. 162.
54. Dáil Éireann Debates, vol. 111, col. 2541, 8 July 1948.
55. Browne, *Against the Tide*, p. 119. As Horgan points out, MacEntee had the ability 'rare in Irish politics, for divorcing the personal from the political' and would later do his best for Browne in the 1954 elections after Browne joined Fianna Fáil (Horgan, *Noël Browne*, p. 55).
56. Dáil Éireann Debates, vol. 111, col. 2539, 8 July 1948.
57. Dáil Éireann Debates, vol. 125. cols 777-778, 12 April 1951.
58. Dáil Éireann Debates, vol. 125, col. 933, 17 April 1951.
59. Browne, *Against the Tide*, p. 127.
60. David Sheehy, archivist, Dublin Diocesan Archives, in conversation with the author, 28 July 2004.
61. Deeny, *To Cure*, p. 178.
62. Dáil Éireann Debates, vol. 117, col. 321, 6 July 1949.
63. Dáil Éireann Debates, vol. 125, col. 797, 12 April 1951.
64. Deeny, *To Cure*, p. 166.
65. Horgan, *Noël Browne*, p. 8.
66. Quoted in Browne, *Against the Tide*, p. 139.
67. Quoted in Browne, *Against the Tide*, p. 139.
68. Browne, *Against the Tide*, p. 107.
69. Accounts and recollections of the dinner vary. MacDermott, *Clann na Poblachta*, p. 146, Whyte, *Church and State*, p. 210, and Jordan, *Seán MacBride*, p. 127.
70. Jordan, *Seán MacBride*, p. 127.
71. Browne, *Against the Tide*, p. 181.
72. *Irish Times*, 12 April 1951.
73. *Irish Times*, 12 April 1951.
74. Dáil Éireann Debates, vol. 125, col. 669, 12 April 1951.
75. Dáil Éireann Debates, vol. 125, col. 758, 12 April 1951.
76. Editorial, *Irish Times*, 12 April 1951.
77. Browne, *Against the Tide*, p. 155.
78. Coogan, *Ireland*, p. 368.
79. Whyte, *Church and State*, p. 370.
80. Inglis, *West Briton*, p. 164.
81. Whyte, *Church and State*, p. 235.
82. Dáil Éireann Debates, vol. 125, col. 749, 12 April 1951.
83. Cruise O'Brien, *Ancestral Voices*, p. 140.
84. Cruise O'Brien, *Ancestral Voices*, pp. 140-141.
85. *Irish Times*, 5 May 1951.
86. *Irish Press*, 17 January 1969.
87. Dáil Éireann Debates, vol. 125, col. 797-798, 12 April 1951.
88. Alvin Jackson, *Ireland 1798-1998* (Oxford, 1998), p. 310.
89. Quoted in Samuel Levenson, *Maud Gonne* (London, 1976), p. 231.

90. Margaret Ward, *Maud Gonne: A Life* (London, 1990), p. 190.
91. William Butler Yeats to Lady Augusta Gregory, 21 August 1917, in Allan Wade (ed), *The Letters of WB Yeats* (London, 1954), p. 630.
92. Gonne later changed her mind after the Civil War began. See Ward, *Maud Gonne*, pp. 133-134.
93. Ward, *Maud Gonne*, p. 191.
94. Conrad A. Balliet, 'Michael MacLiammoir Recalls Maude Gonne MacBride,' in *Journal of Irish Literature*, May, 1977.
95. Ward, *Maud Gonne*, p. 190.
96. Norman Jeffares and Anna MacBride White, introduction to Gonne's *A Servant of the Queen* (Gerrard's Cross, Buckinghamshire, 1994), p. xi.
97. Jeffares and White, *Servant of the Queen*, p. xii.
98. Cooney, *McQuaid*, p. 222.
99. Coogan, *Ireland*, p. 358, Jordan, *Seán MacBride*, pp. 161-162.
100. Jordan, *Seán MacBride*, p. 162.
101. McQuaid to MacBride, 1 November 1947, Seán MacBride file, John Charles McQuaid Papers, Dublin Diocesan Archives.
102. See Cooney, *John Charles McQuaid*, pp. 232-233.
103. Barrington, *Health, Medicine and Politics*, p. 219.
104. *Irish Times*, 12 April 1951.
105. Horgan, *Noël Browne*, p. 152.
106. 'Southern Ireland – Church or State?' p. 2, cited in Whyte, p. 232.
107. *Irish Times*, 13 April 1951.
108. Quoted in the *Irish Times*, 1-2 January 1982.
109. *Belfast Telegraph*, editorial, 12 April 1951.
110. The *Unionist*, editorial, May 1951.
111. Dáil Éireann Debates, vol. 125, 783-784, 12 April 1951.
112. Letter to *Irish Times*, 14 April 1951, signed J.D.
113. *Belfast Telegraph*, editorial, 19 April 1951.
114. Letter to Papal Nuncio Archbishop Ettore Felici, written 16 April 1951, Cooney, *John Charles McQuaid*, p. 252.
115. Cooney, *John Charles McQuaid*, p. 253.
116. Browne, *Against the Tide*, p. 161.
117. Quoted in the *Irish Times*, 1-2 January 1982.
118. The *Unionist*, editorial, May 1951.
119. Barrington, *Health, Medicine and Politics*, p. 211.
120. Coogan, *Ireland*, p. 373.
121. *Irish Times*, editorial, 5 May 1951.
122. *Irish Times*, 14 May 1951.
123. *Irish Times*, 7 May 1951.
124. *Irish Times*, 7 May 1951.
125. *Irish Times*, 29 May 1951.
126. *Irish Times*, editorial, 28 May 1951.
127. *Irish Times*, 19 May 1951.
128. *Irish Independent*, 26 May 1951.
129. *Irish Times*, 28 May 1951, *Irish Independent*, 18 May 1951.
130. *Irish Times*, 2 June 1951.

131. Cruise O'Brien, *Memoir*, p. 154.
132. Dáil Éireann Debates, vol. 125, col. 677, 12 April 1951.
133. *Irish Times*, 12 April 1951.
134. Coogan, *Ireland*, p. 378.
135. *Irish Times*, 2 June 1951, *Irish Independent*, 2 June 1951.
136. Lee, *Ireland 1912-1985*, pp. 317-318.
137. *Manchester Guardian*, 25 April 1951.
138. O'Brien, *Memoir*, p. 160.
139. Cruise O'Brien, *Memoir*, p. 160. Anthony Jordan also includes part of this piece in his book, but attributes authorship to Jack B. Yeats, artist, dramatist, son of the artist, John Butler Yeats and the brother of the poet William Butler Yeats. Jordan does not clarify why Yeats would have written such a piece. (Jordan, *Seán MacBride*, p. 138)
140. *Irish Times*, 17 May 1954.
141. *Irish Times*, editorial, 18 May 1954.
142. *Irish Independent*, 19 May 1954.
143. *Irish Times*, 25 May 1954.
144. *Irish Independent*, 17 May 1954.

Chapter Seven

1. W. Somerset Maugham, *The Moon and Sixpence* (London, 1990), p. 144.
2. Anthony Jordan, *Seán MacBride: A Biography* (Dublin, 1993), Noël Browne, *Against the Tide* (Dublin, 1986), p. 96.
3. See Noël Browne, *Against the Tide*, Phyllis Browne, *Thanks for the Tea, Mrs. Browne: My Life with Noël* (Dublin, 1998), Garret FitzGerald, *All In A Life: An Autobiography* (Dublin, 1991), C.S. Andrews, *Man of No Property: An Autobiography* (Vol. Two) (Dublin, 1982), Brian Inglis, *Downstart: The Autobiography of Brian Inglis* (London, 1990) and *West Briton* (London, 1962), Conor Cruise O'Brien, *Ancestral Voices: Religion and Nationalism in Ireland* (Dublin, 1994) and *Memoir: My Life and Themes* (Dublin, 1998).
4. Sean MacBride Collection, Petronio Room, Iona College Library, New Rochelle, New York.
5. See Jonathan Power, *Like Water on Stone; The Story of Amnesty International* (Boston, 2001) and Egon Larsen, *A Flame in Barbed Wire: The Story of Amnesty International* (London, 1978).
6. Kevin B. Nowlan, 'The Irish Nobel Peace Prize Winners' in Karl Holl and Anne C. Kjelling (eds.), *The Nobel Peace Prize and the Laureates: the Meaning and Acceptance of the Nobel Peace Prize in the Peace Winners' Countries* (Frankfurt, 1994), p. 227.
7. Larsen, *Flame in Barbed Wire*, p. 10.
8. Amnesty International Archives, Oral History Pilot Project, Peter Benenson Memoir, November 1983. However, while researching an article on the beginnings of Amnesty, Tom Buchanan was unable to locate any news items about Portuguese students in the *Daily Telegraph* for November and December 1960. Moreover, their names were never mentioned in the case studies publicised by Amnesty and they were not chosen when the 1961 appeal was launched. The *Times* mentions a few incidents of oppression in

Portugal, but not Benenson's particular case. See Tom Buchanan, 'The Truth Will Set You Free: The Making of Amnesty International,' *Journal of Contemporary History*, October 2002 vol. 37:4, p. 576 (fn).

9. *The Observer*, 28 May 1961.
10. *Irish Times*, 30 May 1961.
11. *The Guardian*, 29 May 1961.
12. Larsen, *Flame in Barbed Wire*, p. 18.
13. Power, *Like Water on Stone*, p. xi.
14. MacBride quoted in Larsen, *Flame in Barbed Wire*, p. 26.
15. Larsen, *Flame in Barbed Wire*, p. 34.
16. Power, *Like Water on Stone*, p. 127.
17. Jordan, *Seán MacBride*, p. 165.
18. Power, *Like Water on Stone*, p. 123.
19. Power, *Like Water on Stone*, p. 179.
20. Power, *Like Water on Stone*, p. 179.
21. 'Report of an enquiry into allegations of ill-treatment in Northern Ireland,' Amnesty International Report, 2nd reprint, June 1975.
22. 'Report of an enquiry into allegations,' pp. 1-3.
23. Power, *Like Water on Stone*, p. 167.
24. Power, *Like Water on Stone*, p. 181.
25. Michael Farrell, 'The Extraordinary Life and Times of Sean MacBride' Part 2, *Magill*, January 1983, p. 36.
26. Farrell, 'Life and Times of Sean MacBride,' p. 36.
27. Sean MacBride, 'Namibia,' in *Bulletin of Atomic Scientists*, vol. 37, no. 6, June/July 1981, p. 22.
28. See also S.C. Saxena, *Namibia and the World: The Story of the Birth of a Nation* (New Delhi, 1991).
29. MacBride, 'Namibia,' p. 24.
30. Cruise O'Brien, *Memoir*, p. 168.
31. *Irish Times*, 9 October 1974.
32. Nowlan, 'Irish Nobel Peace Prize Winners,' p. 233.
33. *Irish Independent*, 11 December 1974.
34. *Irish Times*, 9 October 1974.
35. Dáil Éireann Debates, vol. 275, col. 994, 5 November 1974.
36. *Irish Independent*, 10 December 1974.
37. Nowlan, 'Irish Nobel Peace Prize Winners,' p. 277.
38. Seán MacBride, 'The Imperatives of Survival,' reprinted in *Les Prix Nobel En 1974* (Stockholm, 1975), p. 208.
39. MacBride, 'Imperatives,' p. 209.
40. MacBride, 'Imperatives,' p. 210.
41. MacBride, 'Imperatives,' p. 216.
42. MacBride, 'Imperatives,' p. 219.
43. MacBride, 'Imperatives,' pp. 221-222.
44. Editorial, *Irish Times*, 13 December 1974.
45. Reprinted from *Nobel Lectures, Peace 1971-1980* (Singapore, 1981).
46. *Irish Times*, 2 May 1977.
47. *Irish Times*, 2 May 1977.

48. Inglis, *Downstart*, p. 181.
49. *Irish Times*, 9 October 1974.
50. *Irish Independent*, 10 December 1974.
51. *Irish Times*, 7 October 1991.
52. *Irish Times*, 7 October 1991.
53. New Ireland Forum Report of Public Session, Dublin Castle, 4 October 1983, p. 16.
54. Jordan, *Seán MacBride*, p. 174, J. Bowyer Bell, *The Secret Army: The IRA* (Dublin, 1998), pp. 432-433.
55. Farrell, Life and Times of Sean MacBride', p. 37.
56. See Padraig O'Malley, *Biting at the Grave: The Irish Hunger Strikes and the Politics of Despair* (Belfast, 1990), David Beresford, *Ten Men Dead: The Story of the 1981 Irish Hunger Strike* (London, 1987), Tim Pat Coogan, *The IRA* (London, 2000) and Bobby Sands, *Writings From Prison* (Cork, 1988).
57. Sands, *Writings From Prison*, p. 21.
58. Sands, *Writings From Prison*, p. 14.
59. Andrews, *Man of No Property*, p. 192.
60. New Ireland Forum Report, Stationery Office, Dublin, 1984, Chapter 1, Preface, 1.1.
61. FitzGerald, *All in a Life*, p. 463.
62. Forum Report, Chapter 1, Preface, 1.2.
63. *Irish Times*, 5 October 1983.
64. *Irish Times*, 5 October 1983.
65. *Irish Independent*, editorial, 5 October 1983, *Irish Times*, 6 October 1983.
66. Forum Report, p. 23.
67. *Belfast Telegraph*, 20 November 1984.
68. Richard Bourke, *Peace in Ireland: The War of Ideas* (London, 2003), p. 280.
69. See Bourke, George J. Mitchell, *Making Peace* (London, 1999), Thomas Hennessey, *The Northern Ireland Peace Process: Ending the Troubles* (Dublin, 2000), and Joseph Ruane and Jennifer Todd, eds., *After the Good Friday Agreement: Analysing Political Change in Northern Ireland* (Dublin, 1999).
70. Christopher McCrudden, 'Human Rights Codes for Transnational Corporations: What Can the Sullivan and MacBride Principles Tell Us?' in *Oxford Journal of Legal Studies*, vol. 19, no. 2, Summer 1999, p. 182.
71. Dáil Éireann Debates, vol. 367, cols. 937-938, 4 June 1986.
72. Dáil Éireann Debates, vol. 388, col. 1843, 18 April 1989.
73. McCrudden, 'Human Rights Codes,' p. 184.
74. Paul Routledge, *John Hume: A Biography* (London, 1997), p. 14.
75. McCrudden, 'Human Rights Codes,' p. 197.

76. FitzGerald, *All in a Life*, p. 604.
77. The Background and History, 32 County Sovereignty Movement (http://32csm.netfirms.com).
78. See conclusion.
79. Charles Lysaght email to the author 8 February 2002.
80. Browne, *Against the Tide*, p. 95.
81. Browne, *Thanks for the Tea*, p. 102.

82. *Irish Times,* 7 October 1991.
83. Browne, *Thanks for the Tea,* p. 106.
84. Inglis, *Downstart,* p. 175.
85. Browne, *Against the Tide,* p. 96.
86. Cruise O'Brien, *Ancestral Voices,* pp. 133-136.
87. Browne, *Thanks for the Tea,* p. 101.
88. Andrews, *Man of No Property,* p. 192.

Conclusion

1. Quoted in Stephen Schaefer, 'Michael Collins Film Stirs Controversy' (Reuters, October 8, 1996).
2. *Irish Times,* 16 January 1988.
3. *Irish Times,* 18 January 1988.
4. *Irish Times,* 18 January 1988.
5. *Irish Times,* 18 January 1988.
6. *Irish Times,* 16 January 1988.
7. *Irish Times,* 16 January 1988.
8. *The Times,* 16 January 1988.
9. *The Times,* 16 January 1988.
10. *The Times,* 18 January 1998.
11. *The Times,* 23 January 1988.
12. *The Times,* 16 January 1988.
13. *Irish Times,* 19 January 1988.
14. Haughey later told Tim Pat Coogan that MacBride was 'as crooked as a ram's horn.' [Tim Pat Coogan, *Ireland in the Twentieth Century* (London, 2003), p. 359] One wonders if Haughey then informed Coogan that the kettle was black.
15. *Irish Times,* 16 January 1988.
16. Seanad Éireann Debates, vol. 118, col. 544, 20 January 1988.
17. Seanad Éireann Debates, vol. 118, col. 544, 20 January 1988.
18. Seanad Éireann Debates, vol. 118, col. 545, 20 January 1988.
19. Dáil Éireann Debates, vol. 377, cols. 439-440, 28 January 1988.
20. Dáil Éireann Debates, vol. 377, cols. 440-441, 28 January 1988.
21. Dáil Éireann Debates, vol. 377, col. 443, 28 January 1988.
22. Dáil Éireann Debates, vol. 377, col. 442, 28 January 1988.
23. J.J. Lee, *Ireland 1912-1985: Politics and Society* (Cambridge, 1989), p. 306, Dermot Keogh, *Twentieth Century Ireland* (Dublin, 1994), p. 186.
24. Lee, *Ireland,* p. 307.
25. Kevin B. Nowlan, 'The Irish Nobel Peace Prize Winners' in Karl Holl and Anne C. Kjelling (eds.), *The Nobel Peace Prize and the Laureates: the Meaning and Acceptance of the Nobel Peace Prize in the Peace Winners' Countries* (Frankfurt, 1994), p. 234.

Bibliography

Primary Sources

Private and Unpublished Papers
Dean Acheson Papers, Harry S. Truman Library, Independence, MO
Frank Aiken Papers, University College, Dublin
Clement Attlee Papers, Bodleian Library, Oxford
Clement Attlee Papers, Churchill College, Cambridge
Ernest Bevin Papers, Churchill College, Cambridge
Winston Churchill Papers, Churchill College, Cambridge
John A. Costello Papers, University College, Dublin
Éamon de Valera Papers, University College, Dublin
Paul G. Hoffman Papers, Harry S. Truman Library, Independence, MO
Sighle Humphreys Papers, University College, Dublin
Seán MacEoin Papers, University College, Dublin
Seán MacEntee Papers, University College, Dublin
Patrick McGilligan Papers, University College, Dublin
John Charles McQuaid Papers, Dublin Diocesan Archives, Dublin
Francis Matthews Papers, Harry S. Truman Library, Independence, MO
Philip Noel-Baker Papers, Churchill College, Cambridge
Richard Mulcahy Papers, University College, Dublin
Harry Truman Papers, Harry S. Truman Library, Independence, MO

Government papers
British Parliament
    Cabinet Minutes
    House of Commons Debates
Bunreacht na hÉireann (Constitution of Ireland)
Houses of the Oireachtas
    Dáil Éireann Debates

Seanad Éireann Debates
European University Institute Archives, Florence, Italy
    OEEC Speeches
Macbride Principles
National Archives, Canada
    Department of External Affairs
National Archives, Ireland
    Cabinet Minutes
    Department of Finance,
    Department of Foreign Affairs
    Department of the Taoiseach
National Archives and Records Administration, Washington, D.C.
    US State Department
New Ireland Forum Report
National Archives, Kew
    Commonwealth Office Records
    Dominions Office Records
    Foreign Office Records
    Office of Prime Minister Records
Public Record Office, Northern Ireland
    Cabinet Minutes
    Northern Ireland House of Commons Debates
Franklin Delano Roosevelt Library, Hyde Park, New York
    Vatican Diplomatic Files

Oral Histories
Theodore Achilles, Harry S. Truman Library
Nathan M. Becker, Harry S. Truman Library
W. John Kenney, Harry S. Truman Library

Newspapers and periodicals
Amnesty International (reports, briefs, newsletters, 1962-84)
Belfast Telegraph
The Citizen
The Economist
Freeman's Journal
Irish Echo
Irish Independent
Irish Press

Irish Times
The Leader
Life Magazine
Limerick Leader
Manchester Guardian
The New York Times
The Observer
Our Nation – Clann na Poblachta periodical
Our Policy – Clann na Poblachta periodical, 1948
RTÉ Archives (1979, 1980, 1992)
The Saturday Evening Post
The Times
The Unionist
The Washington Post

Published autobiographies and memoirs

Acheson, Dean, *Present at the Creation: My Years in the State Department* (New York, 1987).

Andrews, C.S., *Man of No Property: An Autobiography (Vol. Two)* (Dublin, 1982).

Attlee, Clement, *As It Happened* (London, 1954).

Browne, Noël, *Against the Tide* (Dublin, 1986).

Browne, Phyllis, *Thanks for the Tea, Mrs. Browne: My Life with Noël* (Dublin, 1998).

Cruise O'Brien, Conor, *Ancestral Voices: Religion and Nationalism in Ireland* (Dublin, 1994).

Cruise O'Brien, Conor, *To Katanga and Back: A UN Case History* (London, 1962).

Cruise O'Brien, Conor, *Memoir: My Life and Themes* (Dublin, 1998).

Deeny, James, *To Cure and to Care: Memoirs of a Chief Medical Officer* (Dublin, 1989).

FitzGerald, Garret, *All In A Life: An Autobiography* (Dublin, 1991).

Gonne, Maud, *A Servant of the Queen* (Gerrard's Cross, Buckinghamshire, 1994).

Inglis, Brian, *Downstart: The Autobiography of Brian Inglis* (London, 1990).

Inglis, Brian, *West Briton* (London, 1962).

Mitchell, George J., *Making Peace* (London, 1999).

O'Neill, Tip and William Novak, *Man of the House: The Life and Political Memoirs of Speaker Tip O'Neill* (London, 1987).

Sands, Bobby, *Writings From Prison* (Cork, 1988).

Thatcher, Margaret, *The Downing Street Years* (London, 1995).

Truman, Harry S., *Memoirs: Years of Trial and Hope, Vol Two* (New York, 1955).

Other published contemporary sources

The Background and History, 32 County Sovereignty Movement (http://32csm.netfirms.com).

Costello, John A., *Ireland in International Affairs* (Dublin, 1948).

Ireland's Position in Relation to the North Atlantic Treaty (Dublin, 1950).

MacBride, Seán, 'The Imperatives of Survival,' reprinted in *Les Prix Nobel En 1974* (Stockholm, 1975).

MacBride, Seán, 'Namibia' *Bulletin of Atomic Scientists* 37:6 (1981).

MacBride, Seán, 'Reflections on Intelligence,' *Intelligence and National Security* 2 (1987).

Jawaharal Nehru's Speeches, vol. 1 September 1946-May 1949 (New Dehli, 1949).

Nobel Lectures, Peace 1971-1980 (Singapore, 1981).

Spaak, Paul-Henri, 'Strasbourg: The Second Year,' Stevenson Memorial Lecture, delivered 30 October 1950, Chatham House (Oxford, 1952).

Wade, Allan (ed.), *Letters of W.B. Yeats* (London, 1954).

White, Anna MacBride and A. Norman Jeffares (eds.), *Always Your Friend: The Gonne-Yeats Letters 1893-1938* (London, 1992).

Secondary Sources

Books and journal articles

Akenson, Donald H., *Conor: A Biography of Conor Cruise O'Brien* (London, 1994).

Akenson, Donald Harmon, *The United States and Ireland* (Cambridge, MA, 1973).

Anderson, Benedict, *Imagined Communities: Reflections on the Origin and Spread of Nationalism* (London, 1983).

Balliett, Conrad A., 'The Lives – and Lies – of Maud Gonne,' *Éire-Ireland* XIV (1979).

Balliet, Conrad A., 'Michael MacLiammoir Recalls Maude Gonne MacBride,' *Journal of Irish Literature* (May, 1977).

Barrington, Ruth, *Health, Medicine and Politics in Ireland 1900-1970* (Dublin, 1987).

Bell, J. Bowyer, *The Secret Army: The IRA* (Dublin, 1998).

Beresford, David, *Ten Men Dead: The Story of the 1981 Irish Hunger Strike* (London, 1987).

Bew, Paul, Ellen Hazelkorn, and Henry Patterson, *The Dynamics of Irish Politics* (London, 1989).

Bew, Paul and Patterson, Henry, *Sean Lemass and the Making of Modern Ireland* (Dublin, 1982).

Bloom, William, *Personal Identity, National Identity, and International Relations* (New York, 1990).

Bourke, Richard, *Peace in Ireland: The War of Ideas* (London, 2003).

Bowman, John, *De Valera and the Ulster Question 1917-1973* (Oxford, 1982).

Boyce, D.G., *The Irish Question and British Politics 1868-1996*, 2nd ed., (London, 1996).

Boyce, D. George and Alan O'Day (eds.), *The Making of Modern Irish History: Revisionism and the Revisionist Controversy* (London, 1996).

Bradshaw, Brendan, 'Irish Nationalism: An Historical Perspective,' *Bullán* vol. V no. 1 (Summer/Fall 2000).

Brown, T.N., *Irish-American Nationalism 1870-1890* (New York, 1966).

Brown, Terence, *Ireland: A Social and Cultural History 1922-1979* (London, 1981).

Buchanan, Tom, 'The Truth Will Set You Free: The Making of Amnesty International' in *Journal of Contemporary History*, October 2002 vol. 37:4.

Bullock, Alan, *Ernest Bevin: Foreign Secretary 1945-1951* (Oxford, 1985).

Cardozo, Nancy, *Lucky Eyes and a High Heart: The Life of Maud Gonne* (New York, 1978).

Carroll, Joseph, 'US-Irish Relations 1939-45,' *Irish Sword* 19 (1993-94).

Carter, Carrolle J., 'Ireland: America's Neutral Ally,' *Éire-Ireland* XII (1977).

Chubb, Basil, *A Source Book of Irish Government* (Dublin, 1983).

Chubb, Basil, *The Government and Politics of Ireland*, 3rd edition (Stanford, 1992).

Chubb, Basil, *The Politics of the Irish Constitution* (Dublin, 1991).

Coakley, John and Michael Gallagher, *Politics in the Republic of Ireland*, 2nd ed. (Limerick, 1996).

Coogan, Tim Pat, *De Valera: Long Fellow, Long Shadow* (London, 1995).

Coogan, Tim Pat, *Ireland in the Twentieth Century* (London, 2003).

Coogan, Tim Pat, *The IRA* (London, 2000).

Cooney, John, *John Charles McQuaid: Ruler of Catholic Ireland* (Dublin, 2003).

Cox, W.H., 'The Politics of Irish Unification in the Irish Republic,' *Parliamentary Affairs* 38 (1985).

Cronin, Mike and John M. Regan, eds., *Ireland: The Politics of Independence, 1922-49* (London, 2000).

Cronin, Seán, *Irish Nationalism* (Dublin, 1980).

Cronin, Seán, 'The Making of NATO and the Partition of Ireland' *Éire-Ireland*, 20 (1985).

Cronin, Seán, *Washington's Irish Policy 1916-1986* (Dublin, 1987).

Cruise O'Brien, Conor, 'Ireland in International Affairs,' in Owen Dudley Edwards (ed.), *Conor Cruise O'Brien Introduces Ireland*, (New York: McGraw Hill, 1969).

Cruise O'Brien, Conor (ed), *The Shaping of Modern Ireland* (London, 1960).

Curtin, Nancy J., *The United Irishmen: Popular Politics in Ulster and Dublin, 1791-1798* (Oxford, 1994).

Davis, Troy D., *Dublin's American Policy: Irish-American Diplomatic Relations 1945-1952* (Washington D.C., 1998).

Dickson, David, Dáire Keogh and Kevin Whelan, eds., *The United Irishmen: Republicanism, Radicalism and Rebellion* (Dublin, 1993).

Dinan, Desmond, 'After the Emergency: Ireland in the Post-War World, 1945-50,' *Éire-Ireland*, vol. 24 (Fall 1989).

Driscoll, Dennis, 'Is Ireland Really Neutral?' in *Irish Studies in International Affairs*, vol. 1 no. 3 (1982).

Drudy, P.J. (ed.), *The Irish in America: Emigration, Assimilation, Impact* (Cambridge, 1985).

Drudy, P.J. and D. McAleese (eds.), *Ireland and the European Community* (Cambridge, 1983).

Dudley Edwards, R. and T.W. Moody, *Irish Historical Studies*, vol. 1, no. 1, March 1938.

Dwyer, T. Ryle, *De Valera's Darkest Hour 1919-1932: In Search of National Independence* (Dublin, 1982).

Dwyer, T. Ryle, *De Valera's Finest Hour 1932-1959: In Search of National Independence* (Dublin, 1982).

Dwyer, T. Ryle, *Strained Relations: Ireland at Peace and the USA at War, 1941-45* (Dublin, 1988).

Edwards, Owen Dudley and David N. Doyle (eds.), *America and Ireland 1776-1976* (Westport, CT: Greenwood Press, 1980).

Edwards, Owen Dudley (ed.), *Conor Cruise O'Brien Introduces Ireland* (New York, 1969).

Fanning, Ronan, 'Anglo-Irish Relations – Partition and the British Dimension in Historical Perspective,' *Irish Studies in International Affairs* vol. 2 no. 1 (1985).

Fanning, Ronan, *Independent Ireland* (Dublin, 1983).

Fanning, Ronan, 'Irish Neutrality: An Historical Perspective,' in *Irish Studies in International Affairs* vol. 1 no. 3 (1982).

Fanning, Ronan, 'The Anglo-American Alliance and the Irish Application for Membership in the United Nations,' *Irish Studies in International Affairs* 2 (1986).

Fanning, Ronan, *The Irish Department of Finance 1922-58* (Dublin, 1978).

Fanning Ronan, 'The Response of the London and Belfast Governments to the Declaration of the Republic of Ireland 1948-1949,' *International Affairs* 58 (Winter 1981-1982).

Fanning, Ronan, 'The United States and Irish Participation in NATO: The Debate of 1950,' *Irish Studies in International Affairs* 1 (1979).

Farrell, Brian, *Chairman or Chief: The Role of the Taoiseach in Irish Government* (Dublin, 1971).

Farrell, Michael, 'The Extraordinary Life and Times of Sean MacBride,' *Magill* (January, 1983).

Fisk, Robert, *In Time of War* (London, 1985).

Fitzpatrick, David, *The Two Irelands 1912-1939* (Oxford, 1998).

Fogarty, M.P., *Christian Democracy in Western Europe 1820-1953* (London, 1957)

Foster, R.F., *The Irish Story: Telling Tales and Making It Up In Ireland* (London, 2001).

Foster, R.F., *Modern Ireland 1600-1972* (London, 1988).

Foster, R.F., *Paddy and Mr Punch* (London, 1993).

Foster, R.F., *W.B. Yeats: A Life, The Apprentice Mage, 1865-1914* (Oxford, 1997).

Foster, R.F., *W.B. Yeats: A Life, The Arch-Poet 1915-1939* (Oxford, 2003).

Fraser, T.G., *Partition in Ireland, India, Palestine: Theory and Practice* (London, 1984).

Gallagher, Michael, *Political Parties in the Republic of Ireland* (Manchester, 1985).

Gallagher, Tom and James O'Connell (eds.), *Contemporary Irish Studies* (Manchester, 1983).

Gallagher, Tom, 'Fianna Fail and Partition 1926-1984,' *Éire-Ireland* 20 (1985).

Garvin, Tom, 'Continuity and Change in Irish Electoral Politics 1923-1969,' in *Economic and Social Review* vol. III (March 1972).

Garvin, Tom, *1922: The Birth of Irish Democracy* (Dublin, 1996).

Garvin, Tom, *The Evolution of Irish Nationalist Politics* (New York, 1981).

Garvin, Tom, *The Nationalist Revolution in Ireland* (Oxford, 1997).

Geiger, Till and Michael Kennedy (eds.), *Ireland, Europe and the Marshall Plan* (Dublin, 2004).

Ginsborg, Paul, *A History of Contemporary Italy: Society and Politics 1943-1988* (London, 1990).

Girvin, Brian, *Between Two Worlds: Politics and Economics in Independent Ireland* (Dublin, 1989).

Girvin, Brian and Roland Sturm, 'Politics and Society in Contemporary Ireland,' *Economic and Social Review* 21:3 (1990).

Hall, H. Duncan, *A History of the British Commonwealth of Nations* (London, 1971).

Hanley, David, (ed.), *Christian Democracy in Europe: A Comparative Perspective* (London, 1994),

Harkness, David, *Ireland in the Twentieth Century: Divided Island* (London, 1966).

Harris, Kenneth, *Attlee* (London, 1982).

Hederman, Miriam, *The Road to Europe: Irish Attitudes 1948-61* (Dublin, 1983).

Heller, Francis H. and John R. Gillingham (eds.), *NATO: The Founding of the Atlantic Alliance and the Integration of Europe* (New York, 1992).

Hennessey, Thomas, *The Northern Ireland Peace Process: Ending the Troubles* (Dublin, 2000)

Hennessy, Peter, *Never Again* (London, 1993).

Hobsbawm, E.J., *Nations and Nationalism since 1780: Programme, Myth, Reality* (Cambridge, 1990).

Hogan, Michael J., *The Marshall Plan: America, Britain, and the Reconstruction of Western Europe 1947-1952* (Cambridge, 1987).

Horgan, John, *Noël Browne: Passionate Outsider* (Dublin, 2000).

Howe, Stephen, *Anticolonialism in British Politics* (London, 1993).

Hutton, Seán and Paul Stewart (eds.), *Ireland's Histories: Aspects of State, Society and Ideology* (London, 1991).

'Ireland and the Commonwealth – Mr. Costello's Government and Partition,' *Round Table* vol. XXXIX (1948-1949).

Irving, R.E.M., *Christian Democracy in France* (London, 1973).

Jackson, Alvin, *Ireland 1798-1998* (Oxford, 1998).

Jordan, Anthony, *Major John MacBride 1865-1916* (Westport, Ireland, 1991).

Jordan, Anthony, *Seán MacBride: A Biography* (Dublin, 1993).

Keatinge, Patrick, *A Place Among the Nations: Issues of Irish Foreign Policy* (Dublin, 1978).

Keatinge, Patrick, *The Formulation of Irish Foreign Policy* (Dublin, 1973).

Kennan, George F., *American Diplomacy 1900-1950* (Chicago, 1953).

Kennedy, Michael, *Ireland and the League of Nations 1919-1946: International Relations, Diplomacy, and Politics* (Dublin 1996).

Kennedy, Michael and Joseph Morrison Skelly (eds.), *Irish Foreign Policy 1919-1969: From Independence to Internationalism* (Dublin, 2000).

Kennedy, Michael and Eunan O'Halpin, *Ireland and the Council of Europe: From Isolation Toward Integration* (Strasbourg, 2000).

Kenny, Kevin, *The American Irish: A History* (Harlow, 2000).

Keogh, Dermot, *Ireland and Europe, 1919-1989: A Diplomatic and Political History* (Cork, 1990).

Keogh, Dermot, 'Ireland, the Vatican and the Cold War: The Case of Italy 1948,' *Irish Studies in International Affairs* 3 (1991).

Keogh Dermot, and Michael H. Haltzel (eds.), *Nothern Ireland and the Politics of Reconciliation* (Cambridge, 1993).

Keogh, Dermot, *Twentieth-Century Ireland* (Dublin, 1994).

Keogh, Dermot, *The Vatican, the Bishops, and Irish Politics 1919-1939* (Cambridge, 1986).

Lamberts, Emiel, *Christian Democracy in the European Union 1945-1995: Proceedings of the Leuven Colloquium* (Leuven, 1997).

Larsen, Egon, *A Flame in Barbed Wire: The Story of Amnesty International* (London, 1978).

Lee, J.J. and Gearóid Ó Tuathaigh, *The Age of de Valera* (Dublin, 1982).

Lee, J.J., *Ireland 1912-1985: Politics and Society* (Cambridge, 1989).

Lee, J.J. (ed.), *Ireland 1945-70* (Dublin, 1979).

Lee, J., *The Modernisation of Irish Society* (Dublin, 1973).

Levenson, Samuel, *Maud Gonne* (London, 1976).

Lipgens, Walter and Wilfred Loth, (eds.), *Documents on the History of European Integration, Vol.3, The Struggle for European Union by Political Parties and Pressure Groups in Western European Countries, 1945-1950* (Berlin, 1988).

Longford, Earl of and Thomas P. O'Neill, *Eamon de Valera* (London, 1970).

Longford, Earl of, *Peace By Ordeal* (London, 1972).

Lynch, P. and J. Meenan (eds.), *Essays in Honour of Alexis Fitzgerald* (Dublin, 1987).

Lyons, F.S.L., *Ireland Since the Famine* (London, 1985).

Mcbride, Ian, (ed.), *History and Memory in Modern Ireland* (Cambridge, 2001).

McCabe, Ian, *A Diplomatic History of Ireland 1948-1949: The Republic, the Commonwealth and NATO* (Dublin, 1991).

McCullagh, David, *A Makeshift Majority: The First Interparty Government 1948-51* (Dublin, 1999).

McCullough, David, *Truman* (New York, 1993).

McCrudden, Christopher, 'Human Rights Codes for Transnational Corporations: What Can the Sullivan and MacBride Principles Tell Us?' in *Oxford Journal of Legal Studies*, vol. 19, no. 2 (Summer 1999).

MacDermott, Eithne, *Clann na Poblachta* (Cork, 1998).

MacEvilly, Michael, 'Sean Macbride and the Republican Motor Launch St George,' *Irish Sword* 16 (1984).

McEvoy, F.J, 'Canada, Ireland and the Commonwealth: The Declaration of the Irish Republic 1948-9,' *Irish Historical Studies* 24 (1985).

McKee, Eamonn, 'Church-state relations and the development of Irish health policy: the mother-and-child scheme, 1944-53,' *Irish Historical Studies*, vol. 25, November 1986.

MacManus, Francis (ed.), *Years of the Great Test 1926-1939* (Cork, 1962).

Maher, D.J., *The Tortuous Path: The Course of Ireland's Entry into the EEC 1948-73* (Dublin, 1986).

Mahoney, Rosemary, *Whoredom in Kimmage: Irish Women Coming of Age* (New York, 1993).

Mansergh, Nicholas, *The Commonwealth Experience*, 2nd edition (London, 1982).

Mansergh, Nicholas, 'The Implications of Éire's Relationship with the British Commonwealth of Nations,' *International Affairs* vol 24 no 1 (Jan. 1948).

Mansergh, Nicholas, 'Ireland: The Republic Outside the Commonwealth,' *International Affairs* vol 28 no 3 (July 1952).

Mansergh, Nicholas, *Nationalism and Independence* (Cork, 1997).

Mansergh, Nicholas, *Survey of British Commonwealth Affairs: Problems of Wartime Cooperation and Postwar Change, 1939-1952* (Oxford, 1958).

Mansergh, Nicholas, *The Unresolved Question: The Anglo-Irish Settlement and Its Undoing 1912-72* (New Haven, CT, 1991).

Milward, Alan S., *The Reconstruction of Western Europe*, 1945-51 (London, 1987).

Mitrany, David, *Functional Theory of Politics* (London, 1975).

Moody, T.W. and F.X. Martin (eds.), *The Course of Irish History* (Boulder, Colorado, 1994).

Moraes, Frank, *Jawaharal Nehru: A Biography* (New York, 1956).

Morgan, Kenneth O., *Labour in Power 1945-1951* (London, 1985).

Moynihan, Daniel Patrick and Nathan Glazer (eds.), *Beyond the Melting Pot: The Negros, Puerto Ricans, Jews, Italians, and Irish of New York City*, (Cambridge, MA, 1963).

Moynihan, Maurice (ed.), *Speeches and Statements by Eamon de Valera 1917-73* (Dublin, 1980).

Murphy, John A., *Ireland in the Twentieth Century* (Dublin, 1975).

Murphy, John A., 'Put Them Out: Parties and Elections 1948-69,' in J.J. Lee, *Ireland 1945-1970* (Dublin, 1979).

Nairn, Tom, *The Break-up of Britain: Crisis and Neo-Nationalism*, 2nd edition, (London, 1981).

Nowlan, K.B. and T.D. Williams (eds.), *Ireland in the War Years and After 1939-1951* (Dublin, 1969).

Nowlan, Kevin, 'The Irish Nobel Peace Prize Winners' in Holl, Karl and Anne C. Kjelling (eds.), *The Nobel Peace Prize and the Laureates: the Meaning and Acceptance of the Nobel Peace Prize in the Peace Winners' Countries* (Frankfurt, 1994).

O'Driscoll, Robert (ed.), *The Celtic Consciousness* (New York, 1981).

O'Grady, Joseph P., 'Ireland and the Defence of the North Atlantic, 1948-1951: The American View' *Éire-Ireland* vol. XXV, no. 3 (Fall 1990).

O'Halloran, Clare, *Partition and the Limits of Irish Nationalism* (Dublin, 1987).

O'Higgins, Brian, Wolfe Tone Annual: Salute to the Soldiers of 1916 28 (1960).

O'Malley, Padraig, *Biting at the Grave: The Irish Hunger Strikes and the Politics of Despair* (Belfast, 1990).

Ovendale, Ritchie, *The Foreign Policy of the British Labour Government 1945-51* (Leicester, 1984).

Pelling, Henry, *The Labour Governments, 1945-1951* (London, 1984).

Pisani, Sallie, *The CIA and the Marshall Plan* (Lawrence, Kansas, 1991).

Power, Jonathan, *Like Water on Stone: The Story of Amnesty International* (Boston, 2001).

Pridham, Geoffrey, *Christian Democracy in Western Germany: The CDU/CSU in Government and Opposition 1945-1976* (London, 1977).

Rafter, Kevin, *The Clann: The Story of Clann na Poblachta* (Cork, 1996).

Raymond, Raymond J., 'Ireland's 1949 NATO Decision: A Reassessment' in *Éire-Ireland*, vol. 20, no 3 (Fall 1985).

Robertson, A.H., *The Council of Europe: Its Structure, Functions and Achievements* (London, 1961).

Routledge, Paul, *John Hume: A Biography* (London, 1997).

Ruane, Joseph and Jennifer Todd (eds.), *After the Good Friday Agreement: Analysing Political Change in Northern Ireland* (Dublin, 1999).

Salmon, Trevor, 'Neutrality and the Irish Republic: Myth or Reality?' *Round Table* 290 (1984).

Salmon, Trevor, *Unneutral Ireland: An Ambivalent and Unique Security Policy* (Oxford, 1989).

Saxena, S.C., *Namibia and the World: The Story of the Birth of a Nation* (New Delhi, 1991).

Seton-Watson, Hugh, *Nations and States: An Enquiry into the Origins of Nations and the Politics of Nationalism* (London, 1977).

Skelly, Joseph Morrison, 'Ireland, the Department of External Affairs and the United Nations 1946-55: A New Look,' in *Irish Studies in International Affairs* vol. 7 (1996).

Skelly, Joseph Morrison, *Irish Diplomacy at the United Nations 1945-65* (Dublin, 1997).

Singh, Kusum and Bertram Gross, 'MacBride: The Report and the Response,' *Journal of Communication* 31 (1981).

Smith, Anthony D., *Nationalism and Modernism: A Critical Survey of Recent Theories of Nations and Nationalism* (London, 1998).

Steiner, Zara (ed.), *Times Survey of Foreign Ministries of the World* (London, 1982).

Stewart, A.T.Q., *A Deeper Silence: The Hidden Origins of the United Irishmen* (Belfast, 1998).

Thompson, John A., *Woodrow Wilson* (London, 2002).

Tiratsoo, Nick (ed.), *The Attlee Years* (London, 1991).

Walsh, James P., *The Irish: America's Political Class*, (New York, 1976).

Ward, Margaret, *Maud Gonne: Ireland's Joan of Arc* (London, 1990).

Ward, Margaret, *Maud Gonne: A Life* (London, 1990).

Webster, R.A., *Christian Democracy in Italy 1860-1960* (London, 1961).

Weight, Richard, *Patriots: National Identity in Britain 1940-2000* (London, 2002).

Whelan, Bernadette, *Ireland and the Marshall Plan 1947-57* (Dublin, 2000).

White, Timothy J., 'Nationalism Vs. Liberalism in the Irish Context: From a Postcolonial Past to a Postmodern Future,' *Eire-Ireland* vol. XXXVII (Fall/Winter 2002).

Whyte, J.H. Church and State in Modern Ireland 1923-1979, 2nd edition (Dublin, 1980).

Unpublished theses

O'Keeffe, Patrick D., 'The Origins and Development of Clann na Poblachta,' unpublished MA Thesis, University College Cork, 1981.